nebraska symposium on motivation
1970

Nebraska Symposium on Motivation, 1970, is Volume XVIII in the series on CURRENT THEORY AND RESEARCH IN MOTIVATION

nebraska symposium on motivation
1970
WILLIAM J. ARNOLD and MONTE M. PAGE, Editors

John A. King

Professor of Zoology
Michigan State University

William A. Mason

Professor of Psychology
Tulane University

Victor H. Denenberg

Professor of Psychology
University of Connecticut

Leonard Berkowitz

Professor of Psychology
University of Wisconsin

Salvatore R. Maddi

Professor of Psychology
University of Chicago

Martin T. Orne

Professor of Psychiatry
University of Pennsylvania

university of nebraska press
lincoln
1970

Publishers on the Plains

UNP

Copyright © 1971 by the University of Nebraska Press
International Standard Book Number 0–8032–0612–7
Library of Congress Catalog Card Number 53–11655
Manufactured in the United States of America

Contents

Introduction, by William J. Arnold and Monte M. Page   vii

ECOLOGICAL PSYCHOLOGY: AN APPROACH TO MOTIVA-
TION: John A. King   1

MOTIVATIONAL FACTORS IN PSYCHOSOCIAL DEVELOP-
MENT: William A. Mason   35

THE MOTHER AS A MOTIVATOR: Victor H. Denenberg   69

THE CONTAGION OF VIOLENCE: AN S-R MEDIATIONAL
ANALYSIS OF SOME EFFECTS OF OBSERVED AGGRES-
SION: Leonard Berkowitz   95

THE SEARCH FOR MEANING: Salvatore R. Maddi   137

HYPNOSIS, MOTIVATION, AND THE ECOLOGICAL VALIDITY
OF THE PSYCHOLOGICAL EXPERIMENT: Martin T.
Orne   187

Chronological List of Contents of the Nebraska Symposia on Motivation   267

Alphabetical List of Contents of the Nebraska Symposia
on Motivation by Author   273

Subject Index   279

Author Index   284

Introduction

This volume is the eighteenth in the series of the Nebraska Symposium on Motivation. Again this year the symposium was arranged by two people. We have found this arrangement to be particularly satisfactory because, as in previous years, the symposium was held in two separate sessions. The first session, experimental in orientation, was arranged primarily by W. J. Arnold and the second session, social-personality in orientation, by Monte M. Page. It seems appropriate at this point to say that next year's symposium will be arranged by Professor James K. Cole, who is now handling the training grant which sponsors the symposium.

The papers of Professors King, Mason, and Denenberg were given during the first session of the symposium. In general, they were centered around aspects of the effects of early experience on later behavior, although this focus was less central in King's paper than in those of Mason and Denenberg.

Professor King opens his paper with a "word picture" of a boy walking through a snow-covered field and finding the tracks of a mouse in the snow. The boy wonders about the motivation of the mouse, being out in the wintry field. King also points out that we might wonder why the boy is out in the snowy, wintry, field, or, for that matter, why human beings are found in other places like crowded cities. He observes that the question of population dispersion is primarily ecological, while the behaviorial factors contributing to dispersion are primarily psychological. He then defines ecological psychology as the study of behavioral determinants affecting the distribution of animals (including man) in space and time. He goes on to point out that the distribution of animals is the end product of many interacting cause-effect systems, but that since the physiological requirements of an animal species are fulfilled over a wider array of environments than those in which the animal is actually found, the presence of an animal at any given time or place depends upon its perception of the environment. For example, a nocturnal mouse will not leave its nest until it perceives a decrease in light intensity, or a bird will not sing until it is located on a perch within its territory. The perception of dusk for a mouse or a song-bird's perch is not determined by the animal's sensory capacity to perceive the intensity of light or to see other trees in the forest, but rather, these animals exhibit a selective perception of their environment. This selectivity of the perceptual world is the principle measure of motivation for the ecological psychologist. When an animal is presented with alternatives of going or not going, going one place or another, going now or later, the probabilities of his choice are the only measure of motivation needed to predict his temporal and spatial locations.

King goes on to say that ecological psychology is primarily comparative and that species' comparisons not only can reveal the perceptual variable which is responsible for their different patterns of distribution but also can reveal how each species selects these perceptual variables. He then presents the results of some of his very interesting work with several species of the deer mouse, *Peromyscus*. He specifically deals with visual perception to illustrate the function of vision in the ecology of these small rodents. He presents the results of work comparing four different species representing those that occupy forests, grasslands, sandpine openings, and deserts. All the mice were born in the laboratory in total darkness where they were raised until tested at 65 to 75 days of age. If visual perception of light does have a function, its function may differ among several species, so despite the difficulties of comparative testing, he devised means of testing the visual reinforcement effects of light in these different species. He found that for some of the species light served as a reinforcer, but not for others.

He was also interested in the effect of early experience with the light on the reinforcing value of light for these four taxa. Although the results were complicated by marked differences between the taxa, he did conclude that the short, mild encounter with light early in life has little effect on light reinforcement relative to the effect of reinforcement as a function of a species' differences.

The second paper in this session was given by Dr. William Mason. In summary, his paper considers psychosocial development with reference to two major developmental trends, each corresponding with a fundamental adaptive problem for the growing primate. Both trends operate throughout life, although their prominence changes as development proceeds. The first trend is inferred from contact-seeking behaviors. These are preadapted patterns which are dominant early in ontogeny and which provide the basis for the adjustment to the mother. They are most likely to occur under conditions of high arousal and their performance leads to arousal reduction, which provides the primary mechanism of reinforcement in the development of the infant's tie to the mother. With respect to this first trend, Mason says that the first task of the infant is to maintain contact with the mother and refers to the mother as a "mobile ecological niche" that is the infant's essential link with the future.

The second major developmental trend is inferred from exploitative behaviors such as social play, motor play, and investigatory activities. Exploitative behaviors are elicited by moderate increments of arousal (in an animal that is not already in a state of excessive arousal), and their performance leads to further increments in arousal. Objects that elicit more sustained exploitative behaviors are effective reinforcers. They are primary agents in moving the infant away from the mother and into the larger world. Because the efficiency of such objects is reduced as a function of repeated exposures, their cumulative effect is to extend the range of objects to which the infant is attracted. Insofar as the exploitative trend brings the growing primate into contact with other individuals, it creates the opportunity and the need for social learning.

The syndrome of aberrations and deficiencies seen in primates raised in social isolation is viewed as a manifestation of these two major developmental trends, operating on reduced or altered environmental input. Similarly, the consequences to exposure to particular classes of social beings and to specific social behaviors are considered to depend on the interaction between these social factors and the current status of the developmental trends.

Mason makes his position quite clear in some of his early introductory statements. He says, "What I am suggesting is that these trends are the outcome of basic developmental programs determined, for the most part, by the biological makeup of the individual. They provide the basic behavioral structure and lay out the major directions along which development must proceed. I *do not* claim that either the trends or the underlying programs are *independent* of experience. On the contrary, determining *how* they are influenced by experience is one of the central tasks of developmental psychology. We are concerned with the phenotypic expression of these programs. How do they manifest themselves under ordinary conditions? How are they modified by the environment and how do they operate upon it?" And then he says, "Having this simple developmental framework before us, we are now ready to look at some of these 'how' questions—at problems of causation and function. In particular, we will be concerned with the motivational determinants and the motivational consequences of filial and exploitative behaviors."

In the third paper of this session Denenberg deals with his program of research concerning the effect of early social variables on subsequent behavioral and physiological processes. His general approach has been to vary systematically the maternal environment of experimental mice as well as the preweaning and postweaning peer group environment of these animals. What makes the work particularly interesting is the manner in which he has manipulated the maternal environment: this has been done by fostering newborn mice to lactating rat mothers who have pups approximately the same age as the infant mice. Even though the rat is a different species than the mouse, they are both rodents and there is sufficient similarity between the two animals for the rat mother to successfully rear mouse young. The importance of this procedure is that it makes it possible to separate experimentally the usual confounding between genetic, prenatal, and postnatal environments which is present in most naturalistic settings and in the great majority of laboratory situations as well.

In summarizing his work, he says that the most general statement he can make is that the adult mother rat, through her behavioral interactions with the mice, will cause a significant reduction in the activity level of these animals both at weaning and in adulthood. This generalization has been found to hold with both of the two strains of mice used in these experiments. With respect to aggression, he says his conclusions must be limited by the genotype of the animal. For one strain of mouse a reduction in fighting results from the mother's behavioral interaction with the pups between birth and weaning. For another strain, however, equivalent experience has no effect upon aggression. Another major finding is that the behavioral interaction of the mother with the pups between birth and weaning is the cause of marked reduction in adreno-cortical reactivity to a novel situation as measured both at weaning and in adulthood. He points out, however, that the generality of this finding is not known since this work has been carried out with only one strain of mouse.

In concluding his paper, he says, "Even though I am a firm believer in motherhood, I must admit that when we started this set of experiments I did not expect to find that the mother's behavior during the nursing period would have such a powerful effect on so many different biobehavioral systems of the animal. Clearly, if these results have any degree of generality to other mammals, the subtle and not so subtle behavioral patterns of the mother during the early stages of a neonate's development have very profound and far-reaching effects."

In the second session of the symposium Professors Berkowitz, Maddi, and Orne presented their papers. Berkowitz led off with a theoretical synthesis and a review of his work in the area of aggression and violence. Beginning with a discussion of the relation between television-portrayed violence and the promotion of aggression in viewers, he takes the position that "rather than pursuing the question of whether media violence does have aggressive consequences, it is time that investigators turned to a more precise analysis of the conditions under which these consequences do or do not arise." He goes on to review relevant data from this perspective. Discussing first the anecdotal and correlational evidence for a connection between publicized violence and further violence, he comes to the conclusion that many kinds of aggresive events seem to be subject to contagious influences.

Berkowitz considers several extant theoretical attempts to explain the contagion of violence, including the concepts of modeling, imitation, and social facilitation. He then presents his own approach, which suggests that a classical conditioning model may be more appropriate than these other instrumental conditioning models. He is struck by the apparent "evoked" character of aggressive stimuli to situational stimuli. The remainder of the paper is a review of his own recent work and that of others which seems to support this S-R mediational paradigm as an explanation of the contagion of violence. In concluding, he emphasizes that his model may not fit all aggressive behavior, but it is particularly appropriate to what he calls impulsive aggression.

Maddi's paper has an intriguing title, "The Search For Meaning." This summarizes his view that the central problem in understanding human motivation is to understand how man searches for and finds meaning. Delving into literature and drama as well as psychology, Maddi creates a theory of personality that uses as its major motivational focus man's search for meaning. It fuses phenomenological and self-actualization themes in psychology with a heavy dose of existentialism. At the conclusion of his paper Maddi expresses some surprise at seeing himself theorizing on such a broad scope, but asserts his belief that some psychologists should engage in this type of activity. What he presents here is a tantalizing and provocative article which may prove to be the prolegomenon to his eventual *magnum opus*.

For Maddi, a complete theory of personality would describe both the structure and the dynamics of personality in terms of the core of personality, or that which is inherent in man's nature, and the periphery of personality, or that which is acquired through experience. It would link up these two levels of personality through a theory of development. Both ideal and nonideal peripheral personalities are functions of the core of personality and the developmental history.

Maddi starts off with a discussion of the psychopathologies of meaning, or *existential sicknesses*. These are vegetativeness, nihilism, and crusadism. In summary, they represent degrees of pathology (with the vegetative being the most profound) and are a result of a comprehensive failure in the search for meaning in life.

From here Maddi turns to the core of personality, which, for him, consists of biological, social, and psychological needs. He spends some time justifying his placement of social needs (involving needs for intimacy and love) on the core side of personality. Then he summarizes his view of man's psychological needs in terms of the urge to symbolize, to imagine, and to judge. Deviant development, particularly regarding psychological needs, results in a premorbid peripheral personality type which Maddi calls conformism. This type of individual is particularly vulnerable to existential sickness. The conformist defines himself as "nothing more than a player of social roles and an embodiment of biological needs." This kind of orientation does not lead to the vigorous search for meaning and individuality. In contrast to the conformist is the individualist, who is Maddi's ideal personality type. The individualist vigorously expresses not only his biological and social needs but his psychological need for meaning as well.

Maddi concludes by discussing his views on development, pointing to some research that is particularly congenial to his position on the nature of man; and finally by addressing himself to some current social concerns, such as black conformism and protest, white humanistic protests, and the hippie movement. In summary, Maddi's is a paper of extraordinary breadth and insight on the topic of a particularly human motivation. It should be of particular interest to those psychologists who are able to pull their noses out of the data occasionally and look at psychology in broad perspective.

Orne's paper represents his most complete statement to date on the social psychology of the psychological experiment. Combined with this is a discussion of the nature of hypnosis and of the hypnotic experiment. Orne thinks that it was no accident that his work in hypnosis led him to focus on the peculiar motivational factors in the psychological experiment itself. In this paper he discusses the problems he has encountered in attempting to work with hypnosis in an experimental setting. What he has to say is very instructive for those of us who work with less spectacular psychological phenomena in the laboratory.

Concerning hypnosis, Orne reviews the historical change that has occurred in the hypnotic phenomena and notes the elusiveness of stable behavior which would define the phenomena. Then he reviews his early and recent research and comes up with the conclusion that the position that he once supported, that hypnosis can be explained strictly in terms of motivation to please the hypnotist, is inadequate. Rather, hypnosis is an intrapsychic state that exists above and beyond the demand characteristics of the situation. The concept of demand characteristics should not be used to indiscriminately explain away all laboratory results, but as a means of purifying research by distinguishing between a psychological phenomenon and the episodic social psychological context of the laboratory situation in which it is studied.

Following the consideration of hypnosis, Orne launches a broader discussion of the psychological experiment and the motivation of the experimental subject. His basic point is that human subjects remain active interpreters of and participators in their environment when they come to the laboratory. They perceive the psychological experiment as episodic and disconnected from the rest of their lives, but they do not become passive responders to stimuli just because they are in an experiment. The fact that subjects do interpret and respond to the demand characteristics of the experimental situation must be taken into account in every interpretation of experimental data. The solution to the problem of demand characteristics is not the abandonment of the experimental method, but the refinement of the experimental method and perhaps the development of something analogous to "correction factors" for translation between laboratory and nonlaboratory behavior. A portion of this latter part of the paper is taken up with the topic of *quasi controls*, which are just such attempts at refining experimental methods.

In summary, Orne's paper is of broad perspective, but will be of particular interest to those concerned with motivation and hypnosis and with the motivation of human subjects in experiments. This latter group should include anyone who ever runs or reads an experimental study using human subjects.

We wish again to express our gratitude to the National Institute of Mental Health and to the University of Nebraska for supporting this series.

WILLIAM J. ARNOLD
Professor of Psychology

MONTE M. PAGE
Associate Professor of Psychology

Ecological Psychology: An Approach to Motivation[1]

JOHN A. KING

Michigan State University

Snow blown off knolls and hilltops by the steady prairie wind left patches of black, tilled soil in the surrounding whiteness. It was cold. The boy stumbled over corn stubble hidden by snow or he pushed through drifts in the depressions. His tracks left an erratic trail down the last slope. He soon discovered he was not alone in this wintry landscape. Trails festooned the snow with lacework. He bent down for a closer look.

"What in the devil is a mouse doing out here in this weather?"

Now that is a good question for a student of motivation. He might also inquire about the presence of the boy out there, or for that matter, about the soldiers in Viet Nam, or about the human concentrations in the inner city. The question of population dispersion is primarily ecological, just as the behavioral factors contributing to dispersion are primarily psychological. Ecological psychology, then, is the study of behavioral determinants affecting the distribution of animals (including man) in space and time. Spatial distribution provides a finite, measurable quantity of the relative numbers of animals at any instant in time. Repeated measures indicate the changes in the population through time (Barker, 1968). What must we know about the behavior of an

1. The original investigations reported here were supported by Research Grant 5 Rol Ey 0447 from the National Eye Institute, U.S. Public Health Service, while the author was on a Research Career Development Fellowship 2 K03 HD 3081 from the National Institute of Child Health and Human Development.

Acknowledgment is given to Martin Balaban and Lynwood C. Clemens for their criticisms of a previous draft of this paper.

1

individual, a group, or a species to predict its presence and abundance at any given time or place?

BEHAVIORAL FACTORS IN DISTRIBUTION

The distribution of animals is the end product of many interacting cause-effect systems, including behavioral systems. If the mechanisms of these numerous systems were known, we could predict when and where the next outbreak of the spruce-bud worm would take place, when the songbird population would be decimated by the application of insecticides, where eutrophic organisms would first appear as the lake became polluted, when highway traffic would become impeded in the urban centers, and at what point human populations would erupt in uncontrollable mass action. At first glance, the distribution of animals in space and time appears unexciting, but upon closer examination this concrete measure reveals one of the most fundamental attributes of animals. The numbers and kinds of animals an ecosystem contains are the final result of all the behavioral, physiological, and biochemical mechanisms of each species interacting with other individuals, species, and the physical universe. Since behavioral interactions compose the subsystem directly involved in the distribution of animals, psychologists have much to contribute to the study of distribution.

Because the physiological requirements of an animal species are fulfilled over a wider range of environments than those in which it actually occurs, the presence of an animal at any given time or place depends upon its perception of the environment. For example, a nocturnal mouse will not depart from its nest until it perceives a decrease in light intensity; a fly will not feed until it perceives the location of a suitable source of food; a bird will not sing until it is located on a perch within its territory. The perception of dusk for a mouse, of sugar for a fly, or a song perch for a bird is not determined by their sensory capacity to see a change in light intensity, to taste other materials, or to see other trees in the forest. Instead, animals exhibit a selective perception of their environment. This selectivity of the perceptual world is the principle measure of motivation for the ecological psychologist. When an animal is provided with the alternatives of going or not going, of going one place or another, of going now or later, the relative probabilities of its choice are the only measure of motivation needed to predict its temporal and spatial distribution. The behavioral study of distribution, then, is ultimately a study of perceptual selectivity exhibited by each individual, each group, and each species. What aspects of an animal's internal and external environment does it select in the process of locating itself in time and space?

Distribution can be studied, without understanding the mechanisms, by descriptive methods, which in the past have characterized much of ecology, including ecological psychology. A high degree of predictability is possible from these descriptive studies, enabling one to predict, for example, the presence of fox squirrels in an oak-hickory forest of the Midwest, the fluctuating changes in abundance of meadow voles in the grasslands, or the migration of songbirds in the spring. Mechanisms for distribution have been proposed and our agricultural productivity attests to the success of manipulating the mechanisms of fertilizers, water, and pests. Not all of our manipulations have proven successful, for example, predator control for increasing game animals; and some manipulations have affected unsuspected mechanisms, for example, pesticides endangering bird and fish populations. Indeed, on the whole, we know very little about the interacting systems controlling the distribution of animals, and perhaps the least understood mechanism involves that of behavior.

One primary aim of ecological psychology is to predict an organism's distribution as a result of manipulating its perceptual selectivity. By changing a mouse's food preferences from grass seeds to nuts, will it then inhabit the forest instead of the field? If the social preferences of an infant mouse can be altered by fostering it on a rat (Denenberg, this volume), will it select the proximity of rats over mice when positioning itself in new surroundings? Will meadow voles disperse over a wide region as a result of their perception of another vole changing from amiable to hostile? The manipulation of perceptual selectivity is, of course, only a means of identifying the significant features an animal selects to respond to in its varied environment. The ethologists have been able to discover the perceptual selectivity of many animals more directly by creating models of releasers or sign stimuli (Tinbergen, 1951). Of all the characteristics of a male stickleback fish that another male can respond to, it selects only the red underparts of its rival to attract it to the boundary of the territory. If we knew how an animal perceived its environment at any given time, its whereabouts would be readily known.

Although the localization of an organism in time and space may appear peripheral to the interests of a behaviorist, it can also indicate the behavior of the organism because feeding, drinking, resting, and other activities are often specific to a particular site. The correlation between site and activity is often so high that an experienced ecological psychologist can direct a person to a particular site in order to observe an animal exhibiting a given pattern of behavior. Behavior is only slightly less *site specific* than *situation specific*. It is possible, however, for an animal to perform several different activities at a given site. The measurable qualities of animal distribution can also serve as a fairly reliable predictor of the type of behavior. Thus, a secondary aim of ecological psychology, in addition to predicting the distribution of animals, is that of predicting what the animals are doing at a particular location.

Temporal units or sequences are critical tools for the ecological psychologists, as shown in the popular textbook by Marler and Hamilton (1966) and the increased interest in periodicity among psychologists (Bolles, 1968; Draper, 1967). For example, the investigator may be concerned with the relative abundance of deer during the next decade of reforestation or with the spatial distribution of age and sex classes of baboons as they progress toward the riparian forests, the temporal units being years or seconds. Similarly, temporal sequences from day to night, summer to winter, will reveal distinctive patterns of distribution for each animal species. I hardly expect a robin to go hopping across my snow-covered lawn in search of earthworms today.

In many respects, temporal units are more readily defined than spatial units; or to put it another way, it is easier to locate an animal in time than in space. If a ground squirrel escapes into one burrow, it is just a matter of time before it will reappear, but a predator would be wasting its time waiting for the squirrel to appear at just any burrow entrance. In the laboratory, we carefully confine

our experimental subjects to their cages or test apparatus, and in
the field we elaborately devise biotelemetry to locate free-ranging
animals (Adams, 1965). Finding a single animal is relatively simple
in comparison to censusing an entire population. Each species
presents special types of problems for its enumeration and ecologists
have developed many different techniques for sampling and
censusing populations (Southwood, 1966). But even with a photo-
graphic record of the distribution of each animal at a given moment,
quantitative descriptions provide further problems. Again ecologists have been at work devising methods of measurement and
mathematically describing the distributions (Lloyd, 1967; Rosenzweig & Winakur, 1969). Despite the limitations of current methods,
the distribution of animals provides a reliable and meaningful
dependent variable for the ecological psychologists.

Comparative Methods

The motivation or perceptual selectivity (these terms are used
synonymously here) that brings adult human beings to the commut-
er train in the morning and later accumulates large numbers of
them in the central city can also be examined in other animals.
Ecological psychology, in fact, is primarily comparative. The
similarities and differences in perceptual selectivity among individuals, groups, geographic races, and species are the basis for their
spatial and temporal distribution. Unlike individuals of the same
species, which often have similar distributions, closely related species
usually have different distributions, which are perceptually distinguishable. For example, a marsh wren's restriction to marsh vegeta-
tion presumably results from its selection of cattails and rushes,
whereas a house wren's distribution is affected by its perception of
orchards and gardens. These habitat differences between species
may be more recognizable than the differences between the specific
nesting sites in cherry or apple trees of individual wrens. Species
comparisons can not only reveal the perceptual variables responsible
for their different distributional patterns, but they can also reveal
how each species selects those perceptual variables.

The goal of the comparative method in ecological psychology is to answer how behavior contributes to the dispersion of animals within their geographic range. This question applies to relative abundance of a species as well as to its presence or absence. Among the many alternative ways of maintaining itself, each species exhibits a different behavioral pattern which gives it a selective advantage over other contending species for the position it occupies. In many species, these alternatives are a matter of choice or preference variously constrained by its ontogeny and phylogeny. In a comparison of several closely related species, the functions of behavior stand out in sharp relief, revealing the limits of generalizations and illuminating the possible mechanisms.

The basis of the comparative method resides in the nature of the comparative material. Comparisons are made among groups of animals with varying degrees of genetic differences. Three broad levels of genetic differences can be used to illustrate the techniques and goals appropriate at each level: (1) *genetic*, (2) *specific*, and (3) *phyletic*.

At the *genetic* level, comparisons are made between experimental subjects, which may differ in only one gene or in several genes as long as these differences do not prevent interfertility. Differences among siblings, litters, families, lines, strains, breeds, races, and subspecies provide the material for most genetic comparisons. Interfertility among the subjects enables hybridization and other genetic manipulations. The chief purpose of comparisons at this level is to understand the genetic mechanisms and the action of the genes upon particular behavior patterns (Bruell, 1967; Broadhurst, 1967; Scott & Fuller, 1965; Wilcock, 1969; Ginsberg, 1967). This is the area of behavior genetics and relatively few studies in ecological psychology have used these techniques (Kettlewell, 1965; Anderson, 1964; Rothenbuhler, 1967).

Species level comparisons overlap with the genetic and phyletic levels, but concentrate on differences within a genus, or those among closely related genera. Interfertility is unusual and two or more similar species may occupy the same area without losing their species integrity by interbreeding. Closely related species often exhibit behavioral differences whose continuity from one species to another can reveal the course of evolutionary modifications (Eisenberg, 1963). Departures in interspecific sequences of behavior suggest recent genetic changes in response to particular types of habitats occupied by related species (Winn, 1958). Since this level provides the principal material for ecological psychology, it will be discussed later.

Phyletic level comparisons are among genera, families, orders, classes, and phyla. Comparisons at this level are of limited scientific value because the groups often differ in too many respects to isolate the significant variable contributing to behavioral differences. Occasionally these comparisons can implicate a significant morphological or physiological variable which differs too subtly at lower levels to be discerned (Bitterman, 1965), but few procedures can carry the implication further (Hodos & Campbell, 1969). It is the dead end which too often characterizes comparative psychology. Among some animal phyla or classes, a judicious selection of orders or families can lead to further comparative refinements because the phylum or class is particularly large and diverse.

Comparisons at any of these levels can suggest the variable responsible for a given behavior and further comparisons with other taxa can strengthen the correlation. Although significant correlations are respectable, experimental manipulations of the suspected dependent variable are more desirable. All the experimental tools of the behavioral sciences are at the disposal of the ecological psychologist, but he fully exploits the comparative method until he can manipulate the genetic variables. Genetic factors related to the behavior of populations are being discovered (Tamarin & Krebs, 1969), but their discovery is not equivalent to their manipulation. One advantage of genetic manipulation is that it provides subjects which reproduce themselves without experimental intervention at each generation. It is not necessary to handle each subject in order to implant electrodes, to inject them, or to train them. If the character breeds true, all subjects or a predicted ratio of the subjects will exhibit the character. If the genotype of the subjects is in doubt, it can sometimes be verified at the termination of the experiment by karyotype examinations, by serum protein analysis, or by laboratory breeding, which are analogous to locating electrode sites by histological examination.

The techniques of genetic manipulation are familiar enough to permit only mentioning them here. Basic to all techniques is the selection of suitable genetic material. The importance of this selection cannot be overemphasized, whether it be among several species, breeds, inbred lines, or even single genes. The investigator, who carefully selects his apparatus, his experimental design, and his treatment procedures, too often blindly grabs his subjects from the bag of genetic differences (McClearn, 1967; Lockard, 1968). The technique of hybridization between different genotypes enables typical Mendelian crosses or diallele crosses, in which several lines are hybridized among themselves. Genetic selection for a given trait is another technique, although many generations of selection may be required to fix a trait. Selection experiments are long term in most vertebrates and the value of the results must be weighed in terms of the time invested. The same is true for inbreeding, which is not a particularly valuable technique for genetic manipulation, although inbred lines provide isogenic stocks suitable for further studies.

After this extended introduction on the characteristics of ecological psychology and the comparative method, let us now turn to the material that generated it. A complete story of how species differences in perceptual selectivity affect species distribution cannot be related because it has been only recently that we began to look for these factors in distribution. Many of the investigations reported below are directed at related problems, which have helped to organize and clarify the aims of ecological psychology.

A GENUS OF RODENT

The subjects of this inquiry into ecological preferences are mice of the genus *Peromyscus*, or deermice. The genus is distributed throughout North and Central America over a variety of habitats. It contains about 57 species, many of which are polytypic with a total of approximately 235 subspecies (Hall & Kelson, 1959). Seven subgenera of varying magnitude are recognized (Hooper, 1968). The type subgenus *Peromyscus* contains seven groups of species, within which species resemble each other more than species of other groups. Species within a species group are also interfertile. Phylogenetically, the genus provides a wide array of divergent forms from local populations, through subspecies, species, species groups, and subgenera. Despite these systematic differences, all members of the genus are recognizable as *Peromyscus*, like all members of *Canis* are recognizable as dogs. The genus provides a rich diversity of comparative material at the genetic and species levels.

One polytypic species, *maniculatus*, is distributed throughout North America, whereas other species, *sejugis* and *guardia*, have geographical ranges limited to a single island. Many species have overlapping ranges and in a few localities as many as five different species occur together. The greatest number of species inhabit Mexico, with decreasing numbers of species occurring northeastward, until only one or two species occur in Maine. Most species live in forests, brush, or rocks, but some species occupy grasslands, beaches, and deserts. Indeed, few places on the continent fail to provide suitable dwelling places for members of this genus, which are often the most abundant small mammal (Baker, 1968). The wide diversity of habitats and species enables an investigator to explore the significant ecological variables contributing to the behavior of each species.

Eyes of Peromyscus

Early in our investigation of this genus, we noted two features of this genus that have concentrated our subsequent efforts on vision: (1) differences in the age of eyelid separation and (2) differences in eye size. One subspecies of *Peromyscus maniculatus* first opened its eyes at approximately 12 days of age (*bairdi*) and another subspecies at 16 days of age (*gracilis*). A genetic difference of this magnitude at the age of eye opening in these closely related subspecies suggested that some selection pressure was differentially affecting the development of these mice. We continued to examine the age of eye opening over a broader spectrum of species (Table 1) and most species opened their eyes within the age range of these two subspecies (Layne, 1968). Regardless of phylogenetic relationship, habitat, body size, or any other variable, the difference between these two subspecies was almost as extreme as that within the entire genus. Age of eye opening also corresponded to other developmental characteristics with *bairdi* generally maturing more rapidly than *gracilis*. Since *bairdi* inhabits the grassland and *gracilis*

TABLE 1

MEAN AGE OF EYE OPENING (DAYS) IN PEROMYSCUS

Species	N	Mean + S.E.
P. maniculatus bairdi	138	13.0 ± 0.1
P. maniculatus gracilis	70	16.1 ± 0.1
P. maniculatus nebrascensis	44	13.1 ± 0.9
P. maniculatus labicula	31	13.9 ± 0.7
P. polionotus	104	13.5 ± 0.1
P. leucopus	279	12.5 ± 0.1
P. crinitus	57	12.3 ± 0.2
P. eremicus	24	11.7 ± 0.3
P. californicus	178	14.7 ± 0.1
P. floridanus	84	14.2 ± 0.4

the forests, it is possible that rate of development is under different selection pressures in these habitats, which could be explored by examining additional forest and grassland representatives of this species. Such comparisons might help locate the significant variable, contributing to the evolution of maturation rates, but an experimental test of that variable might prove difficult.

We decided to take a different tack: What is the genetic variation in age of eye opening and to what extent is eye opening correlated with other developmental characteristics? Answers to these questions would reveal how amenable eye opening was to selection and how well the age of eye opening served as an index for general maturation. Early and late eye opening lines were established in both *bairdi* and *gracilis* and changes in this character were noted over generations—now in the eleventh generation. Ten families were used in each line and at each generation the offspring were outbred to a different family in order to reduce inbreeding and maintain genetic variance. *P. m. gracilis* breed capriciously in the laboratory and this subspecies was discontinued after the seventh generation. Similarly, breeding had fallen off drastically in the late *bairdi* line by the ninth generation and selection was relaxed.

The results have not been completely analyzed, but it appears that both subspecies gave an asymmetrical response to selection (Figure 1). The late eye opening subspecies (*gracilis*) could be retarded in age of eye opening more than it could be accelerated. *P. m. bairdi*, which opened its eyes early, responded more readily

EYE OPENING

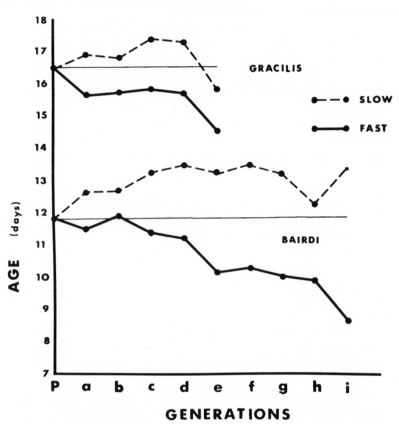

FIG. 1. Age of eye opening response (ordinate) to selection in *P. maniculatus bairdi* and *P. m. gracilis* for fast (early) and slow (late) eye opening over several generations.

to early eye opening selection than to late eye opening selection. Each subspecies contained sufficient genetic variation to respond in the direction natural selection had already operated. Apparently they were preadapted for further selection in the same direction. Whatever the selective force was in nature, it could have produced the subspecies differences rapidly and could continue to do so readily, if the environmental circumstances made further divergence advantageous.

Since early eye opening was associated with a generally accelerated development, we expected to find that the early lines would be more mature than the late lines in their overall development at the same chronological age. Eye opening age could be just one expression of some growth promoting factor: maternal nutrition, thyroid activity, growth hormone, etc. Although we have not studied other aspects of development systematically, it soon became obvious that eye opening was not closely associated with other maturational features. The early eye opening lines were still quite immature in other developmental features; they were infants with their eyes open. The late lines were young adults with their eyelids sealed. Reduced breeding success in the late *bairdi* line suggested that retarded eye opening is related to some biological character which reduced fertility. These lines have not yet been hybridized or cross fostered. The selection did produce experimental subjects within a subspecies exhibiting the same differences that previously occurred between subspecies. Thus, if age of eye opening contributed to some of the behavioral differences between these two subspecies, the variable can now be tested, since the other differences between subspecies are no longer present within a single subspecies. The two selection lines within a subspecies may still differ in some respects other than age of eye opening, but certainly not in all the characters that differentiate *bairdi* from *gracilis*.

Before proceeding to the subject of vision and motivation, let me return to the other distinctive feature of the eyes in these two subspecies: eye size. The entire genus is distinguishable from most other North American mice because of its conspicuously large eyes. The size of the eye itself reveals little about vision except that vision is essential to the organism, that large eyes are effective light-gathering instruments, and that they may provide better resolution than small eyes. What possible function could vision have among the various species to account for the great discrepancy in eye size?

Table 2 illustrates the magnitude of the difference in both absolute and relative eye size among several representative species of the genus. The weight of the crystalline lens is used because it is a discrete morphological organ which can be weighed reliably. In

TABLE 2

MEAN AND STANDARD ERRORS OF BODY AND LENS WEIGHTS IN
PEROMYSCUS

Species	N	Body (gm)	Lens (mg)	$\dfrac{\text{Lens (mg)}}{\text{Body (gm)}} \times 100$
P. maniculatus bairdi	82	18.8 ± 0.3	18.2 ± 0.3	0.97
P. maniculatus gracilis	120	24.0 ± 0.3	26.5 ± 0.2	1.10
P. maniculatus nebrascensis	13	19.1 ± 0.7	18.4 ± 0.8	0.98
P. maniculatus labicula	21	24.6 ± 1.2	27.8 ± 1.1	1.16
P. polionotus	28	13.4 ± 0.3	21.8 ± 0.4	1.63
P. leucopus	26	21.3 ± 1.0	27.2 ± 0.7	1.28
P. eremicus	20	20.0 ± 0.9	17.4 ± 0.3	0.87
P. californicus	22	53.1 ± 1.9	29.4 ± 0.6	0.56
P. floridanus	26	37.8 ± 1.5	46.9 ± 1.2	1.24

comparison to the lens of the house mouse (*Mus*), even the smallest *Peromyscus* lens is twice the weight of those of *Mus*. The weights range from 17.4 mg. to 46.9 mg., but some of these differences correspond to the body weight of the species (King, 1965). Relative lens weight eliminates body weight differences, but it introduces another source of error because body weight is subject to distortions often caused by fat accumulation. Although the smallest species, *P. polionotus*, has relatively large eyes and the largest species, *P. californicus*, has relatively small eyes, that is where this relationship ends (Table 2). For example, *P. leucopus*, which has approximately the same body weight as *P. eremicus*, has lenses which are 36% heavier. *P. leucopus* has a relative lens weight comparable to *P. floridanus*, which is 43% heavier in body weight. Even within the single species *maniculatus*, relative lens weights vary from 0.97 mg. to 1.16 mg., which suggests that ecological variables are more responsible than phylogenetic variables.

VISION

As far as vision is concerned, minor differences in lens weights are probably negligible. The differences do, however, suggest that those features of vision associated with eye size (light gathering and resolution) have been selected independently among the various species of *Peromyscus*. Visual acuity or resolution is one visual parameter associated with eye size that may relate these morphological differences to behavior. Systematic studies of visual acuity among closely related mammals have not been done. At most, we have a scattered array of recorded acuity from the entire class, which allows only a phyletic level of comparison (Lit, 1968; Rahmann, 1967).

Our first studies of visual acuity involved discrimination of minimum separable grid lines with a modified Grice box (Rahmann, Rahmann, & King, 1968). The mice could go through one door with a visual grid of varying densities to the goal, but the other door with an equivalent intensity of overall gray was locked. Five species and subspecies were examined and visual angles ranged from 33′ to 1° 34′, which is a greater difference than has been found throughout all rodents previously tested. This variation in visual acuity among the species tested could not be predicted from eye size, body weight, phylogenetic relationships, or habitat occupied. Does the capacity to resolve visual objects in the environment vary spuriously among these taxa of mice? We are left with this conclusion unless the methods involved in measuring acuity discriminations here were not suitable. Motivation, learning, reaction to the test apparatus, attention to the stimuli, and many other factors affecting discrimination introduce sources of error, even if relative values among species are as acceptable as absolute values. Another technique for visual acuity measures was clearly implicated.

The optokinetic response removes such variables as learning and motivation, while introducing others, such as motion and the problem of the experimenter detecting the optokinetic response. The detection problem could not be solved by electrically recording the oculogram because the electrodes inserted in the eyes of the mice caused them to close their eyelids. The best results were obtained by visually observing the slow rotation of the head and nystagmus of the eyes of a restrained mouse. Our first study of the optokinetic response was related to the age of the eyelid separation (Vestal & King, 1968).

We examined six different genetic stocks of *Peromyscus* including the selection lines, subspecies, species group, and subgeneric comparisons. With one exception, all stocks exhibited an excellent optokinetic response to a revolving striped drum with a visual angle of nine degrees on the same day they first opened their eyes. The onset of vision was perfectly correlated with the separation of the eyelids, unless the capacity to see the revolving drum developed before eyelid separation. If the mice could see prior to the separation of their eyelids, then the early eye opening selected line of *P. maniculatus bairdi* should respond at eye opening. This would mean either that vision developed prior to this age or that selection for early eye opening had also affected the development of vision simultaneously. The early eye opening mice did not exhibit an optokinetic response at the age of eye opening, but did respond approximately 2 to 3 days later when the control stocks responded. These results indicated that the onset of vision was synchronized with eye opening except in our selection line, which affected eyelid separation without affecting vision.

Our comparative studies of visual acuity at present have pushed the resolving power of these mice beyond what we discovered previously by the discrimination technique and to the limits of our test apparatus. The smallest stripes we could readily make produced a visual angle of 14′ at 40 cm. distance. All species we have examined can resolve this angle as indicated by their optokinetic response. A visual angle of 14′ is below those angles previously reported for all rodents and below most mammals except the primates and ungulates (Rahmann, 1967). Furthermore, this level of resolution is attained within 6 days after the eyelids separate (Vestal, 1970). We are currently attempting to use the minimum visible measure of acuity in the optokinetic drum. If this technique will work, we will certainly reach the limits of the mouse's resolving power.

This digression into vision and the eye has simply indicated that the large eyes of *Peromyscus* are suitable visual receptors for something in their environment apparently worth seeing. In a small, nocturnal rodent, we still do not know what it is that makes vision so worthwhile to them. Obviously vision can assist the mice in many different ways, but differences among the species in vision may lead to its function. Let us propose some functions of vision.

Orientation

The mice are small and they inhabit a large area, often up to and exceeding an acre. In this home range, the mice locate food, nests, and refuges. Mice released from traps in their home range appear to be oriented and find refuge immediately in contrast to mice released in strange surroundings. Their tracks on the snow further indicate that they appear to know where they are going, even when the kinesthetic, tactile, and olfactory cues may be eliminated by the snow. The importance of vision in the laboratory rats' maze performance (Honzik, 1936) and track following (Sisemore & Wilcoxon, 1969) is well documented. If visual cues are used to any extent, they must vary among species inhabiting the deserts of Arizona, the cornfields of Nebraska, the chaparral of California, and the deciduous forest of the eastern states. The moon has been implicated as a visual cue in the orientation of these mice, but the test circumstances equally suggest other celestial objects or some terrestrial cues (Kavanau, 1968). In our laboratory, James Joslin is currently investigating the relative use of various visual cues in the orientation of two species.

Locomotion

Associated with orientation, vision could be used by the mice to avoid obstructions, to follow paths, and to climb on trees or rocks. Semiarboreal species, for example, may require better vision to see the limbs of trees they use for a path than a terrestrial species, which could guide itself through narrow runways with its vibrissae. The visual acuity of one semiarboreal species (*P. m. gracilis*) correlated well with that needed to resolve visually a stick of a given diameter, to which the mouse leaped. The mouse refused to leap at distances which reduced the visual angle below its resolving power. Visual cliff studies would be particularly valuable across several species of *Peromyscus* (Walk, 1965).

Habitat Selection

Many regions inhabited by *Peromyscus* have a variegated pattern of heterogeneous habitats, which are occupied or avoided by different species. Mice moving outside of the home range, usually during dispersal, presumably select those habitats most suitable to their way of life. The cues responsible for this selection appear to be predominantly visual (Wecker, personal communication), although similar selection can be achieved in total darkness (Harris, 1952). Perhaps specific visual cues direct the mice to the areas where they can best find food and shelter, such as the lower light intensities reaching the floor of a forest in contrast to those in an open field.

Periodicity

The entire genus is predominantly nocturnal (Falls, 1968), but species may vary in their adherence to daily light schedules. Some species may be crepuscular, whereas other species may restrain their activity on moonlit nights. One might predict, for example, that a nocturnal desert species would become aperiodic under constant dim lights because nocturnal light intensities are brighter in the desert than in other habitats. Perhaps periodicities also change when the mice are exposed to long periods of snow, which increases light intensity by reflection. Good eyesight is not necessary to detect light intensity changes, but each species may be differentially affected by these changes.

Predator Detection

Peromyscus is an important prey species to most predators and each species has a large number of different enemies to escape. Species with predominantly aerial predators might have different visual propensities from those with predominantly terrestrial predators. The large, protruding eyes located high on the head suggest that the wide visual field overhead is a source of important visual cues, such as those provided by an owl making its predatory strike. The function of vision in predator detection is difficult to study, but the selective advantage of an early warning system could account for visual differences among species.

Social Behavior

Although olfaction is predominantly used in many social functions (Whitten, 1966), the nature of the olfactory signal has severe communicatory limitations. In contrast, the sight of another mouse can locate it precisely in time and space, although identity may not be established until it is smelled. James Hill, who has been studying social behavior in our laboratory, has seen one mouse direct its attention to another mouse when it enters the visual field 6 feet away. Once identification is made, probably through olfaction, visually directed pursuit often ensues and a subordinate animal can successfully hide behind some obstruction until it is seen again. Vision may also be important in the sexual pursuit of an olfactory-identified receptive female. Again, species inhabiting areas of unobstructed vision might be more visually oriented toward conspecifics than those species inhabiting grasslands or scrub forests.

The ratio of speculation to fact has been high in the preceding paragraphs in order to illustrate how little we know about the function of vision in the ecology of these small rodents. Indeed, the function of sensory modalities in most mammals has speculation to fact ratios of similar magnitudes. One may conclude that either the problems of function are not worth solving or that we have no techniques for doing so, that is, they are irresolvable. My position is that the problems of function are important and we do have some of the techniques for resolving them. Our concern with mechanisms has often been the easy way out. We know more about the physiology of vision than what vision is used for, or how it is used. We have even been misled in our study of mechanisms because we failed to recognize their function. Once the frog's eye was recognized as a fly-detector, its physiology became clear (Lettvin, Maturana, McCulloch, & Pitts, 1968). The comparative technique is a powerful tool in discerning function and the study of genetic differences in motivation as revealed by stimulus preference is a valuable way of using this tool. The following study illustrates an initial approach to the problem of visual function by comparing species of *Peromyscus* in their response to light reinforcement.

Light Reinforcement

Light detection is a simple visual function. A single photoreceptive cell is sufficient and the eyes of all species of *Peromyscus* can detect light above the skotoptic threshold (Moody, 1929). If light has any function in the life of a mouse, it certainly does not depend on its sensory ability to perceive it. Also, if light served any function in the life of a mouse, it should use the light when given an opportunity to do so. Light reinforcement is consistent with a mouse selecting appropriate visual cues to orient itself, to locate a suitable habitat, or to become active or inactive at a given light intensity, etc. Animals can be expected to prefer those features of the environment which provide them the greatest selective advantage. Of course, they can be tricked or forced into nonadaptive choices, but under most circumstances animals do those things that will keep them alive. Thus, a mouse should select light over darkness, if light serves any function, or if it acts as a token stimulus to any function. Light becomes a reinforcer, capable of increasing the probability of a light-contingent act.

Many experiments have shown that light acts as a reinforcer and many explanations for its reinforcing properties have been proposed: stimulus change (McCall, 1966), light preference (Lockard, 1968), arousal (Berlyne, 1967), and environmental control (Kavanau, 1967). Any one or all of these interpretations may be correct, but none suggests that light may be used by the rat or mouse to see or to govern its periodicity. We ask simply, What function does light provide for the animal? The animal may select light over darkness because it provides some input to the central nervous system, but this interpretation soon brings us to the neurophysiological mechanisms, which are interesting, but have their own types of problems. If light does have a function, its function may differ among several species. In one species, light may enable the mouse to see the limbs of the trees; in another, it may indicate its exposure to a predator; and in a third, it may entrain its periodicity. Species should differ in the amount of light reinforcement exhibited according to its function in each species.

If light has a different function among several species of *Peromyscus*, we can test the hypothesis that species will differ in their frequency of light-contingent responses (King, 1970). Four taxa were examined: *P. m. bairdi*, *P. m. gracilis*, *P. polionotus*, and *P. eremicus*. They represent populations of varying phylogenetic relationships: subspecies in the same species, species in the same group, and species in different subgenera. They also represent species that occupy forests, grasslands, sand-pine openings, and deserts. Six mice from each taxon were tested. All mice were born in the laboratory in total darkness, where they were raised until tested at 65–75 days of age.

Initially we had some difficulty finding a suitable operant because the species varied considerably in the levels of bar pressing, panel pushing, hole poking, and screen climbing. We finally found a suitable operant in licking for water, which all groups performed easily, at about the same frequency, and usually when thirsty. They did not lick, for example, when attempting to escape or when leaping about the cage. The association between drinking and light may tend to confound these two reinforcers, but the association could also reveal a unique function of light. Every time a mouse drank, a light went on for a period of 30 seconds and then automatically turned off. A mouse could drink during the 30 seconds without affecting the light. The mice were left in the test apparatus throughout the entire test period of 24 days, during which time the light intensity was changed from no light to 0.4 ft. candle.

Figure 2 illustrates the results as well as the schedule of light intensity changes. If 100 represents the baseline, then values larger than 100 indicate light reinforcement, and values less than 100 suggest light aversion. *P. polionotus* exhibited no evidence of light reinforcement. *P. m. gracilis* was slightly reinforced by light. *P. eremicus* repeatedly turned the light on. The relationship of *P. m. bairdi* to light was questionable. *P. eremicus* accounted for 96.8% of the variance among species.

After the experiment we continued to test *P. eremicus* on even dimmer lights (0.004 ft. c.) and by offering it alternative sources of water, and even draining the water from the light-contingent tube. Every test indicated that *P. eremicus* was reinforced by the light. This species belongs to a different subgenus (*Haplomylomys*) than the other three taxa and it also inhabits the deserts of the southwestern states. Its level of light reinforcement could correspond to its phylogenetic remoteness from the other species or to its desert environment. The only close relative of *P. eremicus* we had in the laboratory was *P. californicus*, which is so large that it could reach the water without activating the drinkometer. Phylogenetic relationship could not be readily tested and we have learned from previous studies that these relationships within a genus are not reliable predic-

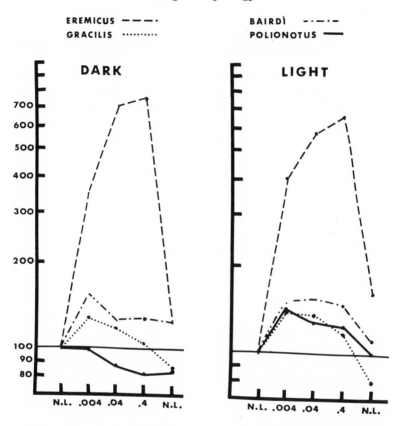

EREMICUS — — —·   BAIRDÌ – · — · –
GRACILIS ··········   POLIONOTUS ▬▬

DARK

LIGHT

700
600
500
400
300
200
100
90
80

N.L. .004 .04 .4 N.L.

N.L. .004 .04 .4 N.L.

FIG. 2. Ratio (ordinate in logs) of the number of 30 sec. light-on periods during the first no light (N.L.) regime to the number of periods with 0.004, 0.04, 0.4 ft. candle and the last N.L. regime in four taxa of *Peromyscus*. Mice raised in total darkness are on the left and those raised with 0.4 ft. candle are on the right.

tors of behavior. Instead, we examined a remote species, *P. crinitus*, which is sympatric with *P. eremicus* and inhabits the same desert regions. If light has a function in desert habitats that it does not have in grasslands or forests, the other desert species should also be reinforced by light. *P. crinitus* was not reinforced by light.

This blow to our hypothesis makes the problem more intriguing. Since the light conditions for both species are similar in the desert, each species must use the light in a different way. We have no firm convictions on how the species differ in this respect, but we do know that sympatric species can compete for the same resources (Sheppe, 1967). Often competition is avoided among similar species by using different parts of the day, that is, they have different diel periodicities. Perhaps *P. eremicus* is more diurnal or crepuscular than *P. crinitus* and light governs its period of activity.

We incidentally collected the periodic activity of *P. eremicus*, but unfortunately did not for *P. crinitus*. This story is only half complete, like the test of another species closely related to *P. eremicus* which will be done now that we have such species in the laboratory. Periodic drinking behavior of *P. eremicus*, during constant darkness prior to the light contingency, exhibited the typical circadian shift of a nocturnal animal in darkness. Its subjective day was a little less than 24 hours long. Shortly after light became reinforcing at about 10 days, the mice began to lengthen their day, thus bringing about a circadian shift associated with a nocturnal animal in constant light (Figure 3). Here, then, was a nocturnal species which not only was reinforced by a dim light, but it also acted as if it was under constant light when it could turn the light on for 30 second periods. None of the other species had such a consistent pattern, although the behavior of some individuals of *P. m. gracilis* (Figure 4) supported the hypothesis that mice reinforced by light will optionally shape their periodicities to a day length longer than 24 hours. This is equivalent to saying that given control over the light cycle, one would lengthen a day beyond 24 hours, but in the absence of this control, one would shorten the day length. Whereas this appears to hold consistently for *P. eremicus*, it is only suggested in some individuals of other species. Circadian periodicities are often quite variable (Aschoff, 1965), particularly in the absence of light reinforcement (Figures 5 and 6).

Another feature of the periodic activity of *P. eremicus* was the amount of drinking activity exhibited during its subjective day. The only other taxon of the four examined that regularly approached this level of aperiodicity was *P. m. gracilis* (Figure 4). This trend of *P. eremicus* toward aperiodicity in addition to its circadian shift with light contingency suggests that its divergence from *P. crinitus* in light reinforcement may enable these sympatric species

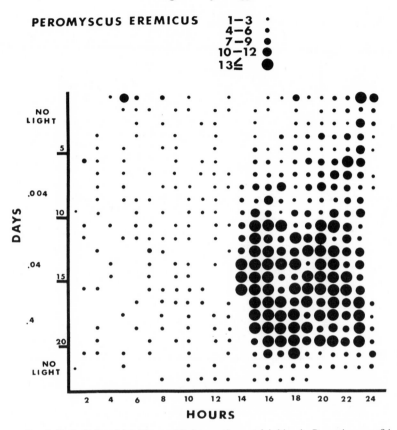

PEROMYSCUS EREMICUS

1–3 ·
4–6 •
7–9 ●
10–12 ●
13≤ ●

FIG. 3. Periodicity of drinking and light-contingent drinking in *P. eremicus* over 24 hours throughout 23 days under various light regimes: no light, 0.004, 0.04, and 0.4 ft. candles. The number of 30 sec. periods of light-on are indicated by the size of the dot.

to avoid competition by either using different parts of the day or different microhabitats of varying light intensity in the desert.

I have purposefully emphasized the comparative aspects of this experiment, but another purpose was to determine the effect of an early light treatment on the light-contingent response of these four taxa. The early treatment consisted of raising mice of the four taxa in a dim light (0.4 ft. candle) from birth to weaning and then

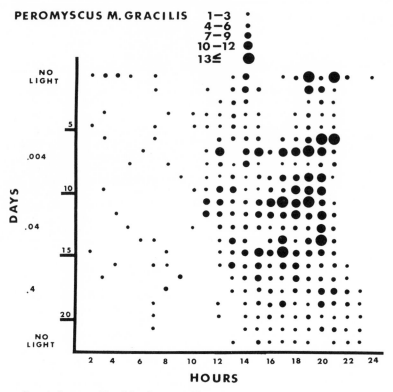

Fig. 4. Same as Fig. 3 for *P. m. gracilis*.

keeping them in darkness until tested at 65 days of age. The effect of this treatment was obscured because *P. eremicus* again contributed so much to the variance that small, but perceptible, differences in the treatment were not significant for the other species (Figure 2). The only significant effect of early light treatment was found in *P. polionotus*, which exhibited no evidence of light reinforcement when raised in darkness, but did show some reinforcement when raised in light. Since the results of this treatment are statistically tenuous, further discussion is not warranted. We did conclude, however, that this short and mild encounter with light early in life has little effect on light reinforcement relative to that of the species differences. The experiment also encouraged us to under-

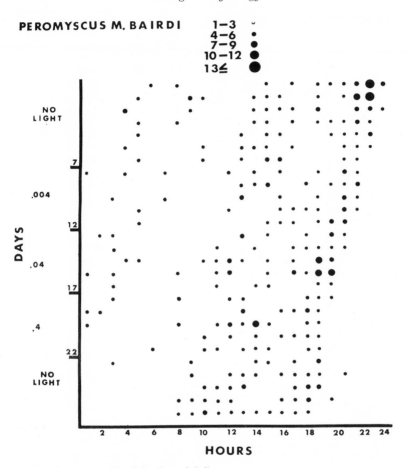

FIG. 5. Same as Fig. 3 for *P. m. bairdi*.

take our current study, which tests the effect of maternally sched-
uled light in the fast and slow eye opening lines of *P. m. bairdi*.
We are asking if maternal control of the light environment will
affect her offsprings' adult response to light. In addition, we are
asking if this experience is affected by the age of eye opening. The
experiment is a "long shot" and the current results suggest that
both questions can be answered negatively.

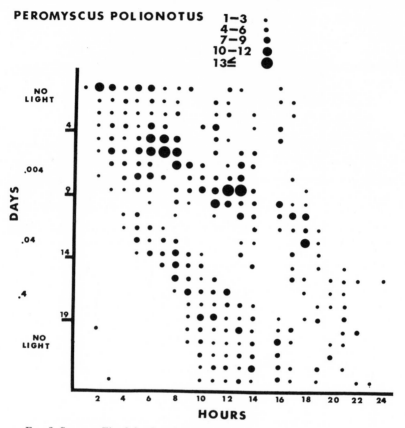

FIG. 6. Same as Fig. 3 for *P. polionotus*.

MOTIVATION AND SELECTION

If an animal selects among several alternative paths of action, and if this selection is not limited by its capacity to perceive or to respond, the animal exhibiting the selection is motivated in the direction of its preference. This substitution of selection (or preference) for motivation may not be applicable to motivation in a fly nor to an animal on the brink of starvation or dehydration, but it does render motivation amenable to study by providing alternative stimuli or responses. Basically this is the "go–no go" situation of many investigations, such as the light–no light experiments reported above. Animals selecting the "no go" alternative do not contribute much to our understanding of motivation (they may not perceive the "go" alternative). Consequently, we often attempt to offer them equally tenable alternatives, such as sucrose concentrations. Any selection among alternatives, however, is a measure of motivation.

Comparative studies of different species of mice within the genus *Peromyscus*, which have been offered alternatives in foods, odors, locations, social relationships, types of activities (digging, gnawing, climbing), lights, sounds, visual patterns, etc. have revealed one basic characteristic of motivation: species, subspecies, local populations, and individuals differ in their motivation. These differences may be disconcerting to an investigator interested in a unifying explanation of motivation, but diversity itself is a unifying concept. The alternative courses of action available to an animal in a heterogeneous and variable environment approach infinity and various types of animals at different periods in their life cycle are motivated to use those alternatives selectively. The motivations of different types of animals do not approach infinity, which means further species diversification is possible, such as that occurring in the tropics (Klopfer, 1969). What kind of selection pressures could bring about a type of mouse that is motivated to hop instead of bound, to construct exposed nests instead of those in crevices and holes, to be diurnal instead of nocturnal, or to turn lights on in darkness?

At the present, we are concerned with the last question: What can motivate a species to turn lights on in darkness? The four taxa of *Peromyscus* differ in their motivation for light from almost none in *P. polionotus* to *P. eremicus*, which turned on the light almost ten times more frequently than the next highest species (*P. m. gracilis*). By raising the mice in a dim light for a few days, we can significantly shift the motivation of one species (*P. polionotus*) for light and apparently increase the motivation of other species. But can we ever make *P. polionotus* perform like *P. eremicus* or vice versa? Substituting the motivation of water for that of light by making water contingent upon light would defeat the purpose of changing motivational levels for light. Different amounts of light at different periods in development might increase the motivation somewhat, but probably not to the extent shown by *P. eremicus*. Perhaps we could find a light intensity and a duration that would motivate the mice to increase the number of light-contingent responses. Again, I doubt if any combination of intensity and duration will bring about the magnitude of change we seek, unless light could be used to govern the periodicity of the mice. Although complete parametric studies of the early exposure to light of various light intensities and durations might alter the frequency of light-contingent responses to a certain extent, this type of approach would probably not contribute significantly to our understanding of the motivation *P. eremicus* exhibits for light.

A more promising approach might be an analysis of visual patterns made possible by the light. Perhaps the mice turn on the light in an effort to see their environment. If so, particular patterns made visible by the light should increase the number of responses. We tentatively found that light-on responses increased when another mouse in an adjoining cage became visible. Responses might also increase if the mouse had an opportunity to see critical features of its habitat (whatever they may be). Also, if light was used for locomotion or orientation, a more complex environment than the present test cages may increase the number of light-contingent responses.

The comparative approach is also amenable to this problem. Our first attempt to use the comparative tool failed when *P. crinitus* did not confirm the hypothesis that the desert environment contributed to light reinforcement. Our stocks of comparative material available in this genus have not been exhausted, however. A careful choice of the next stock to study is necessary. Another desert species closely related to *P. eremicus*, such as *P. guardia* or *P. stephani*, should reveal if *P. eremicus* is unique in its motivation for light or if other species with similar phylogenetic backgrounds and adaptations to the desert respond like *P. eremicus*. Other populations of *P. eremicus* from different parts of its geographic range and from different habitats could also indicate if specific environmental characteristics contribute to the number of responses. Apart from examining the *P. eremicus* complex of species, we could turn to different populations of *P. polionotus* and *P. maniculatus*. If the environment has anything to do with motivation for light, perhaps those populations of *P. polionotus* and *P. maniculatus* inhabiting beaches and other areas with little vegetative cover will perform like *P. eremicus*. The precision of our choices of comparative material can increase with each additional comparison until we can predict with accuracy which populations will exhibit a given number of light-contingent responses.

The comparative approach is not limited to populations genetically fixed by natural selection. The character can also be examined by artificial selection if sufficient genetic variation remains so a segment of the population exhibiting the character can be preserved for producing further generations. Individual variation among the three taxa was great enough to expect a genetic response to selection, if the trait has any genetic components. One further advantage of selection is that it can indicate other characteristics of behavior accompanying light reinforcement. For example, light reinforcement may be just one expression of general activity or aperiodicity, which should also appear in the selected lines of the other species. Genetic selection has been made for many characteristics such as learning (Tryon, 1929), emotion (Broadhurst, 1960), orientation (Hirsch & Erlenmeyer-Kimling, 1961), but not for a character related to motivation.

The ultimate procedure for an ecological examination of motivation quantifies the selective advantage of the trait. This requires measuring the survival (or reproductive) ratio of populations different in respect to the trait. The difficulties in this procedure are measuring survivorship in nature and getting two populations different in a given trait. Estimates of selective advantage have been obtained for morphological traits (Kettlewell, 1965; Brower, Cook, & Croze, 1967), but behavioral differences between populations are more difficult to obtain. Tinbergen, Impekoven, & Franck (1967) used the behavioral artifact of egg placement in gulls by changing the spacing of eggs and then counting the numbers of eggs destroyed by crows in each spatial arrangement. Behavior, in the form of predator evasion, was used to establish the ratio of moths eaten when evading the bats' ultrasonic calls to the numbers eaten by bats when no evasive action was taken (Roeder, 1963). The differential mating success of dominant male fowl (Robel, 1966) has also been determined. Such estimates of selective advantage of a particular behavioral characteristic may eventually replace the intellectual refuge afforded by the concept of adaptation. The estimates will require the combined efforts of the population ecologists and the comparative psychologists.

SUMMARY

Ecological psychology is concerned with the functional aspects of behavior. Since each species is capable of maintaining and reproducing itself, emphasis is given to the behavioral strategy used in selecting among the alternative means of achieving survival. Examination of the differential reinforcing properties of environmental stimuli, which disperse animals in time and space, provide the initial goals. The different levels of reinforcement each species exhibits for specific stimuli can then be manipulated at the genetic or species level of comparison in order to estimate the selective advantage of the species' behavioral strategy.

REFERENCES

Adams, L. Progress in ecological biotelemetry. *BioScience*, 1965, **15**, 83–86, 155–157.

Anderson, P. K. Lethal alleles in *Mus musculus:* Local distribution and evidence for isolation of demes. *Science*, 1964, **145**, 177–178.

Aschoff, J. Circadian rhythms in man. *Science*, 1965, **148**, 1427–1432.

Baker, R. H. Habitats and distribution. In J. A. King (Ed.), *Biology of Peromyscus*. American Society of Mammalogists, 1968. Pp. 98–126.

Barker, R. G. *Ecological psychology*. Stanford: Stanford University Press, 1968.

Berlyne, D. E. Arousal and reinforcement. In D. Levine (Ed.), *Nebraska symposium on motivation*, Vol. 15. Lincoln: University of Nebraska Press, 1967. Pp. 1–110.

Bitterman, M. E. Phyletic differences in learning. *American Psychologist*, 1965, **20**, 396–410.

Bolles, R. C. Anticipatory general activity in thirsty rats. *Journal of Comparative and Physiological Psychology*, 1968, **65**, 511–513.

Broadhurst, P. L. Experiments in psychogenetics: Applications of biometrical genetics to the inheritance of behaviour. In H. J. Eysenck (Ed.), *Experiments in personality*. Vol. 1. London: Routledge and Kegan Paul, 1960. Pp. 1–102.

Broadhurst, P. L. An introduction to the diallel cross. In J. Hirsch (Ed.), *Behavior-genetic analysis*. New York: McGraw-Hill, 1967. Pp. 287–304.

Brower, L. P., Cook, L. M., & Croze, H. J. Predator responses to artificial Batesian mimics released in a natural environment. *Evolution*, 1967, **21**, 11–23.

Bruell, J. H. Behavioral heterosis. In J. Hirsch (Ed.), *Behavior-genetic analysis*. New York: McGraw-Hill, 1967. Pp. 270–286.

Draper, W. R. A behavioural study of the home-cage activity of the white rat. *Behaviour*, 1967, **28**, 280–306.

Eisenberg, J. F. The behavior of heteromyid rodents. *University of California Publications in Zoology*, 1963, **69**, 1–100.

Falls, J. B. Activity. In J. A. King (Ed.), *Biology of Peromyscus*. American Society of Mammalogists, 1968. Pp. 543–570.

Ginsberg, B. E. Genetic parameters in behavioral research. In J. Hirsch (Ed.), *Behavior-genetic analysis*. New York: McGraw-Hill, 1967. Pp. 135–153.

Hall, E. R., & Kelson, K. R. *The mammals of North America*. New York: Ronald Press, 1959.

Harris, V. T. An experimental study of habitat selection by prairie and forest races of the deermice, *Peromyscus maniculatus*. *Contributions of the Laboratory of Vertebrate Biology*, University of Michigan, 1952, **56**, 1–53.

Hirsch, J., & Erlenmeyer-Kimling, L. Sign of taxis as a property of the genotype. *Science*, 1961, **134**, 835–836.

Hodos, W., & Campbell, C. B. G. Scala naturae: Why there is no theory in comparative psychology. *Psychological Review*, 1969, **76**, 337–350.

Hooper, E. T. Classification. In J. A. King (Ed.), *Biology of Peromyscus*. American Society of Mammalogists, 1968. Pp. 27–74.

Honzik, C. H. The sensory basis of maze learning in rats. *Comparative Psychology Monographs*, 1936, **13**, 1–113.

Kavanau, J. L. Behavior of captive white-footed mice. *Science*, 1967, **155**, 1623–1639.

Kavanau, J. L. Activity and orientational responses of white-footed mice to light. *Nature*, 1968, **218**, 245–252.

Kettlewell, H. B. D. Insect survival and selection for pattern. *Science*, 1965, **148**, 1290–1296.

King, J. A. Body, brain and lens weights of *Peromyscus*. *Zoologisches Jahrbuch*, *Anatomie*, 1965, **82**, 177–188.

King, J. A. Light reinforcement in four taxa of deermice (*Peromyscus*). *Journal of Comparative and Physiological Psychology*, 1970, **71**, 22–28.

Klopfer, P. H. *Habitats and territories*. New York: Basic Books, 1969.

Layne, J. N. Ontogeny. In J. A. King (Ed.), *Biology of Peromyscus*, American Society of Mammalogists, 1968. Pp. 148–253.

Lettvin, J. Y., Maturana, H. R., McCulloch, W. S., & Pitts, W. H. What the frog's eye tells the frog's brain. In W. C. Corning & M. Balaban (Eds.), *The mind*. New York: Interscience Publishers, 1968. Pp. 233–258.

Lit, A. Visual acuity. In P. R. Farnsworth, *Annual review of psychology*. Palo Alto: Annual Reviews, 1968.

Lloyd, M. "Mean crowding." *Journal of Animal Ecology*, 1967, **36**, 1–30.

Lockard, R. B. The albino rat: A defensible choice or a bad habit? *American Psychologist*, 1968, **23**, 734–742.

Lockard, R. B. Several tests of stimulus—change and preference theory in relation to light-controlled behavior of rats. *Journal of Comparative and Physiological Psychology*, 1968, **65**, 529–531.

Marler, P. R., & Hamilton, W. J. *Mechanisms of animal behavior.* New York: Wiley, 1966.

McCall, P. B. Initial consequent-change surface in light-contingent bar pressing. *Journal of Comparative and Physiological Psychology,* 1966, **62**, 35–42.

McClearn, G. E. Genes, generality, and behavior research. In J. Hirsch (Ed.), *Behavior-genetic analysis.* New York: McGraw-Hill, 1967. Pp. 307–321.

Moody, P. A. Brightness vision in the deermouse, *Peromyscus maniculatus gracilis. Experimental Zoology,* 1929, **52**, 367–405.

Rahmann, H. Die Sehschärfe bei Wirbeltieren. *Naturwissenshaftliche Rundschau,* 1967, **20**, 8–14.

Rahmann, H., Rahmann, M., & King, J. A. Comparative visual acuity (minimum separable) in five species and subspecies of deermice *(Peromyscus). Physiological Zoology,* 1968, **41**, 298–312.

Robel, R. J. Booming territory size and mating success of the greater prairie chicken *(Tympanuchus cupido pinnatus). Animal Behaviour,* 1966, **14**, 328–331.

Roeder, K. D. *Nerve cells and insect behavior.* Cambridge: Harvard University Press, 1963.

Rosenzweig, M. L., & Winakur, J. Population ecology of desert rodent communities: Habitats and environmental complexity. *Ecology,* 1969, **50**, 558–572.

Rothenbuhler, W. C. Genetic and evolutionary considerations of social behavior of honeybees and some related insects. In J. Hirsch (Ed.), *Behavior-genetic analysis.* New York: McGraw-Hill, 1967. Pp. 61–106.

Scott, J. P., & Fuller, J. L. *Genetics and the social behavior of the dog.* Chicago: University of Chicago Press, 1965.

Sheppe, W. Habitat restriction by competitive exclusion in the mice *Peromyscus* and *Mus. Canadian Field-Naturalist,* 1967, **81**, 81–98.

Sisemore, D. A., & Wilcoxon, H. C. Utilization of visual and tactual cues by the white rat in following a trail. *Psychonomic Science,* 1969, **15**, 151–153.

Southwood, T. R. E. *Ecological methods.* London: Methuen, 1966.

Tamarin, R. H., & Krebs, C. J. *Microtus* population biology. II. Genetic changes at the transferrin locus in fluctuating populations of two vole species. *Evolution,* 1969, **23**, 183–211.

Tinbergen, N. *The study of instinct.* London: Oxford University Press, 1951.

Tinbergen, N., Impekoven, M., & Franck, D. An experiment on spacing-out as a defence against predation. *Behaviour,* 1967, **28**, 307–321.

Tryon, R. C. The genetics of learning ability in rats. *University of California Publications in Psychology,* 1929, **4**, 71–89.

Vestal, B. M. Development of visual acuity in two species of deermice *(Peromyscus).* Unpublished doctoral dissertation, Michigan State University, 1970.

Vestal, B. M., & King, J. A. Relationship of age at eye opening to first optokinetic response in deermice *(Peromyscus). Developmental Psychobiology,* 1968, **1**, 30–34.

Walk, R. D. The study of visual depth and distance perception in animals. In D. S. Lehrman, R. A. Hinde, & E. Shaw (Eds.), *Advances in the study of behavior.* New York: Academic Press, 1965. Pp. 99–154.

Whitten, W. K. Pheromones and mammalian reproduction. In A. McLaren (Ed.), *Advances in reproductive physiology*. New York: Academic Press, 1966. Pp. 155–177.

Wilcock, J. Gene action and behavior: An evaluation of major gene pleiotropism. *Psychological Bulletin*, 1969, **72**, 1–29.

Winn, H. E. Comparative reproductive behavior and ecology of fourteen species of darters (Pisces-Percidae). *Ecological Monographs*, 1958, **28**, 155–191.

Motivational Factors in Psychosocial Development[1]

WILLIAM A. MASON

Tulane University

The central problem of psychosocial development can be stated quite simply: How is it that the newborn individual grows up to become a good member of his society? For "good" you can substitute "adequate," "effective," "normal," "socialized," "civilized," "decent," or "moral" without altering the essential meaning. Whether we are talking about animals or men, the fundamental problem is the same: How does the growing individual reach certain functional endpoints in its development?

The question implies that psychosocial development has a direction and a pattern. Our particular concern here will be the factors that influence that direction and shape that pattern in Old World primates. Let us begin, therefore, by looking at the monkey or ape as it exists in nature and what it must accomplish as it grows up.

ADAPTATION: DEVELOPMENTAL TASKS

From the point of view of adaptation there are two major developmental tasks that the growing primate must complete, and it must complete them at different points in its life cycle. The first task is to maintain contact with the mother. We are so accustomed to thinking of infancy in human terms—in which the mother is able

1. Preparation of this chapter was made possible by NIH Grants FR 00164–08 and HD 03915–02. An earlier version appears in C. R. Carpenter (Ed.), *Regulators of behavior in primates* (University Park: Pennsylvania State University Press, in press).

to delegate her biological functions to other persons, such as pediatricians, grandmothers, older children, and fathers, and to carry them out with the aid of various prosthetic devices, such as cradles, nursing bottles, blankets, and buggies—that we sometimes fail to appreciate the tremendous importance and the intimacy of contact between mother and infant among the simian primates. The monkey or ape can rarely count on anyone or anything to share the burden of motherhood. Also, we must remember that most monkeys and apes are on the move. They have no permanent abode, no nest or lair where they can leave the young.

What this means is that for the infant monkey or ape, "mother" and "nest" are synonymous. She is the infant's ecological niche, its essential link with the future. And adjusting to that niche, making sure that link is not broken, is the first developmental task that the infant must perform. It receives substantial help from the mother, of course, but what the mother provides is complemented by what the infant can achieve on its own.

The infant monkey or ape begins life outside the womb with three main avenues available to it through which it can establish and maintain contact with the mother. These are clinging, sucking, and vocalization. The first two are directly related to contact; the last, vocalization, serves as a kind of emergency channel, its chief function being to arouse the mother, causing her to do whatever is appropriate and within her capabilities to turn off a distressing sound. Usually, this means that contact with the infant is re-established or enhanced.

These are among the first functions of clinging, sucking, and vocalization, and as I have indicated, they are already present at birth. There are other functions, however, that we are just beginning to understand. Having encountered a soft, claspable object that provides nourishment, warmth, and gentle movement, and that responds promptly to whimpers and screams, the infant might be expected to come to perceive all of these attractive attributes as belonging to one object. And this is precisely what happens. Gradually, the mother ceases to be a mobile ecological niche and becomes a single social entity, an object of attachment and a source of emotional security. In an obvious and direct manner, her presence emboldens the infant to engage with the larger world, and at the same time guarantees him a haven to which he can retreat should events prove more than he can manage.

I will turn now to the second major developmental task facing the growing primate. That the close physical and psychological dependence on the mother must wane is as obvious as the need for an effective initial adjustment to her. The growing primate's second developmental task is to prepare itself to function as an adult. In the final analysis, this is what socialization is all about. Our understanding of what it means to be a "civilized" monkey or ape is still far from complete, but it is already clear that in addition to its genetic contribution as parent to the perpetuation of the society, the adult monkey or ape contributes to the welfare of the group in many ways. In such matters as protection from predators, the quelling of intragroup strife, and the transmission of information about travel routes and foodstuffs, the field studies are showing us that the adult members of the primate community have important functions to perform. Preparing itself to assume these functions is the primate's second developmental task.

DESCRIPTION: DEVELOPMENTAL TRENDS

Now let us change focus slightly. Thus far we have looked at psychosocial development in terms of what must be accomplished. Our position was that the two major tasks facing the growing monkey or ape were, first, to make an effective adjustment to the mother, to maintain contact with her, and second, to assume its place as an adult member of the community. Now our attention will shift to the question of how the individual's involvement in these tasks changes during ontogeny, to the question of developmental trends.

There are two major developmental trends, and they roughly parallel the developmental tasks we have already considered. The first trend is inferred from the filial responses, the so-called contact-seeking behaviors of early infancy—sucking, clinging, and the like—that obviously become less frequent as development proceeds. I think that everyone who has had any experience with infant monkeys and apes has been impressed with two things about these behaviors. First, they are highly organized at the sensory-motor level. The responses are functioning and with impressive efficiency, usually within hours of birth. Second, they are highly motivated.

The second major developmental trend must take the infant away from the mother, of course, and bring it into commerce with the rest of the world. There is every reason to suspect that this program is also operating in early infancy, although it is overridden at first by the contact-seeking filial responses. This second major trend can perhaps be described most simply as exploitation of the physical and social environment. We see it reflected in the variety and vigor of motor play, in the growing tendency to investigate and to explore, and in an increase in the scope and amount of social interaction, especially social play.

It is important to recognize that both programs operate throughout development, although their prominence shifts. As a specific illustration, consider Figure 1, which shows the relative frequency of clinging, a typical filial response, and play-fighting, an equally representative exploitative pattern. The subjects were rhesus monkeys, raised individually in wire mesh cages. Starting when they were about 25 days old, these animals were placed in pairs for a

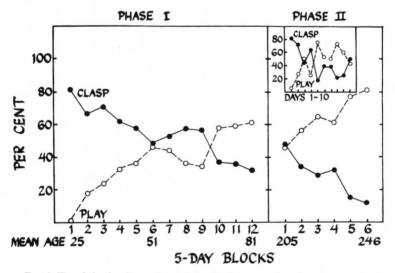

Fig. 1. Trends in clasping and social play in rhesus monkeys housed individually from birth. (From Mason, 1963b)

daily test lasting just 3 minutes. They were tested for 60 days, then given a 120-day break during which they had no opportunity to interact with other animals, and finally were tested for another 30 days. The trends are clear, and they are quite representative of most findings in this area. Similar results have been reported for laboratory infants living with real and artificial mothers (Hansen, 1966), and for free-living infants (Kaufmann, 1966).

It should be noted, however, that the relation between the mother-directed and other-directed trends is not one of simple reciprocity, as Figure 1 might suggest. To be sure, the animal cannot cling and play at the same time. But even when we reduce the likelihood of physical interference between mother-directed and other-directed behaviors by testing the animals individually, the upward trend in other-directed responses is still evident. It is apparent in contacts with the nonsocial environment, as can be seen in Figure 2, which shows age trends in manipulatory behavior. And it can be

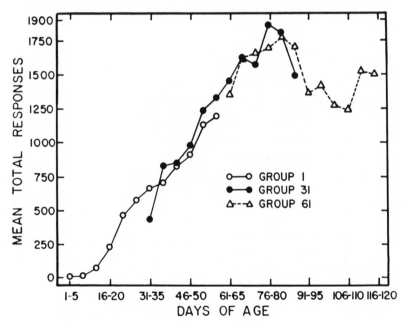

Fig. 2. Development of manipulatory responses in rhesus monkeys. (After Mason, Harlow, & Rueping, 1959)

seen in the frequency of affective-social responses. In one experiment, for example, lab-reared rhesus monkeys encountered fear stimuli as they moved toward them on a continuous belt (Figure 3).

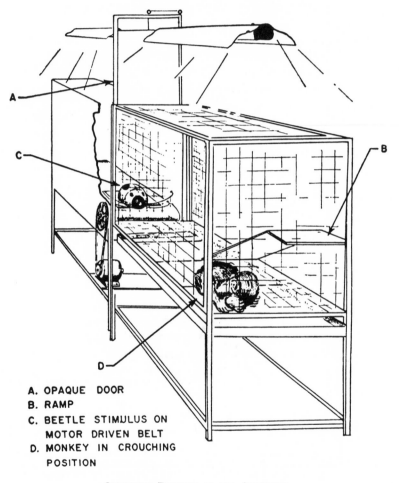

A. OPAQUE DOOR
B. RAMP
C. BEETLE STIMULUS ON
   MOTOR DRIVEN BELT
D. MONKEY IN CROUCHING
   POSITION

SCHEMATIC DRAWING OF THE APPARATUS

FIG. 3. Apparatus for testing affective-social responses in infant monkeys. (After Bernstein & Mason, 1962)

The frequency of affective-social responses characteristic of adult social interactions clearly increased with age (Figure 4).

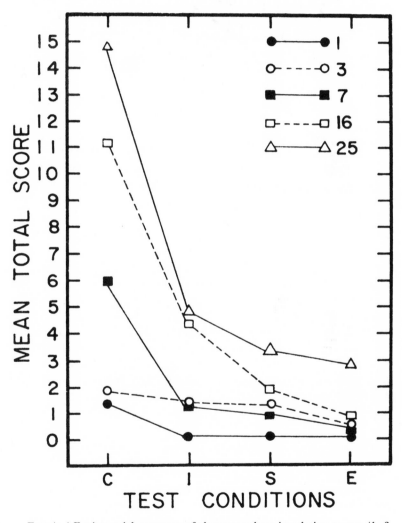

FIG. 4. Affective-social responses of rhesus monkeys in relation to age (1, 3, 7, 16, and 25 months) and stimulus complexity (Complex, Intermediate, Simple, and Empty). (After Bernstein & Mason, 1962)

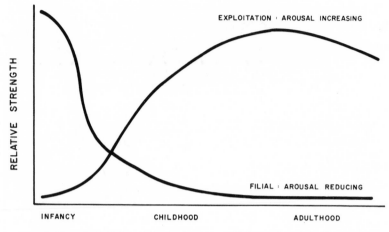

FIG. 5. Hypothetical trends in development of filial and exploitative responses.

Generalizing from such data, we might expect that the relation-ship between trends is something like that shown in Figure 5. What I am suggesting is that these trends are the outcome of basic develop-mental programs determined for the most part by the biological makeup of the individual. They provide the basic behavioral structure and lay out the major directions along which development must proceed. I *do not* claim that either the trends or the underlying programs are *independent* of experience. On the contrary, determining *how* they are influenced by experience is one of the central tasks of developmental psychology. We are concerned with the phenotypic expression of these programs. How do they manifest themselves under ordinary conditions? How are they modified by the environ-ment and how do they operate upon it?

Causation: Motivational Analysis of Filial and Exploitative Behavior

Having this simple developmental framework before us, we are now ready to look at some of these "how" questions—at problems of causation and function. In particular, we will be concerned with the motivational determinants and the motivational consequences of filial and exploitative behaviors.

I mentioned earlier that the filial responses, behaviors which are present at birth, impress one as being highly motivated. With the help of Robert Yerkes I will try to convey that impression to you more clearly: "Something to cling to is essential to the comfort and contentment of the infant. . . . If it be like the mother's coat—soft, pliable, and warm—all the better. But in any case it must be something which can be grasped firmly and made to yield reassuring contact stimuli. A bit of cloth, animal skin, or soft paper will suffice" (Yerkes, 1943, p. 43). I think you can see from this description why contact-seeking has been considered one of the principal "drives" of the infant monkey or ape: the animal shows obvious signs of agitation or distress when contact is prevented and a dramatic reduction of these symptoms when an appropriate outlet is found. Recent efforts have filled out this picture considerably.

We know from Harlow's celebrated experiments that contact is a significant factor in the development of filial attachment, and we have reason to conclude that the effective mechanism is a reduction in emotional arousal.[2] This effect can be demonstrated in many ways. In one experiment we found that an infant chimpanzee that is held in the ventro-ventral position characteristic of clinging makes few vocalizations in response to electric shock, regardless of magnitude, whereas when it is not held, the amount of vocalization increases with increasing shock (Figure 6). We have found a similar effect using heart rate as a measure of arousal. Infant monkeys confined to an unfamiliar room undergo a marked reduction in heart rate when they are given something to cling to (Figure 7). Recently, Hill and McCormack (1969) have obtained similar results with measures of cortisol levels. Infant monkeys, raised on simple artificial mothers (Figure 8), had blood samples withdrawn after they had been confined for 1 hour in an enclosed cage, either alone or with the artificial mother. Samples were obtained at monthly

2. Arousal is here considered a hypothetical physiological variable that is correlated with overt behavior. It is assumed that a given level of arousal establishes a predisposition to engage in certain patterns of behavior rather than serving as a precipitating cause. Specific behaviors are jointly determined by arousal level and by specific features of the stimulus situation. Level of arousal cannot be equated with level of overt behavior inasmuch as such activities as crouching, clinging, freezing, screaming, and frantic running are all expressions of high arousal, in spite of gross differences in motor output.

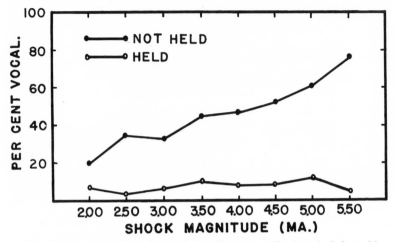

FIG. 6. Percentage of shocks producing distress vocalizations in infant chimpanzees while they were held and while they rested on a bare surface. (After Mason & Berkson, 1962)

intervals for 6 months, beginning in the first week of life. Figure 9 shows that at every age level cortisol levels are lower when the substitute mother is present. Further evidence could be given, but these examples are sufficient to show why I believe the primary motivational consequence of the filial responses is arousal reduction.

The motivational consequences of the exploitative behaviors contrast sharply with this picture. Play, exploration, and the like are characteristically directed toward the novel, variable, or mildly stimulating features of the environment and they serve to increase arousal rather than to reduce it. The character of most exploitative behaviors, associated as they are with violent bursts of motor activity and frequent changes in patterns of stimulation and modalities stimulated, suggests this possibility. Moreover, we have found that responsiveness is elevated following a brief period of play (Mason, Hollis, & Sharpe, 1962), and Berkson (1963) has shown that tickling, a highly effective stimulus for eliciting and sustaining play, does, in fact, produce an increment in arousal as indicated by an increase in skin conductance.

I mentioned earlier that both the filial and the exploitative trends operated throughout development, and I want to return to

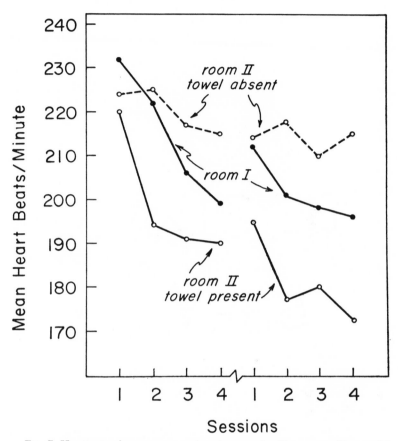

Fig. 7. Heart rate changes over sessions in an unfamiliar room with a social substitute (Room II, towel), in the same room without the social substitute (Room II, no towel), and in a room where the towel was never encountered (Room I). (After Candland & Mason, 1968)

that idea now. It is obvious that if both types of behavior are possible, something must enter the picture to determine which class of behaviors is going to be dominant at any particular moment. Some years ago, we went into this question in a series of experiments with young chimpanzees (Mason, 1965; Mason, 1967). One of the advantages of the chimp over the rhesus monkey for this line of research is that the ape enjoys a rather lengthy childhood—almost

Fig. 8. Monkey on simple artificial mother.

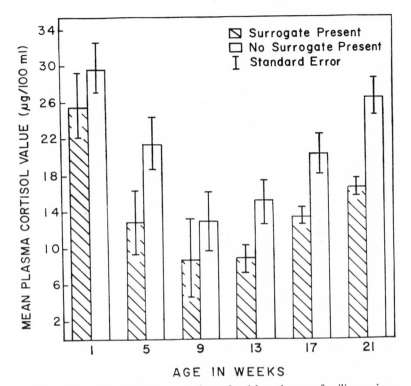

Fɪɢ. 9. Cortisol levels of rhesus monkeys after 1 hour in an unfamiliar environment, alone and with an artificial mother. (After Hill & McCormack, 1969)

as long as our own—and throughout this period, and even into adulthood, it readily displays filial responses right alongside more mature patterns. I have already suggested that mother-directed and other-directed behaviors differ from each other in their motivational *consequences* (effects on arousal level). This also seems to be true with respect to their motivational *antecedents*. As would be expected, filial responses are most likely to occur under conditions of high arousal, whereas the exploitative behaviors are most likely to occur at moderate levels of arousal. Let us consider some of the evidence that led to this conclusion.

If young chimpanzees are given a choice between two costumed stimulus-persons, one who engages the animal in roughhouse play, and another who holds it in a cling position, most animals develop a consistent preference for the play-person. Often they begin a session with a brief bout of clinging, and then switch over to the play-person, with whom they spend most of the time. Once a stable preference is established, one can then look at the effects of motivational factors on this base-line level. Both the experiments I am going to describe dealt with increases in arousal level. In one the agent was amphetamine, and in the other, white noise. As can be seen from Figure 10, contacts with the cling-person increased with noise level. Similar results were obtained with amphetamine: during the 145-minute period following administration of the drug, the duration of play contacts declined, but no such tendency was observed under the placebo (Figure 11); whereas cling contacts increased progressively, and again, no such tendency was observed under the placebo (Figure 12).

Although the instrumental response in these experiments is a very simple one, it is sufficient to affirm that filial responses and exploitative behaviors have reinforcing properties, and to establish that the efficacy of these reinforcers will vary with arousal level.

THE DEPRIVATION SYNDROME: EFFECTS OF ALTERED REARING CONDITIONS

We have seen that the developing primate is a highly motivated and organized system; it is geared to certain adaptive requirements and it is changing through time. What happens to the development of this system when the normal ecology is radically altered? Recent findings suggest that monkeys and apes reared under conditions that prevent contact with the mother and with other significant social objects display a predictable syndrome—the primate deprivation syndrome—which consists of four elements:

1. Abnormal postures and movements (e.g., rocking)
2. Motivational disturbance (e.g., excessive fearfulness)
3. Poor integration of motor patterns (e.g., sexual behavior)
4. Deficiencies in social communication (e.g., threat by aggressive animal A does not produce withdrawal by subordinate animal B)

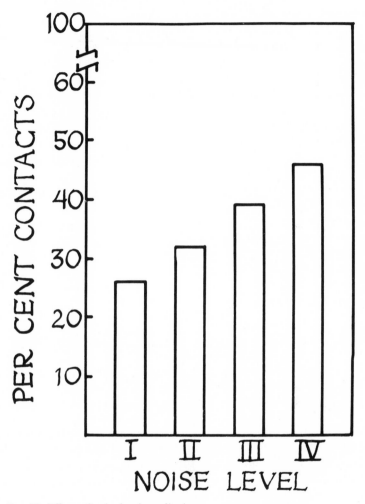

Fɪɢ. 10. Effects of noise level on clinging.

First, the socially deprived primate shows postures or movements that are rare or absent in the wild-born animal. There are several of these, and their interrelations have not been carefully determined. One of the most prominent of the movement aberrations is stereotyped rocking of the trunk. This has been observed in

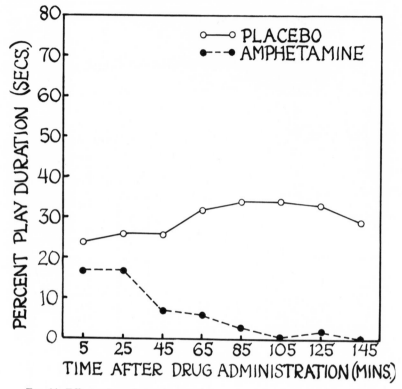

Fig. 11. Effects of amphetamine on play.

isolation-reared chimpanzees, gibbons, baboons, and several species of macaques. The rocking movements of these nonhuman primates bear a striking resemblance to the repetitive patterns of blind and autistic children, and of the severely retarded, suggesting that repetitive stereotyped movements are a primitve reaction to adverse environmental conditions. Discovering the genesis of these behaviors is an area of lively concern in contemporary primate research (Berkson, 1967). Other aberrant patterns that often accompany rocking in rhesus monkeys are self-clasping, thumbsucking, and face-stroking. The second element in the deprivation syndrome is fearfulness or hyperexcitability—some form of gross motivational disturbance—and we see it reflected in many situations in which

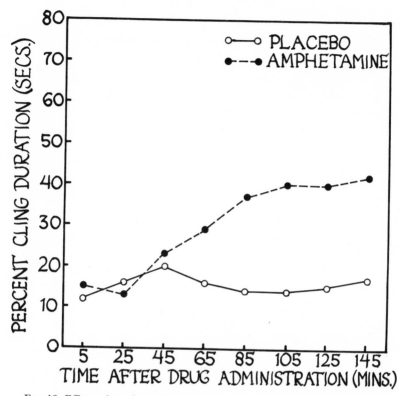

FIG. 12. Effects of amphetamine on clinging.

there is some element of novelty. Third, socially deprived animals often show an absence of certain postures or movements, or fail to form certain movements into larger integrated patterns. Deficiencies in the sexual performance of deprived rhesus monkeys provide one example. Finally, there is evidence of a disturbance in communication. The sounds, postures, and facial expressions that serve as signals in the interaction of normal primates lack this function among socially deprived animals. For example, if a sophisticated and receptive female solicits the sexual attentions of a socially deprived male, he does not respond to it as though it were a signal—which it certainly is for the wild-born male—but instead may initiate play or begin to groom the female, or ignore her altogether.

POSTULATES

You now have before you a fair sampling of the evidence we have to work with. In order to pull it together, fill in a few of the gaps in the argument, and introduce some necessary qualifications, I present a series of postulates dealing with the major events and phases of psychosocial development. They are stated in a form, it is hoped, that can be tested empirically or rendered more explicit as new information becomes available.

A. Development of Filial Attachment

1. *The behaviors and motivations of the newborn monkey or ape include preadapted, organized patterns essential to survival under normal conditions.* The existence of these patterns permits the neonate to adjust to the mother, both as a static object and as a source of varied stimulation. The primary infant responses involved in this adjustment are clinging, rooting, oral grasping, and sucking. Stated in perceptual terms, the monkey or ape enters the world with a schematic (and largely tactile) model of the primate mother.

2. *These early filial patterns, particularly those relating to contact clinging, are highly motivated.* Insofar as the perceptual model is matched by an appropriate object in the environment (that is, when an outlet is available,), the infant is quiescent. The absence of such an outlet leads to increased arousal, as evidenced by heightened vocal activity, generalized motor disturbance, and changes in autonomic activity. Encountering an appropriate outlet leads to a prompt reduction in arousal. The effective characteristics of an adequate outlet are imperfectly understood. With respect to clinging and sucking, however, it is clear that outlets may be found in the nonsocial environment (e.g., a clutch cloth) or on the animal's own body (e.g., self-clasping, thumbsucking).

3. *Any large increment in arousal, whatever its source, increases the tendency to cling.* This phenomenon has the obvious adaptive value of causing the preambulatory infant to cling more tightly to the mother, and the ambulatory infant to seek her under circumstances in which danger is potentially present (for example, the approach of strangers, loud noises, or unusual activity).

4. *Clinging is a reinforcing event.* The evidence that the act of clinging can serve as reinforcer, and that clinging results in a reduction in arousal, suggests that arousal reduction is the effective mechanism of reinforcement (McCulloch, 1939; Mason, 1965). To the extent that an object permits clinging by providing the necessary physical structure or support, it can be considered a reinforcer, in much the same way that a food object can be said to be a reinforcer for the act of feeding.

5. *The effectiveness of an object as a reinforcer for clinging is jointly dependent on its physical properties ("claspability") and upon the subject's level of arousal.* This hypothesis assumes that for all infants some objects are more suitable for clinging than others, and that less appropriate objects will become more acceptable as the subject's level of arousal is increased. The relationship is assumed to be analogous to that prevailing between acceptability of food and level of deprivation.

6. *Any object that is used repeatedly for the performance of clinging can become the focus of emotional dependence (attachment).* The historical basis for an attachment to a particular object is its efficacy as a primary reinforcer for clinging. Other properties associated with the object eventually come to function as discriminanda and as secondary reinforcers, these functions being mediated for the most part by distance receptors (particularly visual). The integration of tactual and visual information results in the emergence of a specific object of attachment (object constancy or object conservation). The *strength* of attachment can be inferred from such measures as the duration of clinging to the object, its effects on autonomic activity, its ability to reduce vocalizations, and its effectiveness as an incentive in certain tasks. The *specificity* of attachment can be assessed using similar response measures to compare the relative effectiveness of different social objects.

7. *The average strength of attachment to a given object is an increasing function of the motivation to cling, the frequency with which the object has served to reinforce clinging in the past, and the efficacy of the object as a reinforcer for clinging.* Individuals can be expected to differ consistently in the tendency to cling and in the vigor of their reactions to separation from an object to which an attachment has been formed, suggesting that attachment to a specific object can be characterized

in terms of its "average" strength. It is assumed that stable individual differences in attachment or emotional dependence reflect, in part, the complex historical relations between the motivation to cling and reinforcement history. Some specific predictions from this hypothesis are: (a) If the frequency and temporal distribution of reinforcements are held constant, the strength of attachment to a specific object will be greater in more highly aroused individuals, that is, individuals displaying a stronger motivation to cling. (b) If the motivation to cling (arousal) is held constant, the strength of attachment to a specific object will vary with the frequency, temporal distribution, or adequacy of the reinforcement for clinging provided by the object.

8. *The effective or manifest strength of attachment is multiply determined.* For any individual, the tendency to cling can be strengthened momentarily by any one of a number of different procedures, including situational novelty, physical restraint, noise, and stimulant drugs (Mason, 1965; Mason, 1967). This leads to the view that momentary variations in the tendency to cling combine with the average strength of attachment to determine the effective or manifest strength of attachment.

9. *The specificity of attachment is multiply determined.* Assuming that an attachment has been formed to a single object, the acceptability of a substitute is jointly determined by the level of arousal (that is, the strength of the tendency to cling), the claspability of the object, and the degree to which it resembles the object on which the original attachment was formed. In other words, it is predicted that some form of generalization gradient will develop around an object of attachment, the slope of which will depend in part on the strength of the motivation to cling.

10. *The tendency to cling declines with age.* It is obvious that clinging and other filial responses become less frequent as development proceeds, as does the intensity of distress reactions to separation from an object of attachment. This occurs in surrogate-reared animals, for which changing patterns of maternal responsiveness can be ruled out, as well as in animals reared by the natural mother. Additional evidence that the tendency to cling decreases gradually is provided by Harlow's delay-group of rhesus monkeys. These animals, given a cloth artificial mother for the first time at 250 days of

age, did not cling to the surrogate when they were placed in an open-field fear situation (Harlow, 1961).

B. *Comment on the Waning of Filial Behaviors*

Although nothing like a sharply delimited critical period for the formation of filial attachments has been demonstrated for monkeys and apes, there is no serious question that such attachments will become increasingly difficult to establish as the animal approaches maturity. There is every reason to believe that intrinsic, maturational changes are important in this trend, modified in varied ways, to be sure, by individual experience.

Few people are likely to take exception to this conclusion, probably because it says very little about the detailed nature of the changes that are involved. One of the reasons that it is difficult to be more precise is that a very large group of related developments can be discerned which may help to bring to a close the period when filial attachments can be easily formed. The motivations and stimulus needs associated with clinging, sucking, and other filial responses are probably strongest early in development and then wane. As they do, other factors increase in frequency, scope, or effectiveness: this can be said of attentional responses, at least in the human infant (Wolff, 1965), tolerance of or attraction toward varied stimulation, "interest" in novel objects, sensory-motor skills, and learning capabilities (Bernstein & Mason, 1962; Fantz, 1965; Harlow, 1959; Mason, 1961; Mason, Harlow, & Rueping, 1959; Zimmermann & Torrey, 1965). These developments contribute to the growth of the exploitative trend, and at the same time they open up new ways of coping with high arousal or stress.

C. *Development of Nonfilial Social Behavior*

11. *Novel or salient stimuli increase arousal.* The infant monkey or chimpanzee responds selectively to its surroundings, and objects that contrast with the general features of the environment are more likely to produce arousal than those that do not.

12. *Repeated presentations of the same stimulus usually lead to a reduction in arousal.*

13. *Stimuli whose novelty or salience is beyond the range to which the organism is habituated produce withdrawal, clinging, and other arousal-reducing patterns.*

14. *Stimuli whose novelty or salience is greater but not too much greater than those to which the organism is habituated lead to approach and contact.* For an organism at a low or moderate level of arousal, moderate increments in arousal are reinforcing. Stimuli that cause a moderate increment in arousal are especially significant in the development of exploitative behaviors since through the process of approach-contact-habituation they have the cumulative effect of gradually increasing the range and complexity of stimuli that the animal will tolerate or approach freely. For this reason, they have been termed pacers (e.g., in Sackett, 1965).

15. *Responsiveness to novel or salient stimuli increases from birth to early adolescence.* It is unlikely that developmental changes in reactions to stimuli can be explained solely in terms of novelty and habituation to novelty. A more reasonable possibility is that the ability of stimuli to provoke attention increases as a function of intrinsic or maturational changes, and that the *degree of arousal* produced by any particular stimulus and the *direction* of the behavioral reaction it elicits (that is, approach or withdrawal) are largely determined by individual experience.

16. *The greater the degree of stimulus deprivation during early development and the longer this condition persists, the greater the likelihood that stimulus change will produce hyperarousal (freezing, flight-fight).* This statement is implied in postulates 8, 9, 10, and 15. Findings on non-primate mammals, especially rodents, show that a variety of behavioral and sympathetico-adrenal changes are associated with early environmental stimulation, and some of these effects appear to be irreversible. The primate data, consisting chiefly of comparisons of gross variations in rearing conditions, are generally consistent with the rodent findings, although little systematic information is available.

17. *The form of social behavior is influenced by the level of arousal.* Menzel (1964) has shown that the development of responsiveness to an entirely novel object in isolation-reared chimpanzees follows a definite sequence in which fear is followed by caution, then aggression, play, and finally satiation or loss of interest. A similar sequence

can be seen in social situations, but seldom with the same clarity because the ongoing patterns of social interactions themselves influence the level of arousal.

18. *The contribution of social interaction to arousal increases with the vigor of the interaction.* In other words, positive feedback is assumed between the vigor of social interaction and its effect on arousal. Play increases the likelihood that aggression will occur; aggression increases the likelihood that one or both participants will withdraw from social interaction or will seek to cling. Both these sequels are, in fact, commonly observed in the social interaction of young primates.

D. *Arousal and Social Learning*

The preceding statements assert that arousal level is a significant determinant of short-term variations in social behavior. They also suggest a mechanism for the development of specific social preferences: in a state of high arousal, the young primate will seek out and cling to the individual that has been most often associated with clinging and arousal reduction in the past. A modest increment in arousal, however, predisposes the animal to play; hence play will be directed toward animals that are moderately unfamiliar, or that provide variable patterns of stimulation, and of course, this last condition is most often fulfilled by animals that meet play overtures with play responses.

Under natural conditions, the relation between arousal level and behavior will become less direct as development proceeds. With increasing experience the animal responds more and more to the information content of the immediate situation (including that provided by its own internal state), and less to the overall level of stimulation. As it becomes more sophisticated, the growing primate learns to terminate play-fighting before arousal reaches the higher levels conducive to aggression or fear; sex objects are selected on the basis of signs of receptivity; dominance is determined on the basis of size and carriage; and an approaching predator causes discreet withdrawal long before it begins active pursuit. To deal with these developments we must extend our concern with arousal level to take conditions of learning into account.

19. *The acquisition of most nonfilial social responses will proceed most rapidly at moderate levels of arousal.* This statement is in accord with the evidence that on most learning tasks, particularly those requiring relatively precise sensory-motor adjustments, acquisition is most rapid when arousal is neither high nor low, but at a moderate level (e.g., Hebb, 1955; Leuba, 1962; Malmo, 1958). One implication of this hypothesis is that the socially deprived primate is more likely to benefit from social encounters if precautions are taken to maintain its level of arousal within a moderate range. High levels of arousal increase the likelihood of fear or aggression (both are characteristic of the deprived animal) and the presence of these behaviors will, of course, work against the development of "constructive" species-typical social patterns.

20. *The acquisition of nonfilial social response patterns in monkeys and apes presents two aspects, response integration and signal learning.* This hypothesis scarcely does more than state what now appears to be an obvious conclusion from the findings on socially deprived monkeys (Mason, 1963a; Mason & Hollis, 1962; Miller, Caul, & Mirsky, 1967).

a. *Response integration.* Most of the response elements that comprise the basic social repertoire of the fully socialized monkey are also seen in the animal reared individually from birth. In the deprived animal, however, these elements are not formed into integrated or biologically effective sequences and patterns. The lack of response integration in the sexual performance of deprived rhesus males has already been cited as one example. Such monkeys show most, if not all, of the essential elements of the male sex pattern—penile erection, thrusting, clasping with the hands, clasping with the feet—but orientation toward the partner is inappropriate and the individual responses are not combined into the unified pattern that is seen in the socialized adult monkey. It is assumed that the integration of these elements into the pattern typical for the species requires rehearsal with and feedback from appropriate objects in the environment. The objects need not be social so long as they provide the proper physical structure for rehearsal, and so long as the animal is appropriately (that is, moderately) aroused. If arousal is too low the behaviors do not appear; if it is too high, they may also fail to appear—or if they appear they do not become integrated into a single pattern.

b. *Signal learning*. In the interactions of adult wild-born monkeys, social coordination and social control are more often achieved by means of distinctive postures, facial expressions, and sounds than by physical contact. There is convincing evidence that socially deprived monkeys are seriously lacking in the ability to "read" these behaviors. Most likely the functions of social signals are learned according to the same principles that are involved in learning that the onset of a light will be followed by shock, or that a red plaque covers a peanut. We can assume that the role of arousal in signal learning will vary according to the "message," that is, it will depend upon whether the appropriate response to the sender is approach or withdrawal. On the one hand, learning to withdraw from a threat gesture should proceed most rapidly when the consequences of not withdrawing produce aversively high levels of arousal (for example, being slapped or bitten) and stand in sharp contrast to the consequences of moving away. On the other hand, learning to discriminate the different messages implied in a "sexual present" and "present for grooming," both of which require approach, will proceed most efficiently when the learner is at a moderate level of arousal.

It should be noted that there is no need to assume that the stimuli involved in "signal learning" are neutral at the onset. On the contrary, it is likely that certain stimulus configurations are analogous to the releasers described by the ethologists. The demonstration by Schiff, Caviness, and Gibson (1962) that fear responses to "looming" occur in laboratory-reared rhesus monkeys under 1 year of age suggests one such possibility, and there are probably others. It seems likely, for example, that the stimulus configuration involved in staring is another pattern possessing a certain potency for macaque monkeys, regardless of specific social history. Sackett (1966) found that monkeys reared in isolation showed more evidence of fear and disturbance in response to colored slides of a threatening monkey than they did when exposed to other monkey pictures. Social facilitation (observing, approaching, and duplicating the manipulatory activities of another) likewise appears to be a "primitive" tendency that can be observed in young laboratory-reared monkeys during their very first social encounters. In such matters as the recognition of predators, the establishment of dominance relations, and the acquisition of information concerning travel routes and foodstuffs, such primitive stimulus-response relations probably provide an initial direction to the learning process which is shaped and refined by the results of individual experience.

E. The Deprivation Syndrome

The behavioral deficiencies and aberrations that describe the deprivation syndrome are viewed here as manifestations of the two major developmental trends, operating on reduced or altered environmental input. Some of the evidence supporting this view is unequivocal. It is clear, for example, that thumbsucking and self-clasping have their origins in response tendencies that are ordinarily directed toward the mother. We have recently obtained evidence that body rocking is also a "substitute" response to a lack of certain forms of stimulation ordinarily provided by the mother.

It is clear from naturalistic studies that the mother ordinarily provides a great deal of passive movement stimulation in the course of her routine activities. It seemed possible that the infant that was deprived of such stimulation would supply it for himself through self-rocking, just as it substitutes self-stimulation for social stimulation in the development of thumbsucking and self-clasping. To test this idea we compared two groups of monkeys, one group reared with a cloth-covered artificial mother that moved freely about the cage on an irregular schedule, and the other group reared with a device identical to the moving dummy, except that it was stationary. All but one of the ten monkeys reared with stationary mothers developed stereotyped rocking as a persistent pattern, whereas none of the nine monkeys reared with robot dummies showed any evidence of this behavior. These results confirm our view that many of the self-directed behaviors appearing in the deprived infant represent the working out of infantile contact-seeking patterns under highly atypical conditions.

In spite of the change in topography, however, their relations to arousal level are similar to those of their normal counterparts. For example, amphetamine, which leads to an increase in clinging in wild-born chimpanzees, leads to an increase in the frequency of rocking in socially deprived chimps (Berkson & Mason, 1964;

Fitz-Gerald, 1966). Similarly, frustration produces an increase in nonnutritive sucking in socially deprived macaque monkeys (Benjamin, 1961).

The remaining elements in the deprivation syndrome are more difficult to interpret on the basis of present evidence. The hyper-arousal that is characteristic of the deprived monkey or ape almost certainly is traceable, in part, to early limitations on the variety and amount of stimulation—to the lack of pacers—and therefore reflects inadequate environmental support of the exploitative trend in development. It is also possible, however, as King (1966) and Bronson (1968) suggest, that the absence of the mother deprives the young primate of an important means of controlling arousal and thereby retards the process of habituation to novelty.

Deficiencies in social communication and sensory-motor co-ordination of social patterns reflect an absence of information and skills that are usually acquired during the give-and-take of social interaction. The primary impetus for such interaction is the exploitative trend, and the primary arena in which such acquisitions occur is interaction with age-mates. We would anticipate, therefore, that deficiencies in social communication and sensory-motor coordination will be somewhat more severe in the animal that has received normal mothering but lacks peer experience, than in the animal that has had no experience with a normal mother but ample contact with peers—although both individuals, of course, would be better off than the animal having no experience whatsoever with other monkeys. The evidence, so far as it goes, is in agreement with this expectation (Harlow & Harlow, 1962).

THE ROLE OF SOCIAL OBJECTS IN PSYCHOSOCIAL DEVELOPMENT

It should be clear, however, that the mother as a social object cannot be aligned simply and directly with either the mother-directed or other-directed trends in primate ontogeny. On the contrary, an important source of her unique position in psychosocial development is that she acts on both trends in multiple ways. She serves many functions, and her role changes progressively over time.

The mother is able to influence the filial, arousal-reducing responses, of course, because circumstances have contrived to make her the object toward which these responses are directed. Inasmuch as she possesses the means to alter motivational factors (that is, arousal level) and to provide reinforcement (that is, arousal reduction), she is in an especially strategic position to shape infant contact-seeking behaviors and to affect the overall strength of filial attachment. According to this view, it would be anticipated that the mother who regularly creates a high level of arousal—whether by threat, physical punishment, or neglect—and follows this regularly by presenting an opportunity to cling, will produce an infant with an unusually strong attachment. In keeping with this expectation, clinging does, in fact, appear to be more tenacious in rhesus infants whose dummy mothers punish them with an air blast than in those whose mothers do not (Rosenblum & Harlow, 1963). It would also be anticipated, however, that *any* condition that creates high arousal (regardless of the specific source) and permits arousal reduction by the mother will strengthen the filial attachment. Thus, if the environment containing the mother-infant pair is stressful and over-stimulating to the infant, its attachment will be stronger than that which develops under less stressful circumstances. The specific source of arousal would thus be a less important determinant of attachment strength, in the present view, than the overall level of arousal and the adequacy and scheduling of arousal reduction.

The mother acts on the exploitative development trend in two ways. First, she influences it indirectly by exposing the infant to varied surroundings as she pursues her daily round. Her function probably goes beyond that of a mere vehicle for bringing the infant into contact with new situations, however, since she also provides a secure home base from which the infant can move and to which he can return for arousal reduction when stimulation becomes excessive. Second, she influences the exploitative trend directly through her interactions with the infant. She transports it using different speeds and gaits; she restrains it; she competes with it; and in some species she may even engage it in play. Increasingly in her interactions with the infant she comes to perform most of the behaviors that the infant will eventually encounter in the larger social environment.

In the light of these observations, it is unlikely that a sharp distinction can be drawn between mothers, siblings, other adults, and peers as sources of important psychosocial variables. For the immature organism these different classes of social beings have overlapping attributes and "object" functions. The degree of functional equivalence among different classes of social objects will be determined by what they do to or for the infant, of course, and this can be expected to vary with the developmental status of the infant and with the objects it has available. The growing primate is characteristically selective in its relations with the social environment. It takes from the environment the best that is available, so to speak, "best" being here defined in terms of the behavioral tendencies dominant at the moment, and the available repertoire of stimulus-response capabilities.

Early in life the absence of the natural mother will lead the newborn monkey or ape to direct filial responses to other adults, to age-mates, to inanimate objects, or to its own body—perhaps in that order of priority. Later, at a time when the growing animal would ordinarily be spending a significant amount of time interacting with age-mates, the absence of peers would lead to altered behavior toward the mother. In all likelihood, the outcome would be circular: changes in infant behavior will modify maternal responses, leading to further modification in infant behavior, and so on and on. If this is the case, it follows that the isolated mother-infant dyad will not yield an undistorted picture of normal patterns of mother-infant interaction or lead to an accurate assessment of the relative importance of the contributions of maternal and non-maternal variables to psychosocial development. The situation is no different, in principle, when access is limited to peers. All such procedures provide a limited and indirect test of equivalence among different classes of social objects.

This is not say that there is no merit in the current concern in primate research with the contribution of different classes of social objects to psychosocial development. On the contrary, because such an approach, which might be called socio-ecological, focuses on real social objects (rather than circumscribed processes or attributes), it can be considered an extension and refinement of the field study and it provides the link with the natural social environment that is required if we are to achieve a valid and comprehensive view of primate psychosocial development. At the same time, however, it is clear that the tendency to conceptualize independent variables in terms of types or classes of individuals places definite limits on the kinds and amount of information that can be obtained. The present theoretical orientation, which directs attention toward specific variables and developmental processes, should be viewed as a complement to the socio-ecological approach.

Epilogue

Systematic data on primate psychosocial development were virtually nonexistent scarcely more than a decade ago. In a comparatively brief period there has been a rapid growth of information on the social development of many different species, observed in a variety of circumstances, natural and contrived. As our knowledge of primate social behavior has increased, so has our awareness that patterns of psychosocial development among different individuals, even individuals from different species, are basically similar. At the same time, it has become quite clear that experience plays a fundamental part in all phases of psychological growth. An adequate model of primate psychosocial development must incorporate both sets of findings. It must provide a framework that reflects the broad regularities that are characteristic of the Old World primates as a whole, and yet it must be able to deal with the specific effects of experience on the course of individual psychological development.

I have attempted such a model here, more in the hope that it will be of momentary heuristic value than out of any suspicion that it will have enduring merit. Since man is a primate too, I would like to believe that the model is also relevant to human psychosocial development. Although I have not tried to establish that relevance here, I have dealt with this problem in some detail elsewhere (Mason, 1968).

Summary

1. Psychosocial development is viewed with reference to two major developmental trends, each corresponding with a fundamental adaptive problem for the growing primate. Both trends

operate throughout life although their prominence changes as development proceeds.

2. The first trend is inferred from the filial contact-seeking behaviors. These are preadapted patterns which are dominant early in ontogeny and they provide the basis for the adjustment to the mother. They are most likely to occur under conditions of high arousal and their performance leads to arousal reduction. Arousal reduction provides the primary mechanism of reinforcement in the development of the infant's tie to the mother.

3. The second major developmental trend is inferred from exploitative behaviors such as social play, motor play, and investigatory activities. Exploitative behaviors are elicited by moderate increments of arousal (in an animal that is not in a state of excessive arousal) and their performance leads to further increments in arousal. Objects that elicit or sustain exploitative behaviors are effective reinforcers and they are primary agents in moving the infant away from the mother and into the larger world. Because the efficacy of such objects is reduced as a function of repeated exposures, their cumulative effect is to extend the range of objects to which the infant is attracted. Insofar as the exploitative trend brings the growing primate into contact with other individuals it creates the opportunities and the need for social learning.

4. The syndrome of aberrations and deficiencies seen in primates raised in social isolation is viewed as a manifestation of these two major developmental trends, operating on reduced or altered environmental input. Similarly, the consequences of exposure to particular classes of social beings and to specific social behaviors are considered to depend on the interaction between these social factors and the current status of the developmental trends.

REFERENCES

Benjamin, L. S. The effect of frustration on the nonnutritive sucking of the infant rhesus monkey. *Journal of Comparative and Physiological Psychology*, 1961, **54**, 700–703.

Berkson, G. Stimuli affecting vocalizations and basal skin resistance of neonate chimpanzees. *Perceptual and Motor Skills*, 1963, **17**, 871–874.

Berkson, G. Abnormal stereotyped motor acts. In J. Zubin & H. F. Hunt (Eds.), *Comparative psychopathology—animal and human.* New York: Grune & Stratton, 1967. Pp. 76–94.

Berkson, G., & Mason, W. A. Stereotyped behaviors of chimpanzees: Relation to general arousal and alternative activities. *Perceptual and Motor Skills*, 1964, **19**, 635–652.

Bernstein, S., & Mason, W. A. The effects of age and stimulus conditions on the emotional responses of rhesus monkeys: Responses to complex stimuli. *Journal of Genetic Psychology*, 1962, **101**, 279–298.

Bronson, G. W. The development of fear in man and other animals. *Child Development*, 1968, **39**, 409–431.

Candland, D. K., & Mason, W. A. Infant monkey heart rate: Habituation and effects of social substitutes. *Developmental Psychobiology*, 1968, **1**, 254–256.

Fantz, R. L. Ontogeny of perception. In A. M. Schrier, H. F. Harlow, & F. Stollnitz (Eds.), *Behavior of nonhuman primates*. Vol. 2. New York: Academic Press, 1965. Pp. 365–403.

Fitz-Gerald, F. L. Effects of d-amphetamine upon behavior of young chimpanzees reared under different conditions. *Excerpta Medica International Congress Series*, 1966, **129**, 1226–1227.

Hansen, E. W. The development of maternal and infant behavior in the rhesus monkey. *Behaviour*, 1966, **27**, 107–149.

Harlow, H. F. The development of learning in the rhesus monkey. *American Scientist*, 1959, **47**, 459–479.

Harlow, H. F. The development of affectional patterns in infant monkeys. In B. M. Foss (Ed.), *Determinants of infant behavior*. New York: John Wiley & Sons, Inc., 1961. Pp. 75–97.

Harlow, H. F., & Harlow, M. K. Social deprivation in monkeys. *Scientific American*, 1962, **207**, 137–146.

Hebb, D. O. Drives and the C.N.S. (Conceptual Nervous System). *Psychological Review*, 1955, **62**, 243–254.

Hill, S., & McCormack, S. The adrenal response of infant rhesus monkeys to an unfamiliar environment with and without a social surrogate present. Paper presented at the annual meeting of the Psychonomic Society, St. Louis, November, 1969.

Kaufmann, J. H. Behavior of infant rhesus monkeys and their mothers in a free-ranging band. *Zoologica*, 1966, **51**, 17–28.

King, D. L. A review and interpretation of some aspects of the infant-mother relationship in mammals and birds. *Psychological Bulletin*, 1966, **65**, 143–155.

Leuba, C. Relation of stimulation intensities to learning and development. *Psychological Reports*, 1962, **11**, 55–65.

Malmo, R. B. Measurement of drive: An unsolved problem in psychology. In Marshall R. Jones (Ed.), *Nebraska symposium on motivation*. Lincoln: University of Nebraska Press, 1958. Pp. 229–265.

Mason, W. A. Effects of age and stimulus characteristics on manipulatory responsiveness of monkeys raised in a restricted environment. *Journal of Genetic Psychology*, 1961, **99**, 301–308.

Mason, W. A. The effects of environmental restriction on the social development of rhesus monkeys. In C. H. Southwick (Ed.), *Primate social behavior*. Princeton: D. Van Nostrand, 1963. Pp. 161–173 (a).

Mason, W. A. Social development of rhesus monkeys with restricted social experience. *Perceptual and Motor Skills,* 1963, **16,** 263–270 (b).

Mason, W. A. Determinants of social behavior in young chimpanzees. In A. M. Schrier, H. F. Harlow, & F. Stollnitz (Eds.), *Behavior of nonhuman primates.* New York: Academic Press, 1965. Pp. 335–364.

Mason, W. A. Motivational aspects of social responsiveness in young chimpanzees. In H. W. Stevenson, E. H. Hess, & H. L. Rheingold (Eds.), *Early behavior: Comparative and developmental approaches.* New York: John Wiley & Sons, Inc., 1967. Pp. 103–126.

Mason, W. A. Early social deprivation in the nonhuman primates: Implications for human behavior. In D. C. Glass (Ed.), *Biology and behavior: Environmental influences.* New York: Rockefeller University Press, 1968. Pp. 70–101.

Mason, W. A., & Berkson, G. Conditions influencing vocal responsiveness of infant chimpanzees. *Science,* 1962, **137,** 127–218.

Mason, W. A., Harlow, H. F., & Rueping, R. R. The devlopment of manipulatory responsiveness in the infant rhesus monkey. *Journal of Comparative and Physiological Psychology,* 1959, **52,** 555–558.

Mason, W. A., & Hollis, J. H. Communication between young rhesus monkeys. *Animal Behaviour,* 1962, **10,** 211–221.

Mason, W. A., Hollis, J. H., & Sharpe, L. G. Differential responses of chimpanzees to social stimulation. *Journal of Comparative and Physiological Psychology,* 1962, **55,** 1105–1110.

McCulloch, T. L. The role of clasping activity in adaptive behavior of the infant chimpanzee: III. The mechanism of reinforcement. *Journal of Psychology,* 1939, **7,** 305–316.

Menzel, E. W., Jr. Patterns of responsiveness in chimpanzees reared through infancy under conditions of environmental restriction. *Psychologische Forschung,* 1964, **27,** 337–365.

Miller, R. E., Caul, W. F., & Mirsky, I. A. The communication of affects between feral and socially isolated monkeys. *Journal of Personality and Social Psychology,* 1967, **7,** 231–239.

Rosenblum, L. A., & Harlow, H. F. Approach-avoidance conflict in the mother-surrogate situation. *Psychological Reports,* 1963, **12,** 83–85.

Sackett, G. P. Effects of rearing conditions upon the behavior of rhesus monkeys (*Macaca mulatta*). *Child Development,* 1965, **36,** 855–868.

Sackett, G. P. Monkeys reared in isolation with pictures as visual input: Evidence for an innate releasing mechanism. *Science,* 1966, **154,** 1468–1470.

Schiff, W., Caviness, J. A., & Gibson, J. J. Persistent fear responses in rhesus monkeys to the optical stimulus of "looming." *Science,* 1962, **136,** 982–983.

Wolff, P. H. The development of attention in young infants. *Annals of the New York Academy of Science,* 1965, **118,** 815–830.

Yerkes, R. M. *Chimpanzees: A laboratory colony.* New Haven: Yale, 1943.

Zimmermann, R. R., & Torrey, C. C. Ontogeny of learning. In A. M. Schrier, H. F. Harlow, & F. Stollnitz (Eds.), *Behavior of nonhuman primates.* New York: Academic Press, 1965. Pp. 405–447.

The Mother as a Motivator[1]

VICTOR H. DENENBERG

University of Connecticut

For the past seven years we have been involved in an interesting program of research concerned with the effects of early social variables on subsequent behavioral and physiological processes. Our general approach has been to vary systematically the maternal environment of experimental mice and also the preweaning and postweaning peer group environment of these animals. What makes this work particularly interesting is the manner in which we have manipulated the maternal environment: this has been done by fostering newborn mice to lactating rat mothers who have pups approximately the same age as the infant mice. Even though the rat is a different species than the mouse, they are both rodents, and there is sufficient similarity between the two animals so that the rat mother can successfully rear mouse young. The rat engages in all the appropriate maternal behaviors with respect to the mouse pups including grooming, licking the anal-genital region, nest building, nursing, and retrieving the young (and the mother adjusts the strength of her bite so that she never breaks the skin of the young mouse even though it is markedly smaller than the same aged rat pups which she also retrieves).

The importance of this procedure is that it enables us to separate experimentally the usual confounding between genetic, prenatal, and postnatal environments which is present in all naturalistic situations and in the great majority of laboratory settings as well. By fostering young mice to rat mothers, with the appropriate controls, we can now begin to separate the genetic-prenatal contributions to behavioral and physiological variance from the postnatal

1. The research described in this paper was supported, in part, by NIH grants HD–02068 and HD–04639 from the National Institute of Child Health and Human Development.

69

maternal contributions. If our experimental animals reared by rat mothers exhibit behaviors different from those of controls reared by mouse mothers, we may conclude that such behaviors are significantly affected by the nature of the postparturient maternal environment. Indeed, if we have an appropriate metric which will allow us to put the mouse and the rat on the same scale of measurement, we can then ask whether the mouse's behavior has become "ratlike" as a function of being reared by a rat mother. However, this is a much more difficult task than is apparent at first glance because of the problems involved in developing measuring instruments which are valid for comparative purposes.

As I indicated above, in addition to manipulating the maternal variable, we have also varied the peer group composition, both before and after weaning. When we worked with mouse mothers we used the presence or absence of peers between birth and weaning as our preweaning variable. We used these same two conditions when rat mothers reared the pups, and we also had conditions in which the rat mother reared both rats and mice. After weaning, mice have been raised in isolation, with other mice of the same sex, or with rats. Even though the nature of the peer composition both before and after weaning does affect subsequent behaviors, we have found that our most potent social variable is the mother. In fact, she is an extraordinarily powerful determiner of the neonatal mouse's future behavior and physiological reactivity. We now have sufficient data to be able to draw some strong conclusions concerning the nature of the mother's influence, and that will be the concern of this review.

DEPENDENT VARIABLES

Now a word about our endpoints. The specific procedures followed may vary from one experiment to another, but the following description will suffice to give a general idea of our techniques.

Our most important behavioral criterion has been a measure of fighting behavior. To study this we take two adult mice and place them into a "fighting box." This is an 11.75-inch by 15-inch by 16.25-inch plywood box divided into two equal-sized compartments by a removable plywood guillotine door. Wood shavings are on the floor, and each compartment is covered by a fiberglass top having externally refillable food and water supplies. Each mouse is placed into a separate compartment where he remains alone for several days. After this, testing begins by removing the partition between the compartments, thus allowing the animals to interact with each other. This continues for a 6-minute period unless a fight occurs, in which case the session is terminated 5 seconds after the fight starts. The animals are then separated into their individual compartments and the partition is restored. This procedure is continued for 7 days. The presence or absence of fighting is recorded for each testing session.

It is quite important to note that this type of fighting differs from the fighting behavior seen in the rat in that it is not necessary to introduce an external noxious stimulus such as electric shock or food deprivation in order to induce aggression. With the mouse, fighting is internally motivated and may fairly be called a species-specific behavior pattern. This is certainly not true for the laboratory rat.

The second behavioral dependent variable which will be covered in this review is activity in the open field. The field is an open box with a 32-inch plywood floor marked off into 64 4-inch squares. The animals are placed in the field and observed for 3 minutes. The number of squares entered are recorded. In some experiments the animals are tested on only 1 day; in others they may be tested on 4 successive days.

The final endpoint to be discussed here is a physiological one— plasma corticosterone. Corticosterone is the primary hormone secreted by the adrenal cortex of the mouse and is one of the major hormones involved in an animal's reactivity to novel or stressful situations. Our procedure is to kill some animals by decapitation as soon as they are taken from their home cage to get a basal or resting level of corticosterone in the blood. Other animals are then exposed to a novel environment (often the open field) and are killed at varying times thereafter. In this manner we can determine their physiological reactivity to this mildly stressful situation as well as the time course of the response.

Procedure during Infancy

Briefly, let me comment on the procedures followed during infantile stimulation. Mouse young are left with their natural mothers usually until 4 days of age, at which time they are reduced to a standard litter size, generally six. Control mice are then returned to their natural mothers and are not disturbed again until weaning. In some instances our controls consist of mice fostered from one mouse mother to another. Experimental animals are fostered at this time to a rat mother, or a rat "aunt" is placed into the nest cage (see below for a discussion of rat aunts). The foster mother has had her own litter from 2 to 6 days at the time that fostering occurs.

Litters reared by mouse mothers live in plastic cages ($6\frac{1}{2}$ inches by 11 inches by 5 inches) filled with shavings while those raised with the rat mother or rat aunt are in an identical but larger plastic cage (9 inches by 18 inches by 6 inches). The reason for the larger cage is to compensate for the much greater size of the rat relative to the mouse mother.

Two strains of mice have been used in these studies: the C57BL/ 10J mouse obtained from the Jackson Laboratory, and the Purdue Rockland Swiss-Albino mouse. The latter animal is heterozygous while the C57 is inbred.

So much, then, for the general details of the procedures. We may now turn to an examination of the experimental findings.

MODIFICATION OF AGGRESSION AND ACTIVITY IN THE C57BL/10J MOUSE

In our first experiment (Denenberg, Hudgens, & Zarrow, 1964), C57BL/10J control mice were reduced to six animals 2 days after birth and were left with their natural mother. Experimental mice were fostered to lactating Purdue-Wistar rat mothers who also had two male and two female rat pups to raise. (This experiment also contained two other groups raised by mouse mothers in which the peer group composition varied. These data will not be discussed here.) Starting at 50 days of age, each mouse was tested for 4 consecutive days in the open field. At least 5 weeks elapsed before the animals were tested in the fighting box situation. The pertinent statistics for fighting behavior are summarized in Table 1 in the first row of that table. Table 2, which parallels Table 1, gives the relevant information for activity in the open field.

TABLE 1

INCIDENCE OF FIGHTING OF C57BL/10J AND SWISS-ALBINO MICE REARED UNDER STANDARD CONDITIONS (CONTROL) OR WITH VARIOUS RAT MOTHERS OR RAT AUNTS (EXPERIMENTAL)

REFERENCE	STRAIN	CONTROL Mouse mother, mouse peers, pre- and postweaning	EXPERIMENTAL Rat mother, rat peers, pre- and postweaning	EXPERIMENTAL Rat mother, mouse peers, pre- and postweaning	EXPERIMENTAL Rat aunt, mouse mother, mouse peers, pre- and postweaning
Denenberg et al. (1964)	C57BL/10J	44% (16)	0% (12)		
Denenberg et al. (1966)	C57BL/10J	77% (13)		9% (11)	
Hudgens et al. (1967)	C57BL/10J	39% (23)		0% (21)	
Hudgens et al. (1968)	C57BL/10J	11% (27)	0% (8)	0% (7)	
Paschke et al. (1970)	C57BL/10J	82% (17)		17% (12)	36% (11)
Paschke et al. (1970)	S-A	80% (40)		82% (17)	84% (19)

NOTE: The number in parentheses is the number of pairs of animals tested in the fighting box situation.

TABLE 2

Open-field Activity of C57BL/10J and Swiss-Albino Mice Reared under Standard Conditions (Control) or with Various Kinds of Rat Mothers or Rat Aunts (Experimental)

Reference	Strain	Age (Age at testing in days)	Control (Mouse mother, mouse peers, pre- and postweaning)	Experimental (Rat mother, rat peers, pre- and postweaning)	Experimental (Rat mother, mouse peers, pre- and postweaning)	Experimental (Rat aunt, mouse mother, mouse peers, pre- and postweaning)	Experimental (Thelectomized rat aunt, mouse mother, mouse peers, pre- and postweaning)	Experimental (Thelectomized and parturient rat aunt, mouse mother, mouse peers, pre- and postweaning)
Denenberg et al. (1964)	C57BL/10J	50	192.49 (34)	141.08 (34)				
Denenberg et al. (1966)	C57BL/10J	40	102.20 (39)		86.60 (31)			
Hudgens et al. (1967)	C57BL/10J	40	233.06 (50)		185.74 (43)			
Hudgens (1965)	C57BL/10J	40	283.76 (35)	226.88 (18)	183.72 (14)			
Denenberg et al. (1968)	S-A	21	170.44 (16)		125.98 (28)			
Denenberg et al. (1969a) Exp. 1	S-A	21	180.90 (30)			160.27 (30)		
Denenberg et al. (1969a) Exp. 2	S-A	200	141.67 (21)			115.46 (13)		
Denenberg et al. (1969b)	S-A	90	157.50 (49)			122.33 (42)		
Rosenberg et al. (1970) Exp. 2	S-A	21	150.2 (16)				140.3 (10)	71.7 (20)

Paschke et al. (1970) Exp. 1	C57BL/10J	21	86.71 (34)	66.50 (26)	71.52 (23)
	C57BL/10J	45	182.41 (34)	131.60 (25)	159.39 (23)
Paschke et al. (1970) Exp. 2	S-A	21	182.20 (40)	130.80 (37)	142.82 (38)
	S-A	45	149.70 (40)	111.71 (37)	129.30 (38)

NOTE: The number in parentheses is *N*.

Of the 16 pairs of control animals which were given the opportunity to fight, 7 pairs fought at least once in the fighting box,[2] resulting in a fighting incidence of 44%. None of the 12 pairs of experimental animals ever engaged in a fight under the same test conditions. In Table 2 we see that the control group of mice entered significantly more squares in the open field than the experimental group.

The activity difference was nice to find, but it was the difference in fighting which struck us as being quite important since this suggested that species-specific aggressive behavior could be drastically reduced by varying the postnatal social environment. However, one experiment does not establish a phenomenon. Also, even if the phenomenon were real, it was not possible from the experimental design to determine how much of this behavioral modification was due to the rat mother, to the presence of rat peers preweaning, to the presence of rats after weaning, or to some interacting combination of these events.

Our next experiment eliminated the peer variable by holding this constant (Denenberg, Hudgens, & Zarrow, 1966). Again C57BL/10J mice were used. The control litters were reduced to six pups 4 days after birth, and were not disturbed thereafter until weaning. Experimental litters of six pups were fostered to Purdue-Wister rat mothers whose own young were removed at this time. Between 40 and 43 days of age all animals were given a daily 3-minute test in the open field. At 50 days males were isolated in the fighting boxes. The findings of this study are summarized in the second row of Tables 1 and 2. Seventy-seven percent of the 13 pairs of control litters fought at least once in the fighting box as compared to only one of 11 pairs (9%) of experimental animals. As in the first study, control mice were more active in the open field than experimental animals.

The second experiment pretty well convinced us that we had a reproducible phenomenon which we thought was quite exciting. We were almost at the point where we could state that being reared

2. The nature of our aggression statistic should be emphasized. For each pair we recorded whether or not a fight had occurred. We then computed the percentage of pairs which had engaged in at least one fight. In this manner each pair is treated as an independent entity.

by a lactating rat mother was sufficient to attenuate and virtually eliminate fighting in the mouse as well as reduce activity. However, there was still one variable that we had not controlled: the act of fostering per se. In our first two experiments control mice had been reared by their natural mothers. The experimental mice, on the other hand, had received two sets of experiences—the act of fostering, and being reared by a rat mother. Thus, it was necessary to foster the control mice as well in order to eliminate this source of contamination from the experimental design. That was one of the purposes of our third experiment (Hudgens, Denenberg, & Zarrow, 1967). C57BL/10J mice were fostered in groups of five to six when they were 4 days of age, either to a mouse mother or to a rat mother. The natural young of these foster mothers were removed at this time. All animals were tested daily in the open field at 40 to 43 days. Aggression testing was done between 55 and 89 days of age.

The results are summarized in the third row of Tables 1 and 2. Of the 23 pairs of fostered control animals, 9, or 39%, fought while none of the 21 pairs of experimental animals fought. As we had previously found, control animals were more active than the experimental animals. However, even though there is a large absolute difference in activity level, there was also a very large error variance in this experiment so that this difference in activity was not statistically significant. But since we had found significant activity differences in our previous experiments, as well as our subsequent ones, we feel that the lack of significance in this particular instance is due to sampling error.

The results of the first three experiments were so consistent with each other on both of our criterion measures as to gladden our collective experimental hearts. It was now time to expand our research horizons. And so we designed and carried out a rather large and complicated factorial experiment, manipulating the maternal variable, preweaning peer group composition, and postweaning peer group composition (Hudgens, Denenberg, & Zarrow, 1968). Only a small part of those findings will be reported here.

The animals were sorted into their various experimental combinations at 4 days of age and again when they were weaned. All animals were tested in the open field from 40 to 43 days of age. Between 90 and 101 days they were placed into fighting boxes. The fourth row of Tables 1 and 2 presents findings of this experiment. Even though the percentage of control animals which fought dropped in an inexplicable manner, we still obtained an 11% incidence of fighting as compared to zero percentages in two experimental groups. In this particular experiment, it will be noted, we had one group which had the same peer group and maternal composition as the experimental group in our first study (Denenberg et al., 1964), in addition to the experimental group raised by a rat mother with mouse peers before and after weaning. The activity data are again consistent with our previous findings in showing that mice raised by mouse mothers are significantly more active than those raised by rat mothers.

This experiment, however, made a much greater contribution than merely replicating our prior findings. As mentioned above, in this study we had a factorial design which varied the peer group composition both preweaning and postweaning. There were four possible preweaning conditions for the mice raised by rat mothers: being raised in groups with other mice, being raised in isolation, being raised with rats, or being raised with rats and mice. After weaning, there were three possible peer group combinations: living with mice, living in isolation, or living with rats. Table 3 presents the number of pairs of animals and the incidence of fighting behavior for the 12 combinations resulting from combining the pre-

TABLE 3

INCIDENCE OF FIGHTING FOR C57BL/10J MICE REARED BY RAT MOTHERS IN VARIOUS COMBINATIONS OF PREWEANING AND POSTWEANING PEERS

Preweaning Peers	Postweaning Peers		
	Mice	None	Rats
Mice	0% (7)	0% (6)	0% (6)
None	60% (5)	0% (5)	0% (5)
Rats	0% (8)	10% (10)	0% (8)
Mice and Rats	0% (4)	0% (1)	0% (6)

NOTE: The number in parentheses is the number of pairs of animals.
From Hudgens et al. (1968).

weaning and postweaning peer group variables. Table 4 presents the same data for the activity variable.

Of the 71 pairs of animals represented in Table 3, only 4 pairs engaged in one or more fights. In other words, regardless of the nature of the peers with which an experimental mouse associates either before or after weaning, if he is reared by a rat mother, this is a sufficient condition to virtually eliminate the probability that he will fight as an adult. (One caution is needed here. In Table 3 the combination of no peers preweaning and mouse peers postweaning resulted in 3 out of 5 pairs, or 60%, fighting. We have similarly found that this particular combination also results in the highest fighting incidence for animals raised by mouse mothers. Therefore, there is some chance that this unique combination of peer experience is sufficient to overcome the powerful effect of the rat maternal variable, but further work is needed for verification.)

A very similar pattern is seen for the activity data in Table 4. The activity level of control mice was given in Table 2 as 283.76 squares. Inspection of Table 4 reveals that in all instances, except when the experimental animals were exposed to both mice and rats between birth and weaning, the activity pattern is markedly depressed when mice are raised by a rat mother.

Therefore, we may draw the rather general conclusion that the role of the mother is an extremely powerful one which can markedly

TABLE 4

MEAN NUMBER OF SQUARES ENTERED IN THE OPEN FIELD FOR C57BL/10J MICE REARED BY RAT MOTHERS IN VARIOUS COMBINATIONS OF PREWEANING AND POSTWEANING PEERS

Preweaning Peers	Postweaning Peers		
	Mice	None	Rats
Mice	183.72 (14)	144.48 (12)	92.84 (12)
None	161.52 (10)	200.20 (10)	94.28 (11)
Rats	136.00 (16)	166.92 (21)	226.88 (18)
Mice and Rats	287.88 (9)	299.52 (2)	219.88 (8)

NOTE: The number in parentheses is N.
From Hudgens (1965).

influence the species-specific aggressive behavior of this particular strain as well as the strain's activity pattern. Furthermore, these are long-term, relatively permanent effects. They are clearly postnatal events and are almost (though not entirely) independent of the nature of the peer group composition before and after weaning.

Modification of Plasma Corticosterone and Activity in the Swiss-Albino Mouse

Having established the critical role of the mother in mediating these behavioral changes, we decided to concentrate our efforts upon a more intensive analysis of the maternal variable and to drop our studies of peer group effects. We also decided at this time to look at a physiological process which might be affected by our rat mother. Our reasoning was as follows: modification of fighting behavior and open-field activity implies changes in the animal's emotional reactivity and, if this is so, it implicates the hypothalamic-pituitary-adrenal axis. Also, in another study we had demonstrated a significant relationship between open-field behavior and adreno-cortical activity in the rat (Levine, Haltmeyer, Karas, & Denenberg, 1967). Thus, we decided to see whether our rat mother would have any effect upon the amount of corticosterone released by the adrenal cortex as a function of exposure to a novel stimulus situation.

But to do this experiment, it was necessary to shift to a different strain of mouse. We wanted to obtain a time-response curve for corticosterone using a within-litter design. Also, we wished to measure our animals at the time of weaning. However, our assay for corticosterone required more blood than we could obtain from one weanling animal, and so it was necessary to pool the blood from two littermates. Because of these experimental demands we had to have a strain of mouse which produced a large-sized litter and one in which the individual animals were also of good size so we could obtain sufficient blood for our assay. Our C57BL/10J mouse fit neither of these requirements, but the Rockland Swiss-Albino mouse did, and so we shifted to it.

It is apparent that by changing both our strain of animal and our dependent variable we had no basis for comparing any new findings with our previous studies. Therefore we tested one group of animals in the open field to provide a comparative link between the Swiss-Albino and the C57BL/10J animals.

We fostered 4-day-old mouse litters to lactating rat mothers. When weaned at 21 days one rat or two mice were decapitated immediately and their blood collected to give us a resting value for the amount of corticosterone present prior to any extrinsic stimulation. The remaining animals were placed into a novel environment for 15, 30, 45, or 60 minutes; they were then decapitated. The amount of corticosterone present in the plasma was determined by a modification of the fluorometric procedure of Silber, Busch, and Oslapas (1958). We did three experiments and the results of those studies are shown in Figure 1.

Our first experiment (the left-hand panel in Figure 1) was a descriptive study of the time course of the corticosterone response to a novel stimulus for mice raised by mouse mothers and rats reared by rat mothers. For both species, introduction into a novel environment causes an activation of the adrenal cortex which results in a rapid production of corticosterone, and there is no habituation to

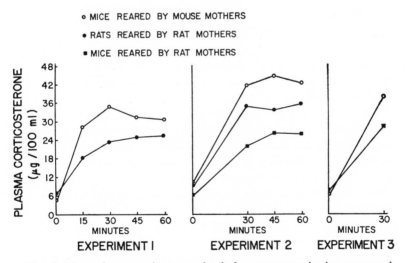

Fig. 1. Mean plasma corticosterone levels for mouse-reared mice, rat-reared rats, and rat-reared mice in three experiments. (From Denenberg, Rosenberg, Paschke, Hess, Zarrow, & Levine, 1968)

the novel environment over a period of 1 hour. In addition, mice have a higher relative amount of corticosterone in their blood than do rats.

In our second experiment (the middle panel in Figure 1) we repeated these two conditions from the first experiment, except that we dropped out the 15-minute interval since it seemed to give us no additional data, and we introduced our experimental group of mice raised by rat mothers. What astonished us was the finding that our experimental mice had the lowest level of corticosterone production of any of the three goups. Going into that experiment our most reasonable assumption was that the genetic effect and the maternal effect would be roughly equivalent. Thus we expected that the mice raised by rat mothers would have an average curve somewhere between our pure mouse curve and our pure rat curve. The results of the experiment are clearly not consistent with such an assumption of additivity of effects.

The findings of Experiment 2 were too important to be published without further verification. In addition, we had not fostered our two control groups in either Experiment 1 or Experiment 2 while, of course, our experimental mice had to be fostered. Even though we had shown that fostering was without effect with respect to our various behavioral measurements (Hudgens et al., 1967, 1968), this did not preclude the possibility that fostering might have an effect upon the corticosterone response. Therefore we did a third experiment fostering mice to mouse mothers or to rat mothers, and at weaning we determined their plasma corticosterone levels 30 minutes after being introduced into the novel environment. Those data are shown in the right-hand panel of Figure 1. Again the mice raised by rat mothers had a lesser adrenocortical response to the novel stimulus than mice reared by mouse mothers.

Since Experiment 3 used only four animals per litter for the corticosterone determinations, we had extra animals left over and these were tested for 3 minutes in our open field at 21 days. Their activity scores are given in the fifth row of Table 2. We were delighted to find that the Rockland Swiss-Albino mouse also had its activity depressed when raised by a rat mother, thus replicating the phenomenon we had obtained with our black mouse.

The finding that the rat mother reduced the adrenocortical

activity of the mouse was almost too good to be true. The reduction of species-specific fighting behavior and open-field activity had been exciting enough, but when we added to that the modification of the adrenocortical response, it was clear that we had a fascinating bio-behavioral preparation which would enthuse any experimenter. Among the many questions which we started asking ourselves at this point, the one which appeared to us to be the most relevant was: by what mechanism does the mother mediate these behavioral and physiological changes upon the young? Our hope was that the mediation was via her behavioral interactions with the young between birth and weaning. However, there were several alternative possibilities to be considered. The most obvious possibility had to do with the milk of the mothers. Perhaps the biochemical differences between the milk of these two species was sufficient to account for the differences in the behavior and physiology of our experimental animals. We spent a lot of time considering various methods of attacking this problem and eventually came up with the idea of using a rat "aunt" in lieu of the rat mother. The reason for choosing this particular preparation is because it is known that the adult rat (male or female) can engage in many of the component acts of maternal behavior if exposed for a sufficient period of time to infant animals (Rosenblatt, 1967). Thus, we expected our rat aunt to perform many of the maternal caretaking activities usually seen when an animal gives birth, with the exception that she would not be able to nurse the young since no milk supply was present.

Several pilot studies confirmed these expectations, and we also verified by means of postmortem examinations that there was no milk in the mammary glands of our aunts. We then did two experiments to determine the effects of the presence of a rat aunt upon the activity and plasma corticosterone response of Swiss-Albino mice (Denenberg, Rosenberg, Paschke, & Zarrow, 1969). In our first experiment each rat aunt was "primed" by being placed with a rat mother and her litter for 6 days, and was then introduced into a litter of 4-day-old mice. At weaning the experimental and control mice were placed into a novel environment for 30 minutes, and then blood was collected. Littermates of these animals were placed into an open field for 3 minutes, and their activity was recorded. Those mice reared in the presence of a rat aunt had a significantly lower adrenocortical response to the novel stimulus than did control mice. We also found that the mice raised in the presence of a rat aunt were less active in the open field than the controls, though this difference was not significant. The activity data are presented in the sixth row of Table 2.

Our second experiment differed from the first in that the rat aunt was placed with a pregnant mouse approximately 3 days before she was expected to give birth. After weaning the males were group housed until 200 days of age. They were then given a 3-minute open-field test after which they were decapitated and the blood assayed for corticosterone. Again our experimental animals had a significantly lesser corticoid response than did our controls. These animals were also less active in the open field (see Table 2, row seven) but here too, the difference was not significant.

These findings gave us strong reason to believe that biochemical differences in the milk of the rat and mouse were not involved in mediating the differences we had found in our prior studies. Both the corticosterone and activity differences were qualitatively the same with our aunt preparation as we had previously found with our mother preparation. The lack of a significant effect for the activity data suggested that the aunt preparation was quantitatively weaker than the mother preparation. Our corticosterone data also suggested this. Even though our differences were significant, the magnitude of difference was generally less than we had found using a rat mother.

Another important finding from this experiment is that the difference in adrenocortical activity was present in adulthood as well as at weaning, thus indicating that the aunt preparation had long-term effects upon the mouse's physiology. However, this conclusion was based upon only one experiment in which the animals were killed approximately 5 minutes after stimulus onset. It was necessary to verify that finding in an independent replication, and it was also quite important to look at the temporal course of the corticosterone response to be certain that our significant effect was not merely a happenstance of the 5-minute interval which we used.

Thus we conducted another study in which rat aunts were primed for 6 days by being placed into a cage containing a rat mother and her litter, and were then transferred to a cage containing a mouse mother and her 4-day-old pups (Denenberg, Rosenberg, & Zarrow, 1969). At weaning the mice were group housed and, when 90 days old, they were given a 1-day test in the open field. Ten to 14 days after this test, mice were killed immediately or else were placed into a novel environment for 15, 30, or 60 minutes and were then killed, and their blood assayed for corticosterone. The corticosterone curves for the two groups are presented in Figure 2. Again the control mice had a significantly greater amount of corticosterone in their blood as a function of exposure to the novel stimulus situation than mice raised by mouse mothers in the presence of rat aunts, and this difference persisted throughout the 1-hour test

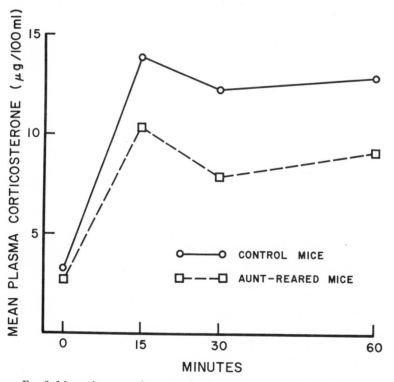

Fig. 2. Mean plasma corticosterone levels as a function of amount of exposure to a novel environment for control and experimental mice. (From Denenberg, Rosenberg, & Zarrow, 1969)

session. The activity findings are in the eighth row of Table 2. For the first time with our rat aunt preparation, we found a significant effect with our experimental animals being less active than the controls.

These data nicely confirmed our earlier finding that the aunt would cause a relatively permanent change in adrenocortical activity and also indicated a long-term effect upon open-field activity which paralleled our results concerning the influence of rat mothers upon our black mice.

These studies have rather conclusively eliminated the possibility that corticosterone and activity changes are brought about by the nature of the mother's milk. Thus, this leaves us with the very strong implication that the changes are mediated through the mother's or aunt's behavior toward the young. Even though this is a reasonable conclusion, it is based upon the elimination of an alternative hypothesis rather than upon direct positive evidence. Our observations were consistent with this conclusion, however. We had noted that some of our aunts did not act very maternally toward the mice, and we had generally found that the difference between control animals and those reared in the presence of rat aunts was less than the difference between controls and mice raised by rat mothers. This suggested that the more maternal the aunt was, the greater was the likelihood that the offspring's behavior and physiology would be changed. Therefore, the experimental question was raised as to how one could systematically vary the amount of rat-mouse behavioral interactions to test the hypothesis that the greater the amount of interaction, the greater would be the magnitude of the observed effect.

One way to maximize the maternal behavior of an aunt is to remove her nipples (technically, to thelectomize her) so that she is unable to nurse, then get her pregnant, let her deliver her young, remove the young at birth, and then place the thelectomized rat into a cage where there is a mouse mother with her young pups. This aunt should be maximally maternal toward the young. We have carried out two experiments using the thelectomized aunt preparation (Rosenberg, Denenberg, & Zarrow, 1970).

Our first experiment measured the corticosterone response to a novel stimulus at weaning with offspring of control mice and mice raised in the presence of postparturient thelectomized aunts. The experimental animals had a significantly lesser adrenocortical response than did the controls, thus establishing the efficacy of the thelectomized postparturient aunt preparation.

We then did a more critical study. In our second experiment we again had thelectomized postpartum animals as aunts, and we also had a second group of rats which had been thelectomized but had not been bred. This latter group is essentially the same as our prior aunts except for the surgery. We made the assumption that the group which had given birth to a litter would act more maternally toward mouse pups than would our usual group of aunts. To test this assumption we took daily observations of maternal involvement between the two groups of rat aunts and the pups. Consistent with our expectations, those females which had given birth to a litter of rat pups acted significantly more maternally toward the mouse young than did the group of control aunts. As usual we also had in the experiment our standard control group of mice reared by mouse mothers. At weaning some of the mice were tested for activity in the open field while others were placed in a novel environment and, 30 minutes later, they were killed and their blood assayed for corticosterone.

The corticosterone data revealed that those animals raised in the presence of a postpartum aunt gave the least response to the novel stimulus followed by the control aunt group, with the mice raised by mouse mothers alone (the control mice) giving the greatest response. The difference between the control group and those mice raised by postpartum aunts was significant, while the intermediate group of animals raised by control aunts did not differ from the two extreme groups. The activity data of the littermates of these animals are presented in the ninth row of Table 2. The control mice were most active, followed by those raised by our standard aunt preparation, with the mice raised by postpartum aunts being the least active. The latter group differed significantly from the other two groups which did not differ from each other.

We also computed correlations between the ratings of maternal activity on the part of each of the aunts and the amount of corticosterone found in the blood of the young at the time of weaning. Within our usual aunt group the correlation was −.16 which is not significant. However, within the postpartum aunt group, which is the group that had the greatest amount of interaction with the pups, the correlation is $-.61$ which is significant. In other words, within this group, the greater the amount of maternal involvement with the pups, the lesser was the pups' adrenocortical response at the time of weaning.

Thus we see for both the activity and the corticosterone data that the postpartum aunt produced a greater effect than did control aunts. This is a confirmation of the hypothesis that the more maternally the aunt acted, the greater would be her effect upon the young. A second substantiation of this hypothesis is seen in our correlation of $-.61$ within the postpartum aunt group.

We felt that these findings, in conjunction with the elimination of the milk as a possible factor, allowed us to conclude that it is the amount of behavioral contact between the mother or the aunt and the pups which is the factor causing the changes in the animal's behavior and physiology. However, we still had one remaining nagging doubt. It is known that the mouse is very sensitive to odors, and there was the possibility that smell or some other distant stimuli could be involved in mediating the observed effects. Therefore, we did an experiment in which all variables were controlled except those stimuli which do not require physical contact between the adult rat and the young mouse (Denenberg, Paschke, Zarrow, & Rosenberg, 1969). Experimental mice were born and reared in a cage where an aunt was present except that in this instance the aunt was separated from the mice by a double wire mesh wall. Under these conditions the young mice could smell the rat aunt, hear her, and see her, but no physical contact was possible. Control mice were reared similarly in the presence of an adult nonlactating mouse. At weaning we tested both groups of animals for their corticosterone response to a novel stimulus since we had previously found that both the rat-mother preparation and the rat-aunt preparation were sensitive to this measure. Our findings are shown in Figure 3. We found absolutely no evidence of an effect here, from which we may conclude that olfactory, auditory, and visual cues are not involved in mediating this phenomenon.

Therefore, we may now draw a reasonably firm conclusion that it is actually the behavior of the adult rat toward the pups which is

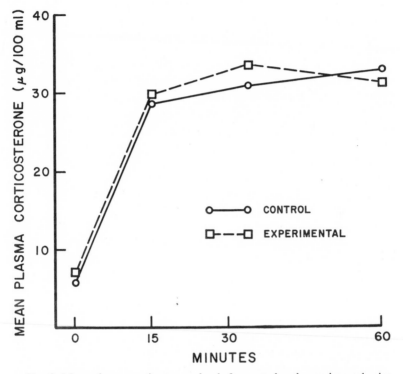

Fig. 3. Mean plasma corticosterone levels for control and experimental mice after exposure to a novel stimulus. (From Denenberg, Paschke, Zarrow, & Rosenberg, 1969)

the critical mediator causing the changes in adrenal activity and in open-field behavior.

Rat Mothers and Rat Aunts: Effects on Aggression and Activity in Both Mouse Strains

And now it is time to complete the circle and return to our original experimental problem. Remember that we started out studying aggression and activity in the C57BL/10J mouse raised by a rat mother. We then shifted to the Swiss-Albino mouse in order to study adrenal physiology and open-field activity when that animal was reared by a rat mother. Still using the Swiss-Albino mouse we moved to our rat-aunt preparation and examined the same dependent variables. Those studies revealed that the aunt preparation was almost as effective as the rat-mother preparation in modifying these two endpoints. But up to this point we did not know whether the aunt preparation affected aggression.

We have just completed a set of experiments on that topic, one with the C57BL/10J mouse and the other with the Swiss-Albino (Paschke, Denenberg, & Zarrow, 1970). Both rat mothers and rat aunts were employed in the same experimental design together with control groups raised by mouse mothers. This allowed us to compare the effects of the mother preparation and the aunt preparation within an experiment. Our usual procedures for housing and rearing the animals were followed. At weaning the males were tested in the open field for 3 minutes, and they were retested at 45 days of age. Starting at 55 days, fighting was measured. The aggression data for the two mouse strains are shown in the last two rows of Table 1. For the C57BL/10J animals we obtained our usual finding that those raised with rat mothers are significantly less aggressive than the control mice. Furthermore, those animals raised by rat aunts did not differ significantly from those raised by rat mothers but they were significantly different from the controls. Therefore, for this strain we may conclude that the aunt preparation is essentially as effective as the rat-mother preparation in attenuating aggression, thereby eliminating the milk factor as a possible variable determining this effect.

An examination of the data for the Swiss-Albino mouse shows quite clearly that the conclusion given above is strain-specific, since no reduction in aggression was found when the white mice were reared with either a rat mother or a rat aunt. In addition to this experiment we have other unpublished data also substantiating this finding of the lack of an effect.

The activity data are in the last four rows of Table 2. The animals were tested at weaning and retested later on. Here we have a very clear pattern which generalizes across strains. In both the Swiss-Albino and the C57 we found, as we had previously, that being raised by a rat mother reduces activity. In addition, we now see that being raised by the rat aunt also reduces activity. The aunt-tended animals are significantly different from controls but do not differ from rat-mother reared mice. However, in all four instances the aunt-reared group's score is higher than the rat-mother group, which is consistent with our findings that the rat aunt is somewhat less maternal than the rat mother.

THE MOTHER AS A MOTIVATOR

Let me now summarize. First of all, our most general statement is that the adult rat, whether mother or aunt, through her behavioral interactions with mice, will cause a significant reduction in the activity level of these animals both at weaning and in adulthood. This generalization has been found to hold with both strains of mice used in our experiment.

Our conclusion concerning aggression must be limited by the genotype of the animal. For the C57BL/10J mouse, a reduction in fighting results from the mother's behavioral interactions with the pups between birth and weaning. For the Swiss-Albino mouse, equivalent experience had no effect upon aggression.

Our third conclusion is that the behavioral interactions of the mother between birth and weaning are the cause of a marked reduction in adrenocortical reactivity to a novel situation, as measured both at weaning and at adulthood in the Swiss-Albino mouse. The generality of this finding is not known since all of our experiments have been carried out on the Swiss-Albino mouse.

Even though I am a firm believer in motherhood, I must admit that when we started this set of experiments I did not expect to find that the mother's behavior during the nursing period would have such a powerful effect upon so many different biobehavioral systems of the animal. Clearly, if these results have any degree of generality to other mammals, the subtle and not so subtle behavior patterns of the mother during the early stages of the neonate's development have very profound and far-reaching effects.

The next task we have before us is to find out what are the particular behavior patterns which the mother engages in that actually cause the behavioral and physiological modifications. In addition, the question of why one genotype is affected while another one is not, in our fighting test, should throw light on the problem of genetic-environmental interactions. Hopefully, an analysis of the maternal behavior patterns which affect and change the offspring's performance will allow us to isolate some of the crucial dimensions of maternity.

SUMMARY

A series of experiments are described in which newborn mouse pups are fostered to a lactating rat mother or are reared by mouse mothers in the presence of a rat "aunt." Both the C57BL/10J mouse and the Rockland Swiss-Albino mouse have been used in these studies. This review is concerned only with the effects of maternal variables upon fighting, open-field activity, and the plasma corticosterone response from the adrenal cortex.

The open-field activity of both mouse strains was significantly depressed when animals were raised in the presence of a rat mother or a rat aunt. The aggression of the C57BL/10J mouse was reduced almost to zero by the rat mother. The rat aunt had a similar effect, though not so marked. However, no attenuation of aggression was found when the Swiss-Albino mouse was studied. Only the Swiss-Albino mouse has been used in investigations of the adrenocortical response to a novel stimulus. In all these experiments, the experimental animal gave a lesser corticosterone response to novelty than did control mice.

Biochemical differences in the milk supply between the mouse mother and the rat mother have been eliminated as a possible causal factor underlying these events. Likewise, distant stimuli such as odors, and auditory and visual cues have also been eliminated. We may conclude that the differences obtained are caused by the mother's or aunt's behavioral interaction with the pups between birth and weaning. Direct tests have substantiated this hypothesis.

REFERENCES

Denenberg, V. H., Hudgens, G. A., & Zarrow, M. X. Mice reared with rats: Modification of behavior by early experience with another species. *Science,* 1964, **143**, 380–381.

Denenberg, V. H., Hudgens, G. A., & Zarro, M. X. Mice reared with rats: Effects of mother on adult behavior patterns. *Psychological Reports,* 1966, **18**, 451–456.

Denenberg, V. H., Paschke, R. E., Zarrow, M. X., & Rosenberg, K. M. Mice reared with rats: Elimination of odors, vision, and audition as significant stimulus sources. *Developmental Psychobiology*, 1969, **2**, 26–28.

Denenberg, V. H., Rosenberg, K. M., Paschke, R. E., Hess, J. L., Zarrow, M. X., & Levine, S. Plasma corticosterone levels as a function of cross-species fostering and species differences. *Endocrinology*, 1968, **83**, 900–902.

Denenberg, V. H., Rosenberg, K. M., Paschke, R. E., & Zarrow, M. X. Mice reared with rat aunts: Effects on plasma corticosterone and open-field activity. *Nature*, 1969, **221**, 73–74.

Denenberg, V. H., Rosenberg, K. M., & Zarrow, M. X. Mice reared with rat aunts: Effects in adulthood upon plasma corticosterone and open-field activity. *Physiology and Behavior*, 1969, **4**, 705–707.

Hudgens, G. A., Denenberg, V. H., & Zarrow, M. X. Mice reared with rats: Relations between mothers' activity level and offspring's behavior. *Journal of Comparative and Physiological Psychology*, 1967, **63**, 304–308.

Hudgens, G. A., Denenberg, V. H., & Zarrow, M. X. Mice reared with rats: Effects of preweaning and postweaning social interactions upon adult behaviour. *Behaviour*, 1968, **30**, 259–274.

Levine, S., Haltmeyer, G. C., Karas, G. G., & Denenberg, V. H. Physiological and behavioral effects of infantile stimulation. *Physiology and Behavior*, 1967, **2**, 55–59.

Paschke, R. E., Denenberg, V. H., & Zarrow, M. X. Mice reared with rats: An interstrain comparison of mother and "aunt" effects. *Behaviour* 1970, in press.

Rosenberg, K. M., Denenberg, V. H., & Zarrow, M. X. Mice (*Mus musculus*) reared with rat aunts: The role of rat-mouse contact in mediating behavioral and physiological changes in the mouse. *Animal Behaviour*, 1970, **18**, 138–143.

Rosenblatt, J. Non-hormonal basis of maternal behavior in the rat. *Science*, 1967, **156**, 1512–1514.

Silber, R. H., Busch, R. A., & Oslapas, R. Practical procedure for estimation of corticosterone or hydrocortisone. *Journal of Clinical Chemistry*, 1958, **4**, 278–285.

The Contagion of Violence: An S-R Mediational Analysis of Some Effects of Observed Aggression[1]

LEONARD BERKOWITZ

University of Wisconsin

In the fall of 1969 the National Commission on the Causes and Prevention of Violence published a strong indictment of the television industry:

> Each year advertisers spend $2½ billion in the belief that television can influence human behavior. The television industry enthusiastically agrees with them, but nonetheless contends that its programs of violence do not have any such influence.
>
> The preponderance of the available evidence strongly suggests, however, that violence in television programs can and does have adverse effects upon audiences—particularly child audiences. [Eisenhower et al., 1969, p. 5]

Without going into any detailed review of the entire body of research on this topic, I should like to offer several reasons why these adverse effects occur and thus also suggest some conditions under which they arise. There has been a great deal of controversy about the consequences of media violence since the 1930s and a good many arguments have been advanced as to why the portrayal of aggression on movie and TV screens might influence people in the audience. The analysis to be presented here will emphasize certain

1. The author's research reported in this paper has been supported by grants from the National Science Foundation and the National Institute of Mental Health.

psychological processes that have been neglected unduly in most of these discussions. By considering these processes, I think we will gain a better understanding of the contagion of violence—why the sight of violence at times ignites other aggressive outbursts.

To be fair, we must acknowledge some arguments on the other side of this issue. Defenders of TV and movie programming often object that the mass media are being singled out unfairly. They say that television and the movies have been chosen as the scapegoat for society's ills, and point out quite correctly that violence usually has far more complex and profound causes than the fleeting images flashing across the tube or screen.

It certainly is true that there are no simple solutions for our domestic turmoil, crime, and violence. There is no one villain whose eradication will bring peace and harmony. Oversimplified diagnoses of our troubles are easily understood but are only illusory guide-posts for action. Saying all this, however, does not mean that I disagree with the Violence Commission: I am convinced that aggressive scenes shown or even reported in the communications media *can* have violent consequences under some circumstances. But here, too, it is best to acknowledge the complexities governing these aggressive consequences. Media-portrayed violence does not inevitably promote aggression; violent aftereffects emerge under some conditions but not under others. Rather than pursuing the question of whether media violence does have aggressive conse-quences, it is time that investigators turned to a more precise analysis of the conditions under which these consequences do or do not arise. We cannot fully understand the role of the mass media in influencing social behavior, or institute policies to minimize social violence at the lowest cost to our cultural values, unless we recognize these exceptions.

Some media effects are recognized by all but television's staunchest defenders. The mass media help determine children's attitudes toward other people and contribute to their expectations of how other persons will act. Back in 1933, Peterson and Thurstone demonstrated that one showing of a movie (such as the silent film *The Birth of a Nation*) can produce long-lasting changes in children's attitudes toward other groups. Similarly, Alberta Siegel showed in 1958 that young children developed beliefs about how certain people (in this case taxi drivers) would generally behave after listening to a single radio story about these persons. As the Violence Commission has noted, television programs can also mold youngsters' ideas regarding the best way to solve interpersonal problems. Children from low-income families are evidently particularly susceptible to this kind of influence. In one study cited by the Violence Commission, 40% of the poor black adolescents and 30% of the poor white teenagers interviewed believed that the people portrayed on TV programs are just like people in real life, as compared with only 15% of the middle class white youngsters (Eisenhower et al., 1969).

Well, how do people act in real life—as shown on television? According to a content analysis of the 1968 TV programs carried out for the Violence Commission, most people use violence to solve their problems and are rarely punished for such actions. More than half of the leading characters in the programs analyzed acted violently toward other persons, whether these characters were "good guys" or "bad guys." In the majority of instances studied, aggressive behavior led to a happy ending; violence is evidently a good way to get what we want. Furthermore, people are rarely arrested for acting violently, at least on television, and relatively few TV victims of violence suffer a physical injury or death. Not only is violence effective and socially acceptable, but it is also remarkably painless (Eisenhower et al., 1969). At least this is what television teaches.

The television industry is responsible for promulgating this kind of lesson. It alone cannot be faulted, however, for other effects produced by all of the mass media and perhaps even by informal conversations. Sometimes, perhaps more frequently than we care to admit, violence seems contagious. Crime stories reported in newspapers, or on radio or TV, appear to spark other persons into violent action. These are the consequences I would like to discuss particularly in this paper.

CONTAGIOUS VIOLENCE

Writing over 80 years ago, the French sociologist Gabriel Tarde described what he called "suggesto-imitative assaults." Epidemics of crime, he proposed, "follow the line of the telegraph." News of a spectacular crime in one community suggests criminal ideas to others and can even produce imitative crimes. Tarde pointed to the after-effects of the Jack the Ripper murders as a notable example. The lurid news stories about these crimes evidently inspired a series of female mutilation cases in the English provinces (Tarde, 1912, pp. 340–341). Police in this country have at times offered similar obser-vations. According to Commander Francis Flanagan of the Chicago Police Department (*Look*, Sept. 19, 1967), Richard Speck's murder of eight nurses in Chicago in July, 1966, and Charles Whitman's shooting of 45 people from the University of Texas Tower the next month instigated a rise in homicides in Chicago. At least five murders in Arizona were apparently influenced by the Texas Tower shootings. In November, 1966, Robert Smith, an 18-year-old high school senior, walked into an Arizona beauty school and shot four women and a child. He told police he had gotten the idea for a mass killing from the news stories of the Speck and Whitman outbursts. He had been planning his murders from the time his parents gave him a target pistol 3 months earlier (*Ithaca Journal*, Nov. 14, 1966).

Many other illustrations of apparently contagious violence can also be cited. To single out just a few, in the winter of 1966–1967 a televised dramatization of a fictitious plot to blow up an airliner led to a sharp increase in hoax telephone calls warning about bombs aboard airliners (*Ithaca Journal*, Dec. 20, 1966), and in the spring of 1968 a German housepainter shot the student radical Rudi Dutschke, saying he had gotten the idea from the assassination of Martin Luther King (*Madison Capital Times*, Apr. 13, 1968). The news stories may even instigate crimes that do not closely resemble the instigating event; in Gravesend, England, probation officers re-ported a sharp rise in offenses by local delinquents after a sex killing of two teenagers (*London Sunday Times*, Apr. 24, 1966). Urban riots in this country also show a pattern suggestive of a contagious spread of violence. According to Lieberson and Silverman (1965), American race riots tend to be clustered together in time. No detectable riot occurred in 26 of the 51 years between 1913 through 1963, while there were two or more such riots in 15 of the years in this period, and 5 years actually had seven or more riots—all of this before Watts exploded into our awareness. Can it be that any one racial flare-up somehow makes it easier for another similar outburst to take place soon after?

Some time ago I wondered if these seeming "imitative" effects would be revealed in crime statistics. Through the cooperation of the Federal Bureau of Investigation, my associate, Dr. Jacqueline Macaulay, and I obtained the number of aggressive crimes in each month of 1960 through 1966 for 40 cities across the country. We were particularly interested in the possibility of increases in the frequency of these offenses after John Kennedy's assassination in late November, 1963, and after the Speck-Whitman murders in the summer of 1966. The data for each city were first transformed into Z scores using the mean and standard deviation for that city over the 84 months, and a statistical analysis was then performed employing a least-squares model. The most reliable measure is the sum of the scores for the four violent crimes (murder, rape, aggravated assault, and robbery) and many criminologists have worked with an unweighted sum of these offenses as an index of total violent crimes. Analyses were also carried out for the separate crimes, but I will here focus my attention on the total score measure.

We found a significant, positively accelerated trend for these aggressive crimes across the 84 months and no reliable differences from one area of the country to another. More important, the analysis revealed a significant rise from the general linear trend after each of the sensational murders.

Two analyses actually were carried out to test the effects of President Kennedy's assassination. The more conservative method computed the overall trend *from the months following this crime* as well as from the preceding months.[2] Here there was no reliable increment in December, 1963, the month after JFK's murder, but there was a significant and a sharp jump in January, as if a numbing shock or anxiety had worn off. The second procedure based the overall trend only on the months *before the assassination* and showed

2. Although many economists compute trend lines in just this manner in searching for unusual occurrences, this procedure might mask relatively slight but significant effects. To use a rough analogy, it is as if we tested an experimental treatment by comparing the experimental group with a combination of the control group and the experiment condition.

that the December rise was significant as well as the January one. The total incidence of violent crimes then declined in February and was significantly above the overall trend only when we used the less conservative method. In either case, however, President Kennedy's murder evidently had its strongest effect about a month or more after this tragic event. The FBI does not know of any widespread changes in police procedures that could have accounted for this jump. Going on to the summer of 1966 (and again computing the overall trend from the full 84 months), there was a reliable increase in violent crimes above the trend line in 4 of the 5 months following the slaying of the Chicago nurses. The other destructive outbursts occurring that summer probably strengthened the aggressive consequences of the Speck murders.

A graphic analysis of changes in the frequency of violent crimes also shows these effects (Figure 1). For these data we first calculated the mean number of aggressive crimes over all 40 cities in each of the 12 months. Using these monthly averages as a base, we then plotted the deviation from the monthly average for each month in the period from January, 1960, through December, 1966. Here we saw the sharp and startling rise in January, 1964, after John Kennedy's assassination, the decline from January through July of that year, and then the gradual increase until the tragic summer of 1966. Another rise in violent crimes occurred at that time, but the Speck and Whitman violence evidently increased the incidence of aggressive crimes still further.

Many other examples of behavioral contagion could be provided if we were to get away from violence. It is enough for my purposes, however, merely to show that many kinds of aggressive events seem to be subject to contagious influences: reactions to filmed aggression, urban disorders, and violent offenses following sensational crimes. The problem now is to account for these violent outbursts. Why does the depiction of violence in the mass media so often incite people to act violently themselves? In answering this question many contemporary psychologists would employ such concepts as modeling, imitation, and social facilitation. I would like to examine some of the ideas involved in these usages and, as I indicated earlier, emphasize the role of a process that I believe has been unduly minimized by other writers.

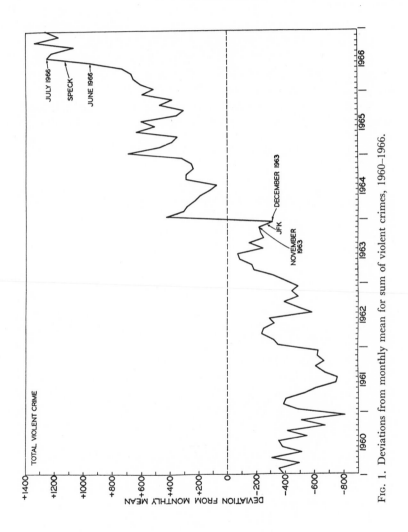

Fig. 1. Deviations from monthly mean for sum of violent crimes, 1960–1966.

Several Theoretical Analyses

The terms "modeling" and "imitation" are usually confined to those cases in which the observer's actions closely resemble the witnessed or reported behavior. Influenced greatly by "social-learning" considerations, psychologists such as Bandura (1965), Walters (1968), and Aronfreed (1969) generally attribute this behavioral correspondence to learning, although they also differentiate between the conditions governing the acquisition of a response and the determinants of its performance. As Bandura and Walters have discussed imitation, the observer acquires imaginal and verbal representations of the depicted event which can later be retrieved by the re-presentation of any of the stimuli associated with this image-thought configuration. This perceptual-cognitive structure guides behavior through providing discriminative stimuli for the direction and control of instrumental responses (cf. Bandura, 1965, pp. 10–11). Put more simply, the observer has obtained information which he can later employ if he has sufficient incentive to carry out the witnessed actions.

The aggression-enhancing effect of observed violence has to be explained in a somewhat more complicated manner, according to these writers, especially when the observer's hostile behavior does not resemble the portrayed aggression. For Bandura (1965) and Walters (1968), media violence serves primarily to influence the strength of the audience's inhibitions against aggression. They apparently assume that viewers typically want to attack someone (evidently even when they have not been angered or emotionally aroused) but restrain themselves in fear of some unpleasant consequence. If the observed aggressor is rewarded, or even if he is only not punished, the audience is informed that the anticipated danger may not arise after all—and that there may even be some benefit from aggression. As a result, the viewers' inhibitions against aggression are lowered and they attack the available target. Wheeler (1966) has offered a similar analysis of behavioral contagion. Contagion arises, he says, when the observer is in a conflict between wanting to perform a certain action and being afraid to do so. The model's behavior presumably reduces this fear, whether he is rewarded or only not punished. Since Wheeler cites an experiment employing nonprovoked subjects (Walters, Thomas, & Acker, 1962), he apparently also assumes that these people had wanted to injure the available target even when this person had not angered them before.

Aronfreed (1968, 1969) generally accepts this reasoning and also suggests that the observer behaves aggressively because he anticipates the gratifications this action will bring. He contends, however, that the aggressive model's influence is best described "as the effect of a generalized social facilitation" (1968, p. 95). Being a descriptive label rather than a hypothesized mechanism, this term seems to refer to any process that produces "an indifferent and nonimitative correspondence between observed and elicited behavior" (1969, p. 214). His discussion of social facilitation includes such notions as a "generalized arousal or motivational effect" (apparently akin to Hull's concept of a general drive), and a "releasing stimulus for the subject's own aggressive dispositions," but excludes the idea of discriminative informational control over the subject's behavior. "Behavior that is released or enhanced by social facilitation," he says, "is relatively insensitive to the informational and affective value of its outcomes" (1969, p. 217).

Bandura's (1965, p. 32) discussion of facilitating effects, on the other hand, emphasizes the discriminative nature of the model's actions. Here the model's behavior presumably signals those occasions in which the observer is likely to be reinforced for following the model, or directs the observer's attention to particular environmental stimuli to which he then responds.

THE CLASSICAL CONDITIONING MODEL OF IMPULSIVE AGGRESSION

It should be clear from this brief review that many of the leading theoretical analyses of the effects of observed aggression have emphasized three things: (1) the information provided by the model's conduct, (2) changes in the strength of the observer's inhibitions against aggression, and (3) the degree to which the witnessed event has produced a generalized emotional or motivational arousal. My own approach has been somewhat different. While I do, of course, recognize that the three types of reactions just summarized play an important part in determining the consequences of media violence, I have also been struck by the extent to which aggressive behavior occasionally seems to function like a conditioned response to situational stimuli. There are times, I suggest, when a classical conditioning model appears to be better than the more popular operant notions used in this area. On these occasions the observer reacts impulsively to particular stimuli in his environment, not because his inhibitions have been weakened or because he anticipates the pleasures arising from his actions, but because situational stimuli have evoked the responses he is predisposed or set to make in that setting. Contagious violence often comes about in this way.

Before I embark on an examination of some of the relevant evidence, I should acknowledge several problems and even questions in my own mind. For one thing, it is obviously often difficult if not impossible to distinguish between elicited and disinhibited reactions. We frequently cannot tell whether the individual had wanted from the outset to display as much aggression as he subsequently showed (the "pent-up drive" notion and also the idea implicit in operantlike formulations), or whether at least part of his aggressive behavior was influenced by evoked aggressive responses. Instead of assuming that nonprovoked people have an urge to attack that is only released by the model's action—the type of assumption made by Bandura, Walters, and Wheeler—I suggest that much of their aggressive reaction to the model was elicited in them.

Then too, I wonder if learning is always the basis of contagious imitation. There may well be a "monkey see, monkey do" tendency under some conditions, but is this tendency always an outgrowth of prior experiences? Upon reviewing various discussions of social facilitation in the animal research literature, Tolman (1968) has noted that some instances of contagious behavior can be described as a "reflex." This reflexive copying of another animal's behavior may emerge when the organism is closely attending to the other, is not engaged in any interfering activity, and perhaps is set to perform the responses the model is carrying out. Berger (1966) has reported an experiment with human adults that appears to demonstrate this kind of phenomenon. His subjects watched another person practice the manual alphabet for the deaf and always knew the intended letter. Most of the subjects began to perform the model's actions themselves as they watched—*even when they had been told they would not have to learn the hand signals*. Although these responses might have been made because the observers had established incentives and criteria for themselves, as Aronfreed (1969) maintains, I suspect the reflexive imitation was not governed by any such ideas. It came about, in part at least, I believe, merely because the subjects paid close attention to the model's behavior without having any interfering thoughts and actions. (I think I show essentially the same behavior on Sunday afternoons when I watch professional football on TV and lunge into the opponent's line along with the Packers' fullback.) If so, this tendency may not have been learned, although learning may add to and complicate the reaction.

Evidence of S-R Generalization and Aggressive "Meaning"

The violent aftereffects of the Kennedy assassination and the Speck-Whitman slayings can easily be attributed to a lowering of restraints in particular segments of the American populace—at first thought. Other findings pose difficulties for this simple explanation. The consequences seem to be fairly specific to certain crime categories but not to others. Aggravated assaults, robberies (which involve the use of force) and, to a less clear-cut extent, murders followed the pattern I described earlier, but rapes, manslaughter, and property crimes did not. The simple disinhibition or general emotion-arousal notions do not explain why the sensational crimes apparently had the strongest influence on those crimes in which the threat or commission of bodily harm was a major component.

However, the case for the present analysis must rest on a firmer foundation than a lack of a good explanation. We must also have some positive evidence that the classical conditioning model is applicable to these instances of contagious violence. Since aggravated assaults and robberies do not resemble the presumed stimulating crimes, it is particularly necessary to show that these different events could have been connected along S-R generalization gradients. I will argue that reported or portrayed violence in the mass media is associated with other violent scenes the individual had encountered previously—there is a response-mediated stimulus generalization—and these stimuli, in turn, can evoke a range of aggressive responses.

Whatever else is involved here, a broad variety of aggressive occurrences and reactions are tied together semantically as "aggression." Lang, Geer, and Hnatiow (1963), among others, have demonstrated the existence of such a dimension of hostile meaning. In their study, GSR responses which had been conditioned to words having a highly hostile meaning were also evoked by other highly hostile words but not by words lacking this connotation.

Similarly, several experiments have shown that the reinforcement of one kind of aggressive response increases the likelihood of other types of aggressive reactions as well. In one of the first of these investigations, Lovaas (1961b) reinforced young children for making aggressive verbal responses and then found that they subsequently were more likely to activate a toy on which two dolls fought. Several years later, Loew (1967) reinforced a group of college students whenever they spoke a hostile word aloud and showed that they later administered more intense electric shocks to another person engaged in a learning task (as punishment for his supposed errors) than did other subjects reinforced for speaking nonaggressive words. Geen and Pigg (1970) reversed this sequence in a recent investigation. After their college men were given verbal approval for administering shocks to a fictitious learner, the subjects had a higher frequency of aggressive word associations on a later word-association task than did a nonreinforced control group.

It would seem that the first responses made by the subjects (whether verbal or electrical aggression) had elicited other aggressive response tendencies as well so that at least some of these were also strengthened by the reinforcement. But as the classical conditioning model requires, the heightened tendency is the probability of making a particular class of responses (aggressive ones in this case) *to a particular class of stimuli* (stimuli associated with aggression). Geen has provided evidence on this point. In his study with Pigg, the reinforced men gave more aggressive word associations only to words having an aggressive meaning and *not* to nonaggressive words. Moreover, in a later study (Geen, 1970), when the subjects had an opportunity to shock the supposed learner upon the presentation of a stimulus word, the men who had been reinforced for giving shocks gave stronger shocks to aggressive words than to nonaggressive ones. The reinforcement had strengthened a tendency to react aggressively to aggressive cues. Probably because of this kind of reinforcement history, when hyperaggressive people display their hostility, they do so in reaction to stimuli that for them are associated with aggression (Simpson & Craig, 1967).

This heightened probability of reacting aggressively to particular stimuli can come about through classical conditioning as well as through the selective application of rewards. Extending the earlier research by Staats and Staats (1958), Berkowitz and Knurek (1969) conditioned subjects to dislike a certain name by pairing the name with unpleasant words. When this attitudinal training was completed, each subject participated in a brief discussion with two fellow students, actually the experimenter's confederates, one of whom bore the critical name. Each of these people later rated how friendly or hostile the subject had been toward him. As these ratings indicated, the subjects had exhibited greater hostility toward the person having the disliked name than toward the confederate bearing the neutral name. The unpleasant affect evoked by the name had generalized to the man carrying this label.

To return to stimuli associated with aggressive meaning, the argument I have been spelling out has an obvious implication: stimuli having aggressive meaning should be capable of eliciting aggressive responses from people who, for one reason or another, are ready to act aggressively. Weapons are prime examples of such stimuli, and an experiment by myself and Le Page (1967) demonstrates that even their mere presence can instigate violent reactions for angry people. For many men (and probably women as well) in our society, we reasoned, these objects are closely associated with aggression. Assuming the weapons do not produce inhibitions that are stronger than the evoked aggressive reactions (as would be the case, for example, if the weapons were labeled as morally bad), the presence of the aggressive objects would generally lead to more intense attacks upon an available target than would occur in the presence of a neutral object.

To test this hypothesis, male undergraduates were made to be angry with the experimenter's confederate who was posing as another subject. This was done by having the confederate give the subject seven electric shocks, supposedly as the confederate's evaluation of the subject's solution to an assigned problem. The other subjects received only one shock—the minimum number possible—as their evaluation. All of the men were then given an opportunity to administer electric shocks to the confederate, but some of the men saw weapons lying on the table near the shock apparatus. (Half of these people were informed the weapons belonged to the confederate in order to test the hypothesis that aggressive stimuli which also were associated with the anger instigator would evoke the strongest aggressive reaction from the angered subjects. The other people seeing the weapons were told the weapons had been left there by a previous experimenter.) Another group of subjects in both the angered and nonangered conditions gave the shocks without anything being on the table besides the shock key. Finally, for yet another group of subjects, two badminton rackets and shuttlecocks were close to the shock key. This condition asked whether the presence of any object near the shock apparatus would reduce inhibitions against aggression, even if the object were not connected with aggressive behavior.

The hypothesis guiding the study received good support, as can be seen in Table 1. The strongly provoked men delivered more frequent electrical attacks upon their tormentor in the presence of a weapon than when nonaggressive objects (the badminton rackets and shuttlecocks) were present or when only the shock key was on the table. The angered subjects gave the greatest number of shocks

TABLE 1

MEAN NUMBER OF ELECTRIC SHOCKS GIVEN
IN WEAPONS AND NO WEAPONS CONDITIONS

	Shocks Received	
	1	7
Associated Weapons:	2.60_a	6.07_d
Unassociated Weapons:	2.20_a	5.67_{cd}
No Object:	3.07_a	4.67_{bc}
Badminton Rackets:	—	4.60_b

NOTE: Cells having a common subscript are not significantly different at the .05 level.
Data from Berkowitz and LePage (1967).

in the presence of the weapons associated with the anger instigator, as predicted, but this group was not reliably different from the other weapons condition. Both of these groups having weapons nearby were significantly more aggressive than the Angered–Neutral Object condition.

Fraczek and Macaulay recently extended this study by inquiring into some of the individual differences in reactions to weapons. All of their subjects were angered, as in the earlier experiment, and then had an opportunity to shock the confederate. This was done either in the supposed accidental presence of weapons or with nothing but the shock key on the table. The investigators also divided their subjects into highly emotional and less emotional groups depending upon the emotionality of their word associations to aggressive words in a prior assessment. As is indicated in Table 2, the less emotional men were the ones who showed a significant weapons effect, perhaps because the highly emotional subjects had become very anxious in the presence of the weapons and suppressed any unusually strong aggressive reactions. Questionnaire evaluations demonstrated that the less emotional men were not merely responding more energetically to the weapons. Thus, in the absence of weapons, 70% of the less emotional subjects indicated their partner (the confederate) had performed well on his assigned problem in comparison to their own work. When the guns were nearby, however, none of the unemotional men said their partner had done as well as they. The relatively unfavorable evaluation of the confederate's performance cannot be

TABLE 2

Aggressive Responses Toward Partner (p)
in Presence or Absence of Guns

Measure	Guns Present	No Guns Present	p-value
Mean No. Shocks			
High Emotional Ss	5.5	5.9	n.s.
Low Emotional Ss	5.6	4.6	0.05 (t test)
Proportion saying Ps work better than their work			
High Emotional Ss	30%	38%	n.s.
Low Emotional Ss	0%	70%	0.001 (x^2)

Note: Data from Fraczek and Macaulay.

due solely to a generalized arousal. Such an arousal would not in itself have led the subjects to rate their partner unfavorably; a favorable evaluation was also possible. It was the guns' aggressive meaning that had steered the responses in this direction.

AGGRESSIVE STIMULI IN THE MASS MEDIA

A methodological note might be inserted here before we consider some of the substantive implications of the present reasoning for the mass media. Several critics of laboratory research on media effects have objected to the "unreality" of the electric shock measures used in many of the experiments in this area (Hartley, 1964; Klapper, 1963; Weiss, 1970). Nobody gives electric shocks in real life, they say, so the shocks cannot possibly be representative of naturalistic aggression. The evidence I have just summarized argues against this naive dismissal of the laboratory findings. Subjects clearly do regard giving electric shocks as aggressive acts and seem to label the behavior as aggression, implicitly if not explicitly. Because of this labeling, indeed, various possible measures of aggression are psychologically equivalent. Whether based on questionnaire evaluations, electric shocks, or blasts of noise, all refer to responses that, the subject knows, can hurt the target-person in one way or another. All of these actions have an aggressive meaning.

Following the principles outlined earlier, stimuli presented in the mass media that also have this kind of aggressive meaning should also elicit aggressive reactions in audience members. It is for this reason that I believe Frederick Wertham (1954) is essentially correct in criticizing comic books that feature violent crimes. With Wertham, and extrapolating from Bandura as well, I suggest that these violent scenes can give rise to aggressive ideas and images in the reader even though the scenes are portrayed only on the printed page. An unpublished experiment by Parker, West, and myself demonstrates that comic book violence can stimulate aggressive ideas even in "normal" people. Third-, fourth-, and fifth-grade school children were asked to select words completing a series of incomplete sentences both before and after they read a particular comic book. The results are summarized in Table 3. The youngsters given a war comic book to read (*Adventures of the Green Berets*) were much

TABLE 3A

NUMBER OF AGGRESSIVE RESPONSES
TO FIVE INCOMPLETE SENTENCES

	Before Reading	After Reading
War Comics	0.87_a	1.73_b
Gidget	1.20_{ab}	1.27_{ab}

NOTE: Cells not having a subscript in common are significantly different at 0.05 by Duncan test.

TABLE 3B

FREQUENCIES SHOWING CHANGE IN NUMBER OF AGGRESSIVE RESPONSES TO INCOMPLETE SENTENCES

	Increase	No Change or Dec.
War Comics	9	6
Gidget	3	12

NOTE: Chi-square = 4.66, p = .05 (Aggressive responses: spank, accidents, scold, tear, beat up, break, murders, punish. E.g., "I want to—tear, read—the book.")
Data from Parker, West, and Berkowitz.

more likely to have an increase in their use of hostile words to finish these sentences than the control children required to read a non-aggressive comic book (*Gidget*). For example, if the subjects had to complete a sentence such as "I want to ——— the book," and could choose between "read" and "tear," the children who had read the war comics were more apt to select "tear."

These aggressive ideas and images evoked by violent scenes are probably usually too weak and short lived to influence the behavior of most viewers. Under some conditions, however, these implicit reactions might lead to fairly open attacks upon an available target even by people who ordinarily have strong inhibitions against direct aggression. This is shown in an experiment in which college girls listened to a humorous tape recording (Berkowitz, 1970). The co-eds were required to rate another girl's suitability for a job as

TABLE 4

AGGRESSION MEASURES YIELDING SIGNIFICANT DIFFERENCES
BETWEEN AGGRESSIVE AND NEUTRAL HUMOR CONDITIONS

Measure	Insulting Job Applicant		Non-Insulting Job Applicant	
	Aggressive Humor	Neutral Humor	Aggressive Humor	Neutral Humor
Adjectives Attributed to Job Applicant				
No. Moderately Hostile	5.35_a	4.20_b	0.75_c	0.65_c
No. Friendly	1.35_a	1.80_a	9.40_b	12.15_c
Questionnaire Evaluation	79.70_a	75.20_a	43.60_b	$34.95_b{}^a$

NOTE: Cells having different subscripts are significantly different by Duncan test at the .05 level.
On the final questionnaire evaluation, the higher the score the greater the expressed hostility toward the job applicant.
Data from Berkowitz (1970).
[a] This mean is different from 43.60 at the .06 level.

dormitory counselor after they heard a brief excerpt from a comedian's routine. Half of the subjects listened to a nonaggressive comedian (George Carlin), while the other girls heard the very hostile comedian, Don Rickles, in an aggressive routine. As Table 4 demonstrates, the female undergraduates were much more hostile toward the job applicant after hearing the aggressive humor than after the neutral humor. Moreover, contrary to some recent studies purporting to demonstrate the supposedly beneficial effects of aggressive humor, there was no evidence of a cathartic reduction of hostility in the aggressive humor condition; Don Rickles's comic routine led to heightened hostility whether or not the job applicant had previously provoked the subjects. In both cases, as can also be seen in the table, the hostile jokes had stimulated aggressive reactions in the listeners which then caused them to evaluate the job applicant less favorably.

Perceived Aggressiveness of Contact Sports

An external stimulus obviously does not have "meaning" in itself; the meaning is imparted to the stimulus by the perceiver. To recite a truism, where one person might regard an event as an aggressive encounter, someone else could view the same scene as a nonaggressive situation. This implicit labeling could determine whether a witnessed occurrence will evoke aggressive reactions. Football is often called an aggressive sport, but not everyone thinks of it as such, and it is those people who do define the game as "aggression" who should be most likely to attack someone after seeing a gridiron contest. Berkowitz, Alioto, and Turner recently carried out an experimental test of this reasoning.

After being informed that he and his partner (actually the experimenter's accomplice) were participating in a study of physiological reactions to complex stimulus situations, each subject was hooked up to supposed recording wires and was given a problem to solve. His partner angered the subject by giving him a relatively high number of shocks as the partner's judgment of the quality of the subject's work. The confederate then left the room, ostensibly to think up answers to his own problem, and the subject was shown either our standard boxing film or an equally long movie of a professional football game. A tape-recorded voice provided a brief introduction to the film, supposedly so that the subject would have a better understanding of what he saw. In half of the cases, for each type of movie the voice indicated that the contest winner (either the boxer or the football team) had wanted to hurt the opponent because of some earlier insults. In other words, the winner in the filmed encounter was intentionally aggressive toward the opponent. The remaining subjects were told that the participants were professionals unemotionally engaged in their business, and did not have any particular feelings towards their opponent, thus defining the contest as essentially nonaggressive in nature. At the end of the movie the partner returned to the room, went into a cubicle where he could not be seen, supposedly was reattached to the physiological apparatus, and read aloud his answers to the four problems he had been given. The subject was to give him one to five shocks on each problem solution.

Several aggression measures yielded the predicted significant effect for the perceived aggressiveness of the contact sport as is shown in Table 5. Thus, the first time the shocks were given, but *not* on the other shock trials, the men who had been induced to think of the filmed contest as an aggressive competition gave their partner reliably more shocks than did the subjects who had been led

TABLE 5

AGGRESSION MEASURES SHOWING SIGNIFICANT MAIN
EFFECT OF PERCEIVED AGGRESSIVENESS OF FILM

Film	Boxing Film		Football Film		
Definition	Aggressive	Non-aggressive	Aggressive	Non-aggressive	*p*-value for main effect
No. Shocks[a] Trial 1	2.62	2.31	2.75	2.12	(*p* .036)
Total Duration of Shocks, All Trials (Sec.)	3.99	2.43	3.98	2.19	(*p* .001)
Want to serve with P again[b]	11.31	7.69	10.88	10.31	(*p* .012)

NOTE: Data from Berkowitz and Turner.
[a] Not more than 5 shocks or less than 1 could be given on any trial.
[b] The higher the score, the less S wanted to serve with P again in another experiment.

to define the encounter as nonaggressive.[3] The former subjects also gave the accomplice significantly longer shocks over the four trials, and on the final questionnaire indicated a reliably weaker desire to serve with him again in another experiment. All in all, the movie had an aggression-enhancing effect when it had an aggressive meaning for the subjects. The boxing match and the football game evoked the strongest aggressive responses in those angry men who thought the people they watched wanted to hurt their opponents.

Characteristics of the Available Target

The general line of reasoning I have advanced here also suggests that aggressive reactions can be governed by the available target as well as by the events portrayed on the screen. For example, in considering the consequences of filmed violence, I have proposed that the aggressive responses elicited by the movie or TV program are often relatively weak and do not show up in overt behavior unless the viewer happens to encounter someone associated with the witnessed violence (cf. Berkowitz, 1962). (The Bandura and Walters analysis might lead to a similar prediction; they, too, probably

3. This finding is consistent with my description of cue-elicited aggression as "impulsive aggression." I wonder if any proponent of the demand-characteristics view of experimental–social psychological results would have predicted this outcome—or the finding that total shock duration was significantly affected but not the total number of shocks.

would hypothesize that the later occurrence of stimuli associated with the imaginal-verbal representation of the observed aggression would tend to evoke this perceptual-cognitive configuration, assuming it had been fairly well learned, and might thereby influence the observer's behavior.)[4]

A series of experiments conducted in our Wisconsin laboratory has been guided by this kind of analysis. What we have found is that a target-person tends to draw the strongest attacks if he is associated with the victim of the witnessed aggression.

Typically in these studies, the subject, a male college student, was first angered or treated in a neutral fashion by the experimenter's accomplice. Under a pretext appropriate to the ostensible purpose of the study, the subject was then shown a brief film, either a prize fight scene or an exciting but nonaggressive film of a track race between the first two men to run the mile in less than 4 minutes. About 7 minutes later, at the conclusion of the film, the subject was given an opportunity to administer shocks to the other person (the confederate) as a judgment of this person's performance on a task that had been assigned to him.

As I indicated before, the general hypothesis with which we began this research was that the anger-instigating confederate would receive more attacks if he was also associated with the witnessed aggression. In the first experimental test of this idea (Berkowitz, 1965), the confederate's degree of association with the aggressive prize fight film was manipulated by means of the role he occupied when he was introduced to the subject. Since the crucial scene was a prize fight, the accomplice had been introduced in half of the cases as a "college boxer." For the other subjects, those for whom the confederate was to have a low association with the aggressive movie, he had been introduced as a "speech major." In accord with prediction, the target-person received the strongest attacks when he had provoked the subjects, they had seen the boxing film, and he had been identified as a college boxer. The findings are summarized in Table 6.

4. At least some of the aggression displayed by Hicks' (1965) children 6 months after they had watched a filmed aggressive model could be due to the presence of the same cues in the retest situation that had existed in the original setting.

TABLE 6

MEAN AGGRESSION DIRECTED TO AVAILABLE TARGET

	Angered Subjects				Nonangered Subjects			
	Boxing Film		Track Film		Boxing Film		Track Film	
	Boxer	Speech Major	Boxer	Speech Major	Boxer	Speech Major	Boxer	Speech Major
No. Shocks	5.35_d	4.90_c	4.94_c	4.78_c	4.42_{abc}	3.92_a	4.37_{abc}	4.16_{ab}
Duration of Shocks	16.56_d	11.90_c	11.47_c	11.16_{bc}	10.15_{bc}	6.67_a	12.04_c	8.15_{ab}

NOTE: The shock data were subjected to an $\sqrt{x} + \sqrt{x+1}$ transformation. Cells having different subscripts are significantly different at the .05 level by Duncan test.

Data from Berkowitz (1965).

However, the data given in this table actually are equivocal regarding the major hypothesis. We cannot be sure that the insulting accomplice was attacked so strongly because he was associated with the observed prize fight. As Table 6 also indicates, the boxer drew more and longer shocks than the speech major regardless of the film shown the subjects or his earlier treatment of them (and this difference was reliable in the case of the duration measure in the nonangered condition). The aggressive-cue value of the boxer role might have been responsible for—or could have contributed to— the high level of punishment given the angering accomplice after the subjects had watched the prize fight. Although this possibility supports my notion of the aggression-eliciting ability of objects having aggressive meaning, it clouds the interpretation of the present findings. The research therefore turned to labels that would not necessarily have an ability to evoke aggressive reactions: names.

Specifically, we made use of the name of the protagonist in the fight film. The movie showed the actor, Kirk Douglas, taking a very bad beating. Thus, in the next experiment (Berkowitz & Geen, 1966), the accomplice was introduced either as Kirk Anderson or as Bob Anderson. Our theoretical expectation was upheld. The angered subjects gave a reliably greater number of shocks to the confederate named "Kirk" than to the confederate introduced as Bob, but only after they had seen Kirk Douglas being beaten. These groups did not differ in how angry they felt just before they administered the shocks.

In yet another study (Geen & Berkowitz, 1966), the association with the aggressive film made use of the names employed in the film story. Kirk Douglas played the part of a boxer called Midge Kelly, so the confederate was at times introduced as Bob Kelly. The character who punished him severely was called Dunne, and in another condition the confederate was introduced as Bob Dunne. In yet another group, the confederate was introduced as Bob Riley, a name not used in the film scene. Finally, as a check on the first experiment, one group of subjects shown the prize fight scene were told that the confederate's name was Kirk Anderson. Unlike the earlier study, all of the subjects were angered by the confederate before seeing the film.

Again our reasoning was upheld, as can be seen in Table 7. The

TABLE 7

Mean Number of Shocks Given to Confederate

Confederate's Name	Boxing Film	Track Film
Kelly	5.40_a	3.60_b
Dunne	4.15_b	3.87_b
Riley	4.40_b	4.00_b
Kirk	5.27	

Note: Cells having different subscripts are significantly different at the .05 level by Duncan test. The "Kirk" group mean is significantly different, by 2-tailed t test, from all Track Film group means and the "Dunne" group mean in the Boxing Film condition. The "Kirk" and "Riley" difference in this condition is at the .07 level of significance.

Data from Geen and Berkowitz (1966).

greatest number of shocks was given by the angered subjects who saw the aggressive film to the confederate who was associated with this film by means of his name, either Kelly or Kirk. We can even see indications of a generalization gradient based on the "Irishness" of the confederate's name. The men witnessing the prize fight attacked the confederate somewhat more frequently when his name was Riley than when it was Dunne. Furthermore, if this generalization gradient is a reliable phenomenon, we might even conclude that the important association is with the victim of the observed aggression. That is, the available target is likely to be attacked to the extent that it is associated with the observed victim of the witnessed aggression.

As encouraging as these results appear to be, there are always alternative explanations. The experiments just described created only name-mediated associations with the prize fight scene; the confederate was not connected with the nonaggressive track race. Is it not possible that the results are really due to associations with an exciting event, whether this occurrence is aggressive or not? To test this alternative hypothesis, another experiment was run in which the confederate's name-mediated connection with the track film was varied. All of the subjects were provoked, but in one-third of the cases, the anger-arousing confederate was given the name of the race victor, Bannister, while for another third he was introduced as Landy, the name of the person who lost. For the remaining subjects, he was called Kelly. Half of these groups saw the track race, while the other men read a magazine for the equivalent time. Our results indicated that the track film in itself did not affect the number of shocks given to the confederate, nor did the confederate's association with this film. There is no good reason, then, to attribute the prior findings to the confederate's connection with some source of excitement, regardless of the nature of the excitement.

Other alternative explanations remain, however. In the interests of simplicity, the subject was introduced to the other person in the first studies at the very start of the experimental session, before seeing the film. This means, of course, that the people in the "high association" conditions may well have been reminded of the anger instigator. The person being beaten up in the film had the same name as the man who had angered them. Instead of being led to a "symbolic catharsis," the subjects could have been stimulated to make fractional anticipatory aggressive responses themselves. For example, they may have thought how they would punish this person when they had the opportunity. These anticipatory aggressive responses could have then set off strong overt aggression by the subjects. Or, to put this in another language, the sight of someone associated with their frustrator could have stirred them up all the more.

Another experiment (Berkowitz & Geen, 1967) was carried out in order to investigate this possibility. Again, all of the subjects received seven shocks from another person, actually the experimenter's accomplice, supposedly as a judgment of their performance on an initial problem. Each individual then was shown either our standard prize fight scene or the track film. When this was over, and after the subjects had rated their mood, the experimenter said he had forgotten to get the subjects' names and asked the two people who they were. The subject first gave his name, and then the confederate identified himself either as *Kirk* Anderson or *Bob* Anderson. This meant, in the case of the men shown the aggressive film, that the accomplice named Kirk was connected with the film *after* it had been seen. As before, the tormenting confederate generally drew the greatest number of aggressive responses from the angered men when he was closely associated with the victim of the previously witnessed aggression. The restriction on this finding should be clear, however; the importance of the available target's stimulus qualities became most apparent when inhibitions against aggression were lessened. But even with this qualification, it seems clear that the high-cue value target automatically elicited the strong aggression from the subjects who were ready to act aggressively because of their immediately preceding experiences.

GENERAL AND EMOTIONAL AROUSAL

Many of the findings I have reported here cannot be explained solely in terms of a generalized arousal state produced by the aggressive stimuli in the situation. For one thing, the subjects often exhibited highly selective behavior; in some studies they carried out one action rather than another or gave one type of questionnaire rating rather than another. Moreover, Zillman and Tannenbaum have reported (unpublished study) that the track film used as a control movie in most of our studies is just as arousing physiologically as the boxing film. However, a generalized arousal *can* enhance aggressive behavior. In the research I have described so far, the effects of aggressive cues were detected primarily when the subjects had previously been angered by the person they were permitted to attack. This anger arousal could have done several things: lowered restraints against aggression; decreased the utilization of peripheral, non-aggression-associated stimuli which might have evoked responses incompatible with aggression; and heightened responsivity to the dominant, aggression-connected cues in the environment.

Frustrations probably increase the likelihood of aggression for all of these reasons—and also because they are aversive, unpleasant events. Thinking along these lines, Geen and Berkowitz (1967) hypothesized that thwarted subjects would be relatively prone to attack a target-person having strong aggressive-cue properties even when their frustration had not been deliberate and aggressive in nature.

The subjects in this study were first given a jigsaw puzzle to assemble in 5 minutes. In the Control condition the subjects were able to do this task, but in the Insult condition the men had an insoluble puzzle and also were insulted by a confederate for not being able to do the job. In the Task Frustration condition, on the other hand, the subjects could not assemble the puzzle but the confederate acted neutrally toward them. After this, the subjects were shown either the boxing film or our track film, and then, at the end of the movie, the men learned that the confederate's name was either Kirk or Bob. All subjects were then given a socially sanctioned opportunity to shock the confederate on 12 different trials (out of 20 trials) on which the other person supposedly made a mistake. The intensity of the shocks could be varied on a 10-step continuum, and each person's score is the median intensity he gave. Analysis of the shock intensity data revealed a significant Film × Arousal Treatment interaction.

The multiple-range tests revealed that in the Track Film condition only the insulted group gave significantly more intense shocks than the Control subjects. In the Boxing Film condition, however, both arousal treatments led to significantly more intense shocks than those given in the Control group. Thus, while insult aroused the strongest aggression, the task frustration evidently also created a readiness for aggression. The justified violence the men witnessed enabled this readiness to show up in overt aggression. But is this overt aggression directed against the high-cue target, Kirk, more than against Bob?

Looking at the findings summarized in Table 8, there are no reliable differences among any of the four Control groups; the intensity of the electrical attacks was not greatly affected by the target's name or the nature of the film witnessed when the subjects were not emotionally aroused. As expected, however, the strongest aggression in the experiment was exhibited by the insulted men shown the boxing film who had an opportunity to attack a person with the same name as the film victim. Futhermore, after the task frustration,

TABLE 8

INTENSITY OF SHOCKS DELIVERED BY SUBJECTS

	Boxing Film		Track Film	
Target Name:	Kirk	Bob	Kirk	Bob
Control	3.07_{de}	2.60_e	3.34_{cde}	3.01_{de}
Task Frustration	4.49_{bc}	3.84_{cde}	3.91_{cd}	2.98_{de}
Insult	6.20_a	5.41_{ab}	3.99_{cd}	4.23_{cd}

NOTE: Means having common subscripts are not significantly different from each other at the .05 level of confidence by Duncan test.
Data from Geen and Berkowitz (1967).

as after the insult, the most intense aggression was directed against the person having the same name as the victim of the observed aggression. While the Frustrated-Boxing-Film-Kirk subjects did not differ significantly from the Bob subjects receiving the same arousal and film treatment, only the former were significantly different from the Control-Boxing Film conditions. All in all, then, we have at least suggestive evidence here for the present theoretical analysis; the task frustration led to stronger aggression than that displayed by a nonaroused group when the thwarted men were provided with an opportunity to attack a person having high-cue value for aggression because of his name-mediated connection with the victim of the observed aggression.

At least part of the effect of frustration can be traced to the general arousal state created in the thwarted person. Other sources of heightened arousal could well have the same consequences if there were clearly defined aggressive stimuli in the environment. Two interesting experiments are illustrative. Geen and O'Neal (1969) recently found that men who heard a loud but not painful white noise after seeing the prize fight film attacked their partner more strongly than did other subjects who had not watched the fight or who had not heard the sound. The excitation resulting from the noise had evidently strengthened the aggressive reactions stimulated by the aggressive movie. As this experiment suggests, anger is not the only arousal state that can facilitate aggressive responses to aggressive stimuli. Similarly, when Tannenbaum and Zillman showed a brief sex film to one group of men who had been provoked by a partner, these sexually aroused subjects gave him stronger electric shock punishment than did similarly angered but non-sexually aroused men in the control group. The sexual arousal had evidently helped "energize" the aggressive responses elicited by the provocation and the opportunity to attack the partner. In a later variation on this study, these researchers obtained results consistent with the previously cited Berkowitz-LePage (1967) experiment. The strongest electric attacks on the tormentor were given by men who watched the sex film and at the same time heard a tape recording of the woman character's thoughts about killing her lover. Here the viewers' sexual arousal apparently also strengthened the aggressive responses elicited by the aggressive tape recording.

This kind of phenomenon, in which sexual arousal functions like other arousal sources to facilitate aggressive responses to aggressive cues, could contribute to the apparent connection between sexual and aggressive motivation posited by some writers.

Judging the Propriety of the Observed Aggression

We have already seen that the observer cannot be viewed as merely a passive recipient of the stimuli presented to him. He imparts meaning to these stimuli, sometimes classifying the witnessed event as "aggressive" and sometimes as "nonaggressive." He may also judge any observed violence he sees as "good" or "bad," "moral" or "immoral," "justified" or "unjustified." Five separate experiments employing college students have demonstrated that this interpretation of the propriety of the witnessed aggression can influence the observer's own aggressive behavior immediately after the movie.

In four of these studies (Berkowitz & Rawlings, 1963; Berkowitz, Corwin, & Heironimus, 1963; Berkowitz, 1965; Berkowitz & Geen, 1967) the "Champion" prize fight scene was introduced to deliberately provoked students in one of two ways: by varying a supposed summary of the plot, the fight loser (the main character in the movie) was portrayed either in a favorable or relatively unfavorable manner so that the beating he received was generally regarded as either unjustified or justified aggression. Immediately afterwards, when the men had an opportunity to attack their tormentor, they displayed weaker aggression towards him after seeing the film victim get the less justified beating than following the more justified injury to the movie character.

The previously cited experiment by Berkowitz & Geen (1967) is illustrative. It will be recalled that at the end of the film the insulting confederate was introduced to some of the subjects as Kirk and to the others as Bob. In addition, for the two-thirds of the men shown the prize fight movie, the story synopsis used to introduce the scene led the subjects to regard the film violence as either justified or less justified aggression. Table 9 reports the mean number of shocks given to the confederate in each condition. The top half of the table presents the findings with all of the subjects. Here we can see that

TABLE 9

MEAN NUMBER OF SHOCKS GIVEN TO CONFEDERATE

Confederate's Name	Justified Film Aggression	Less Justified Film Aggression	Track Film
Total Sample ($N = 15$)			
Kirk	5.87_a	5.13_{ab}	4.13_b
Bob	5.00_{ab}	4.67_{ab}	4.60_{ab}
Omitting 5 most anxious men in group			
Kirk	6.40_a	5.00_b	4.40_b
Bob	4.80_b	4.30_b	4.70_b

NOTE: Cells having different subscripts are significantly different at the .05 level by Duncan test.

Data from Berkowitz and Geen (1967).

the condition differences were in the direction predicted by our theoretical reasoning, with the greatest number of shocks being transmitted in the Kirk-Justified Film Aggression group. However, this condition was significantly different from only the Kirk-Track Film group. A subsidiary analysis was then conducted in which the five most highly anxious men in each condition were excluded. The subjects had rated their mood on a series of scales after seeing the film but before they administered shocks, and we assumed that those people who felt highly anxious would inhibit their subsequent aggressive responses. (The self-report anxiety index was based on the sum of three interrelated scales: tension, anxiety, and worry.) As is shown in the bottom half of Table 9, omitting the highly anxious subjects increased the mean number of shocks in the Kirk-Justified Film Aggression condition so that this group was now reliably different from all of the other conditions. Thus, the attacks received by the present frustrater depended to a considerable extent upon his possession of the appropriate stimulus properties—and also on whether or not inhibitions against aggression had been lowered in the angry subjects by showing them justified film aggression.

But were the differences between the Justified and Less Justified Film Aggression groups due to stronger inhibitions in the latter condition? I have assumed throughout this section that aggressive reactions had been elicited by the witnessed violence but had been suppressed as a consequence of the observers' definition of the aggres-

sion as "unjustified." Table 10, reporting findings obtained by
Berkowitz, Corwin, and Heironimus (1963), contains some suggestive evidence on this point. The questionnaire assessing the subjects'
attitudes toward their frustrator (the main aggression measure) also
asked the men to rate how much other students of their sex would
enjoy the film and how hard they had worked on the assigned task.
Both of these items apparently functioned as indirect measures of
resentment.

Looking at the responses to the first of these questions, we see
that the neutral film (which, in this study, had been about English
canal boats) was not particularly enjoyable. More important, the
nonangered subjects seemed to like the boxing film less when Kirk
Douglas was portrayed in an unfavorable manner than when he was
said to be a "good guy." Most subjects apparently liked him and
wanted him to play a likable character. This difference is reversed,
however, in the case of the angered subjects; here the men given the
Less Justified introduction—which described Kirk Douglas favorably—said they had enjoyed the film less. It may be that these
people were inclined to derogate the fight movie because their self-
induced restraints had not permitted them to devalue the person
who had insulted them. The angered men seeing the Less Justified
Film Aggression also seemed to be expressing resentment in their
high level of rated indifference toward the experiment (Item 2 in
Table 10). Perhaps here the inhibited subjects were indicating their
dislike for the experiment (in a restrained and indirect way).

TABLE 10

INDICATIONS OF RESTRAINT-PRODUCED HOSTILITY
DISPLACEMENT AFTER SEEING LESS JUSTIFIED AGGRESSION

	Justified Film Aggression	Less Justified Film Aggression	Neutral Film
1. *Others would enjoy film*			
Angered *S*s:	4.20$_{ab}$	5.13$_{ab}$	7.73$_c$
Nonangered *S*s:	5.47$_b$	3.53$_a$	8.27$_c$
2. *Indifference toward Experiment*			
Angered *S*s:	6.7$_{bc}$	8.4$_c$	5.8$_{ab}$
Nonangered *S*s:	4.3$_a$	5.2$_a$	6.2$_{abc}$

NOTE: For both questionnaire measures the higher the score the greater the
expression of hostility or resentment.
Data from Berkowotz, Corwin, and Heironimus (1963).

In the fifth and most recent inquiry into the effects of the judged propriety of the witnessed aggression, Hoyt (1967) extended the earlier findings. In his study, subjects in the crucial condition were told that the witnessed fight was a "grudge match" because the winner had wanted revenge for Kelly's (that is, Kirk Douglas's) earlier unfair treatment of him. These people then gave the angering confederate stronger punishment than did the control subjects. The definition of the filmed violence as justified vengeance had evidently made the subjects more willing to attack the villain in their own lives.[5]

This last-mentioned study obviously raises a question about my earlier interpretation of the aggression-enhancing consequences of the perceived aggressiveness of contact sports. Rather than the sport movies serving to elicit hostility because they had shown "aggressive" actions, the films could have lowered inhibitions because they portrayed justified vengeance. It clearly is extremely difficult to untangle these possibilities at present, but in either case, the findings highlight the important role played by the way the observer labels and understands the witnessed violence.

Whatever the exact thoughts that went through the subjects' minds, the justified aggression (or justified vengeance) on the screen may have conveyed the lesson that violence is sometimes good; they may think that a villain can properly be given the beating he deserves. But by the same token, showing that aggression can be bad, or can have bad consequences, depresses aggressive reactions. Richard Goranson (unpublished Ph.D. dissertation) found that angry college men restrained their attacks upon their tormentor

5. As this is being written, the present findings were again confirmed (for the sixth time) in an experiment employing juvenile delinquents at a state reformatory. The boys were either deliberately insulted or treated in a neutral manner by a same-aged confederate and then saw our standard boxing film or did not view any movie. The fight scene was introduced with either the justified or less justified aggression story summary. When the subjects were given an opportunity to shock the confederate at the end of the film, the weakest attacks were made by the insulted youngsters not seeing any movie. They had apparently suppressed their aggressive inclinations. More important, as we had expected, the strongest punishment (reliably different from the Insulted–No Film group) was given to the insulting confederate by the boys who had watched the justified film aggression. For these juvenile delinquents, then, as for our Wisconsin college students, the observed "proper" aggression had evidently lowered their inhibitions against their own aggression.

after learning that the loser in the filmed prize fight had died later because of the beating he had received in the fight. These people apparently held back their aggression somewhat when they were reminded that violence can lead to very serious injury or even death. At least part of this inhibition of aggression stems from the arousal of death-related anxiety. Goranson also found that the reporting of a death not connected with the witnessed fight—the character played by Kirk Douglas supposedly died in an auto accident—also served to inhibit the subjects' later attacks upon the insulting confederate.

IDENTIFICATION WITH FILM CHARACTERS

In addition to defining the meaning of the actions he sees and judging their moral rightness, the observer may play a fairly active role in the situation by imagining himself to be one of the film characters. This process, often termed "identification," has frequently been discussed by film writers but has received surprisingly little systematic research attention. Tannebaum and Gaer (1965) have reported one of the few studies of identification with a movie character. Male and female students rated their mood before a brief film was shown, then again after they had seen almost the entire movie except the ending, and finally again after the end of the story. The viewers who had identified most strongly with the film protagonists, as determined from the similarity between their semantic differential ratings of themselves and the film hero, were most strongly affected by the movie ending.

When a person identifies with someone on the screen, he does more than watch the individual closely. In imagining himself to be this character, he is also thinking of doing what he believes the other is doing. He is implicitly copying the actions he observes. As a result, we might say, he is also particularly ready to carry out the same kind of behaviors openly and should be highly responsive to those situational cues which could evoke these responses. Turner and Berkowitz applied this reasoning to film violence.

After each subject was informed that the study was an investigation of physiological reactions to complex stimulus situations and was hooked up to supposed autonomic recording apparatus, the experimenter's accomplice deliberately angered the subject by giving him a high number of shocks as his "judgment" of the subject's work. For the second stimulus situation, the subject and the confederate then watched the "Champion" boxing scene. Instructions written on an index card that had been given to the subject (without being seen by the experimenter) created the set the subject was to employ in watching the violent film. One-third of the men were asked to think of themselves as the character named Dunne, Kirk Douglas's opponent in the movie fight. Another third were to think of themselves as a judge watching the fight whose job was to observe Dunne specifically and judge his performance. Finally, the control group was given no specific "imagine self" instructions.

When the film had ended the confederate was given 2 minutes ostensibly to think up answers to his own problem. He was to propose five ideas and, the experimenter explained, the subject was to give him from one to five shocks for each idea as the subject's judgment of the quality of each problem solution.

The results, summarized in Table 11, indicate that identification with the movie fight winner had heightened the aggression-evoking effect of the witnessed violence. The men who were asked to imagine themselves as Dunne (the winner) administered a greater mean number of shocks for each idea evaluated, and inflicted reliably longer punishment in doing so, than either the subjects who had only watched Dunne or the control subjects not given any particular

TABLE 11

Aggression Expressed in Different Imagine-Self Conditions

	Imagine as:		
	Dunne (winner)	Judge	Watch Only
Mean No. Shocks	2.58_a	2.33_b	2.32_b
Duration Shocks (Secs.)	5.05_a	3.42_b	3.62_b
Mood: Forgiving . . .[a]	6.73_a	8.88_b	7.96_{ab}
Experimenter delivered instructions well[b]	4.19_a	2.58_b	2.35_b
Expt. worthwhile	4.65_a	3.46_b	3.46_b

Note: Data from Turner and Berkowitz.

[a] On the self-rated mood scale, forgiving-kindly-affectionate, the lower the score the less the scale applies.

[b] On the other items, the higher the score the more unfavorable the rating.

instructions. This increased aggressiveness evidently also produced a greater general hostility toward the experimenter and the experiment. Thus, the subjects identifying with Dunne also rated themselves on the Nowlis Mood Scale as less "forgiving-kindly-affectionate" than the other subjects, were more critical of the way the experimenter had delivered his instructions, and were less inclined to regard the experiment as a worthwhile endeavor. Here, as in the other experiments in the Wisconsin program, observed violence did not have a cathartic effect. Rather than lessening hostile desires, identification with an observed aggressor led to stronger displays of aggression.

The Reinforcing Quality of Aggression

Many people like to see other persons fight. Over the centuries, crowds have gathered excitedly to watch gladiators kill each other, fighting cocks maim each other, boxers pummel each other, and wrestlers twist each other into agonizing shapes. Since the sight of aggression is enjoyable, it must be need-satisfying, many writers have insisted, and obviously must have reduced the audience's hostile urges. However, contrary to conventional thinking, we have seen that observed violence often leads to more, not less, aggression. Is this a paradox? Why do people like to watch aggression if it doesn't reduce their aggressive "drive"?

One clue to the answer can be found in the nature of those persons who are particularly drawn to violent scenes. At least two studies dealing with teenagers, one carried out in upstate New York (Eron, 1963) and the other in the English Midlands (Halloran, Brown, & Chaney, 1969), have come up with somewhat similar observations: it is the extremely aggressive adolescent who is most strongly attracted to violence in the mass media. People who are violence prone themselves evidently enjoy seeing violence. Moreover, it also appears that aggressive scenes do not relax and calm them (the English study has some pertinent evidence on this point). Instead, they become excited as the observed aggression elicits implicit aggressive reactions, including hostile ideas and fantasies. This excitement might be pleasant in itself, but I suspect these people also find the internal aggressive reactions enjoyable because these specific responses have been frequently associated with rewards in the past. They will, therefore, seek out aggressive situations because of the pleasant excitement they think watching these encounters will generate in them.

These exciting internal aggressive reactions may be particularly pleasant for people who have been frequently rewarded for acting aggressively, but may also be somewhat enjoyable for other persons as well. As long as the observed aggression does not provoke anxiety, or violate our moral and/or esthetic standards, we may like the sensations the aggressive scenes arouse in us. I can even suggest (if I may mix my senses) that many of us have developed a taste for the sight of aggression. Like other forms of appetitive behavior, furthermore, a little taste of observed violence can arouse a desire for still more of this pleasant fare—up to the point where satiation or anxiety or moral revulsion sets in. Findings obtained by Lovaas (1961a) suggest just this. In comparison to other youngsters shown a neutral film, nursery school children shown an aggressive cartoon movie had a greater urge to activate a toy causing one doll to hit another rather than another attractive but nonaggressive mechanical toy. The aggressive cartoon had evidently awakened a greater liking for the sight of still more aggression.

Observations obtained by Boyanowsky and Newtson (unpublished study) are also suggestive of this type of process at work. They examined attendance at two Madison, Wisconsin, movie theaters before and after a co-ed was brutally murdered on the campus. One theater was showing a film about lesbians (*The Fox*), while the other had a movie about a true-life murder case (*In Cold Blood*). Attendance declined from the level of a week earlier in both theaters the day the campus murder was reported in the papers, perhaps because of the usual drop in interest after a film had been running for a week. This reduced attendance, moreover, was about the same in both theaters. The next day, however, there was a further decline in attendance at the film about the lesbians but a sharp rise in the number of people going to see the murder movie. The killing of the co-ed had apparently created a heightened interest in the violent picture.

Let me again spell out the principle I have developed so far: the stirring of mild aggressive responses within us produces an increased striving for those environmental stimuli which would produce a still greater surge of these internal aggressive reactions (as long as these sensations are not expected to be anxiety-arousing). These environmental stimuli can also be regarded as reinforcing stimuli; like other reinforcements, they are sought out. Equally important, as is also the case for other reinforcing stimuli, they are capable of eliciting the responses for which they are the reinforcement. The sight of someone being hurt aggressively—assuming the injury is not too extreme—is evidently a reinforcement for angry people, and as such, may be enjoyable for them. But seeing someone being hurt may also evoke aggressive reactions.

Evidence for this can be found in an experiment by Hartmann (1969) in which one of three different films was shown to juvenile delinquents. In one condition the film was about two youngsters fighting, and the greatest attention was given to the fight winner's aggressive actions. The same fight was depicted in a second condition but this time the camera focused on the fight loser and showed him being beaten and hurt. In the control film, by comparison, the same two boys played a basketball game. Immediately after the movie, each subject was required to give another boy in the next room electric shocks each time that person made a mistake on a learning task. The subject could select the intensity of the shocks he wanted to deliver. Those adolescents who had watched the brief fight film administered significantly stronger shocks to the boy next door than did the control subjects. This difference occurred, moreover, for both youngsters who had been insulted by the other boy just before the movie started and subjects who were not angry with the other boy. More important, however, the strongest attacks were made by angry subjects who had been shown the violent picture focusing on the fight victim's pain. The sight of someone being hurt was apparently a stimulus that had drawn particularly strong aggressive reactions from the provoked subjects, and these responses had then added to the intensity of the electric attacks upon the subjects' insulting partner.

Conclusion

The present paper does not pretend to be an analysis of all human aggression or even necessarily of the most dramatic forms of violence. Nor does it offer a comprehensive interpretation of all of the influences the mass media can have. I have dealt only with relatively quick, impulsive reactions to events portrayed in the media. Much of the speculation advanced here, however, probably applies to other forms of impulsive aggression as well. Although they are often called "expressive" behaviors, these outbursts are governed by environmental cues as well as by internal excitation. The classical conditioning model appears to be more appropriate for an understanding of these reactions than the more frequently employed operant notions. Situational stimuli have elicited aggressive responses from people who were predisposed to display this behavior.

Viewing impulsive aggression as something like a conditioned response to a particular stimulus does not imply that cognitive processes have no part in this behavior or that the human being is merely a passive responder to the world around him. He quickly categorizes the stimuli impinging on him and then reacts, even when this seems fast and spontaneous, in terms of the meaning the dominant stimuli have for him. Even very rapid explosions of violence can be governed by the aggressive meaning the individual has imparted to aspects of the situation confronting him as well as by his level of emotional arousal.

We do not know just what ideas are involved in the notion of "aggressive meaning" although they probably have to do with intentional injury to another. Other kinds of ideas also influence the individual's reactions to witnessed violence. It may be that the sight of aggression, or of an object associated with aggression, elicits aggressive thoughts (together with an imaginal representation of the stimulus) in virtually everyone. However, this perceptual-cognitive reaction will not necessarily lead to open attacks upon available targets. Other cues in the environment may tell the person his aggression will bring unpleasant consequences, so that he inhibits this response, or that the behavior will be rewarded, and the action comes forth. Furthermore, as I tried to show earlier, the viewer may also think of the observed violence as "good" or "bad," "justified" or "unjustified," and these ideas will also influence what he does.

The role of thinking must not be exaggerated, however. Impulsive behavior is not carried out with deliberation and forethought. It bursts forth, relatively free of control by intellect and cognitive processes. When this happens, man is more like the lower animals than he is otherwise and is subject to many of the same influences that operate on them. One of our most important tasks as psychologists is to determine the conditions that govern these different levels of human functioning. What makes a person respond impulsively, automatically, and with a minimum of thought, and when are his cognitive processes more dominant in regulating his actions?

REFERENCES

Aronfreed, J. *Conduct and conscience.* New York: Academic Press, 1968.

Aronfreed, J. The problem of imitation. In L. P. Lipsitt and H. W. Reese (Eds.), *Advances in child development and behavior.* Vol. 4. New York: Academic Press, 1969.

Bandura, A. Vicarious processes: A case of no-trial learning. In L. Berkowitz (Ed.), *Advances in Experimental social psychology.* Vol. 2. New York: Academic Press, 1965.

Berger, S. M. Observer practice and learning during exposure to a model. *Journal of Personality and Social Psychology,* 1966, **3**, 696–701.

Berkowitz, L. *Aggression: a social psychological analysis.* New York: McGraw-Hill, 1962.

Berkowitz, L. Some aspects of observed aggression. *Journal of Personality and Social Psychology,* 1965, **2**, 359–369.

Berkowitz, L. Aggressive humor as a stimulus to aggressive responses. *Journal of Personality and Social Psychology,* 1970, in press.

Berkowitz, L., Corwin, R., & Heironimus, M. Film violence and subsequent aggressive tendencies. *Public Opinion Quarterly,* 1963, **27**, 217–229.

Berkowitz, L., & Green, R. G. Film violence and the cue properties of available targets. *Journal of Personality and Social Psychology,* 1966, **3**, 525–530.

Berkowitz, L., & Geen, R. G. Stimulus qualities of the target of aggression: A further study. *Journal of Personality and Social Psychology,* 1967, **5**, 364–368.

Berkowitz, L., & Knurek, D. A. Label-mediated hostility generalization. *Journal of Personality and Social Psychology,* 1969, **13**, 200–206.

Berkowitz, L., & Le Page, A. Weapons as aggression-eliciting stimuli. *Journal of Personality and Social Psychology,* 1967, **7**, 202–207.

Berkowitz, L., & Rawlings, E. Effects of film violence on inhibitions against subsequent aggression. *Journal of Abnormal and Social Psychology,* 1963, **66**, 405–412.

Eisenhower, M. S. et al. *Commission statement on violence in television entertainment programs.* Washington, D.C.: National Commission on the Causes and Prevention of Violence, 1969.

Eron, L. D. Relationship of TV viewing habits and aggressive behavior in children. *Journal of Abnormal and Social Psychology*, 1963, 67, 193–196.

Fraczek, A., & Macaulay, J. R. Some personality factors in reaction to aggressive stimuli. *Journal of Personality*, in press.

Geen, R. G. Generalization of an aggressive response to a verbal stimulus. *Journal of Personality and Social Psychology*, in press.

Geen, R. G., & Berkowitz, L. Name-mediated aggressive cue properties. *Journal of Personality*, 1966, 34, 456–465.

Geen, R. G., & Berkowitz, L. Some conditions facilitating the occurrence of aggression after the observation of violence. *Journal of Personality*, 1967, 35, 666–676.

Geen, R. G., & O'Neal, E. C. Activation of cue-elicited aggression by general arousal. *Journal of Personality and Social Psychology*, 1969, 11, 289–292.

Geen, R. G., & Pigg, R. Acquisition of an aggressive response and its generalization to verbal behavior. *Journal of Personality and Social Psychology*, 1970, in press.

Goranson, R. E. Observed violence and aggressive behavior: The effects of negative outcomes to observed violence. Unpublished doctoral dissertation, University of Wisconsin, 1969.

Halloran, J. D., Brown, R. L., & Chaney, D. *Mass media and crime.* Leicester, England: Leicester University Press, 1969.

Hartley, R. *The impact of viewing aggression.* Multilithed. Columbia Broadcasting System, Office of Social Research, 1964.

Hartmann, D. P. The influence of symbolically modeled instrumental aggressive and pain cues on aggressive behavior. *Journal of Personality and Social Psychology*, 1969, 11, 280–288.

Hicks, D. J. Imitation and retention of film-mediated aggressive peer and adult models. *Journal of Personality and Social Psychology*, 1965, 2, 97–100.

Hoyt, J. L. Effects of justification of film violence on the instigation of aggressive behavior. Unpublished master's thesis, University of Wisconsin, 1967.

Klapper, J. T. The social effects of mass communication. In W. Schramm (Ed.), *The science of human communication.* New York: Basic Books, 1963.

Lang, P. J., Geer, J., & Hnatiow, M. Semantic generalization of conditioned autonomic responses. *Journal of Experimental Psychology*, 1963, 65, 552–558.

Lieberson, S., & Silverman, A. The precipitants and underlying conditions of race riots. *American Sociological Review*, 1965, 30, 887–898.

Loew, C. A. Acquisition of a hostile attitude and its relation to aggressive behavior. *Journal of Personality and Social Psychology*, 1967, 5, 335–341.

Lovaas, O. I. Effect of exposure to symbolic aggression on aggressive behavior. *Child Development*, 1961, 32, 37–44. (a)

Lovaas, O. I. Interaction between verbal and nonverbal behavior. *Child Development*, 1961, 32, 329–336. (b)

Peterson, R. C., & Thurstone, L. L. *Motion pictures and the social attitudes of children.* New York: Macmillan, 1933.

Siegel, Alberta E. The influence of violence in the mass media upon children's role expectations. *Child Development*, 1958, 29, 35–36.

Simpson, H. M., & Craig, K. D. Word associations to homonymic and neutral stimuli as a function of aggressiveness. *Psychological Reports*, 1967, **20**, 351–354.

Staats, A., & Staats, C. Attitudes established by classical conditioning. *Journal of Abnormal and Social Psychology*, 1958, **57**, 37–40.

Tannenbaum, P. H., & Geer, E. P. Mood changes as a function of stress of protagonist and degree of identification in a film-viewing situation. *Journal of Personality and Social Psychology*, 1965, **2**, 612–616.

Tarde, G. *Penal philosophy*. Boston: Little, Brown, 1912.

Tolman, C. W. The role of the companion in social facilitation of animal behavior. In E. C. Simmel, R. A. Hoppe, and G. A. Milton (Eds.), *Social facilitation and imitative behavior*. Boston: Allyn and Bacon, 1968.

Walters, R. H., Thomas, E. L., & Acker, C. W. Enhancement of punitive behavior by audiovisual displays. *Science*, 1962, **136**, 872–873.

Walters, R. H. Some conditions facilitating the occurrence of imitative behavior. In E. C. Simmel, R. A. Hoppe, and G. A. Milton (Eds.), *Social facilitation and imitative behavior*. Boston: Allyn and Bacon, 1968.

Weiss, W. Effects of mass media on communication. In G. Lindzey and E. Aronson (Eds.), *Handbook of social psychology*. (2nd Ed.) Boston: Addison-Wesley, 1970.

Wertham, F. C. *Seduction of the innocent*. New York: Rinehart, 1954.

Wheeler, L. Toward a theory of behavioral contagion. *Psychological Review*, 1966, **73**, 179–192.

The Search for Meaning

SALVATORE R. MADDI[1]

University of Chicago

It seems to me that the ultimate problem of motivational psychology is to understand how man searches for and finds meaning. One cannot reach adulthood without having considered what is worthwhile, what is interesting, what is true, what is worth doing. If a person works, raises a family, joins clubs, gives parties, falls in love, or meets challenges, it is because these are the activities that have somehow achieved meaning for him. As soon as we accept that any activity may or may not have meaning for us, we can no longer avoid the existential question of why we get out of bed in the morning at all and, just beyond that, of why we continue to live.

In general, psychologists have not given the problem of meaning sufficient attention, being apparently content either to leave it to the philosophers or to chip away at the smallest corner of it with the rudimentary tools of memory drum and semantic differential. If the existential question were pressed on them, I suspect many psychologists would contend, with the Skinnerians, that men perform the activities that lead to rewards, nothing more and nothing less. But the term reward is just a magic label, for it is generally given no more definition than that which increases the probability of the activities leading to it. This is not much to go on in confronting the problem of meaning. A Skinnerian will readily say that he can shape a person's behavior in any direction if what constitutes rewards for him are known. This is surely a marvelous engineering feat, but it leaves untouched the basic and difficult task of supplying the Skinnerian with an articulate understanding of the very rewards the existence of which he has so blithely assumed.

What is needed, it seems to me, are serious, empirically promising

1. Paul T. Costa, Jr., and Marvin Frankel have my thanks for useful suggestions incorporated in this paper.

137

theoretical efforts at understanding the content and development of
the various orientations toward meaning that can be observed in the
lives of people. As I am a personologist, my way of contributing to
this endeavor takes the form of the rudiments of a theory of personality. Among other things, I will consider the ways in which the
inherent nature we all share compels us to search for meaning. I will
also delineate some learned personality states differing importantly
in meaning orientation. Do not expect blazing originality, for my
effort has been to use all the resources and information I could
muster to say what really seems basic, whether or not it has been
said before in some sense. Indeed, I will be referring to some ancient
concepts. But perhaps in their particular definition, interrelation-
ship, and research implications, there will be enough that is new to
stimulate you to rethink the problem of meaning.

A Model for Understanding Personality and Psychopathology

Before going any further, I should tell you about the model for
personality theorizing that has guided my efforts. The model is
simple, coming directly out of current usage, and yet general enough
to cover not only psychological health but sickness as well. First, it
is important to know that personality, for me (Maddi, 1968),
includes a core and a peripheral level. The *core of personality* is
essentially man's inherent nature—that set of characteristics and
directional tendencies which each man shares from birth with
all other men. The *peripheral personality* is the learned type or life-
style that develops in a person as the result of the interaction of
his expressed inherent nature and the environmental events he
encounters.

In order to make statements about both psychological health
and illness, it is necessary to distinguish among the postulated
peripheral personality types one that is ideal and one or more that
are not. As the core of personality is the same for all peripheral
types, it must be development which determines whether or not the
periphery is ideal. In other words, the *ideal peripheral personality is
some function of the core of personality and ideal development*. In contrast,
the *nonideal peripheral personality is some function of the core of personality*

and nonideal development. What makes a peripheral personality ideal is that it is fully congruous with, or maximally expressive of, the core personality. Nonideal peripheral personalities express only part of the core, with the rest defended against because of its anxiety-provoking nature. It is the circumstances of development that are considered to instill the potential for anxiety and defense.

The nonideal peripheral personality is considered premorbid in the sense that it is vulnerable to stress. When the content and degree of stress are sufficient to undermine premorbid adjustment, there is a breakdown into a psychopathological state. In contrast, the ideal peripheral personality constitutes psychological health, for no kind or degree of stress is considered sufficient to precipitate breakdown. But the premorbid state should also be considered within the boundaries of normalcy because if no stress is encountered there will be a fairly adequate, if precarious, life.

The assumption that psychopathology is some function of premorbidity and stress may seem a rather static construal, but I encourage you to recognize that stasis is not at all a necessary attribute of the model. Psychopathology comes about only when the necessary stress conditions exist. And when the stress recedes, so too may the psychopathology, permitting a reconstitution of the premorbidity. In principle, one could oscillate back and forth between sickness and premorbidity. Finally, there is the possibility of shifting a premorbid personality in the direction of something more ideal through psychotherapy, which in this context would be considered a special case of ideal development.

As you can imagine, the framework outlined above is general enough to be applied to many content considerations. In this paper, however, I am mainly concerned with a view of personality in which the search for meaning, with its successes and failures, is paramount. This concern dictates many of the topics I will cover.

EXISTENTIAL SICKNESS

There is no more apt, if unpleasant, place to start the substantive part of this paper than with the psychopathologies of meaning. I shall call these ills *existential sickness* to emphasize that what is wrong has to do with a comprehensive failure in the search for meaning in life. In a general sense, we can probably all agree that existential problems form the sickness of our time. But further analysis of the phenomena considered relevant is necessary if we are to achieve understanding.

Let me suggest that the most extreme, or *vegetative*, form of existential sickness has widespread cognitive, affective, and actional expressions (Maddi, 1967). Cognition in this disorder expresses *meaninglessness*, or the chronic inability to believe in the truth, importance, usefulness, or interest value of any of the things one is engaged in or can imagine doing. The things that one perceives, reflects upon, remembers, and anticipates all seem trivial and stupid. The affective tone in this vegetative sickness is *blandness* and *boredom*, punctuated by periods of depression which become less frequent as the disorder is prolonged. It is the general absence of emotions, pleasant or unpleasant, with the exception of boredom, that is characteristic. Apathy and boredom, and more apathy and boredom, in a humdrum cycle of indifference. Such a break with indifference are the occasional stabs of depression that they are actually greeted with something like pleasure, in one of those paradoxes which abound in the psyche. But if existential sickness continues for any length of time, even the depression recedes, and the person becomes settled in his indifference. As to the realm of action in this disorder, one observes an activity level that may be low to moderate, but more important than amount of activity is the introspective and objectively observable fact that activities are not chosen. There is little selectivity, it being immaterial to the person what if any activities he pursues.

It is important to recognize that the syndrome described above refers to a chronic state of the person. I do not refer to stabs of doubt or occasional indifference or passivity, but rather to a settled, continuous state of meaninglessness, apathy, and aimlessness, such that the contradictory state of commitment, enthusiasm, and activeness is the exception rather than the rule. Once this sickness gets well established, doubt, like depression, becomes less and less likely. The person who is convinced that nothing has meaning, who has no vivid emotions, and who floats through life, is not prone to doubting. In order to doubt one must also believe, or at least believe in the importance of believing. Indeed, I shall refer to doubt later as a by-product of vigorous mental health, however painful it may be.

Even though the vegetative form of existential sickness may seem like an extreme thing, it is apparently quite common these days. The writings of many psychotherapists, sociologists, and social critics abound with references to meaninglessness, apathy, and aimlessness, as does fiction, poetry, and drama. An especially clear example of existential sickness from fiction is the character of Meursault in Camus's *The Stranger*. This character frequently says that he believes life to be meaningless and his activities to be arbitrary. He is virtually always bored and apathetic. He never imagines or daydreams. He has no goals. He makes only the most minimal decisions, doing little more than is necessary to keep a simple job as a clerk. He walks in his mother's funeral cortege and makes love to a woman with the same apathy and indifference. His perceptions are banal and colorless. The most difference anything makes is to be mildly irritating. He has this reaction, for example, to the heat of the sun, but then does nothing about it. Although it might seem remarkable that a novel about such a person would have any literary power at all, it is precisely because of the omnipresence of the symptom cluster we have been calling existential sickness that the reader is intrigued and shocked. When Meursault finally murders a man—without any emotional provocation or reaction, without any premeditation or reason, without any greater decision than is involved in resolving to take a walk—the reader is not even surprised. Anything is possible for Meursault, specifically because nothing is anything of importance. His is a vegetative existence that amounts to psychological death, and that is a very apt description of existential sickness. The body lives on, but thoughts, evaluations, and decisions are not made; no vivid or unusual emotions are felt, and little is carried out.

In contemporary cinema, Antonioni's work is particularly noteworthy for its exploration and depiction of existential sickness. In *L'Avventura*, the hero and a girl he meets embark on a movie-long search for his fiancée, who has mysteriously disappeared. As the film progresses, the fiancée recedes as the object of the search. For a while, one is still reasonably sure that some sort of search is going on, even though the fiancée seems somehow unimportant. But by the end, the viewer has become uncertain even about why the characters go through their actions at all. In the course of the film, the similarities of this hero to Meursault become apparent. The hero of *L'Avventura* has nothing much to say when his female companion questions him concerning his career, aspirations, and supposed love for his fiancée. He actually has intercourse with this companion, and she runs disappointed from the room because he is so cold and apathetic that he cannot even rejoice with her over their supposed new-found closeness. He walks through endless scenes in town after town and city after city and countryside after countryside, expressionless and distant and indifferent. In a cinematic tour de force, Antonioni is actually able to make the audience understand what is going on by feeling as apathetic as the hero does. Something analogous to the murder committed by Meursault takes place when Antonioni's hero deliberately spills ink on the architectural drawing being attempted by a young student he has been watching. He continues to watch impassively and indifferently while the student sputters in impotent rage and frustration, a whole morning's work unaccountably destroyed. Near the end of the film, the hero aimlessly makes love to a prostitute in the lobby of a hotel and is discovered by his female companion, who has somehow fallen in love with him by now. She is shaken and in great pain, but it becomes apparent in a dramatically understated ending that she is grieving for him as much as if not more than for herself. And the audience grieves for him too, for he feels nothing and believes nothing.

There are many additional examples, with varying degrees of aptness, that could have been chosen from contemporary art. In one way or another, all the films of Antonioni are relevant, as are Arthur Miller's *After the Fall*, T. S. Eliot's *The Wasteland*, Edward Albee's *Zoo Story* and *Who's Afraid of Virginia Woolf?*, Genet's *The Balcony*, and Ionesco's *Rhinoceros*. Even the recent film *Easy Rider* reflects meaninglessness, boredom, and aimlessness in some ways. But artistic productions are by their nature inventions, not literal descriptions of actualities. How do we know that the preoccupations of the contemporary artist express an actual problem shared by people in general? Even if there were no further evidence to be scrutinized, it could well be argued that art is always of important diagnostic value, is always a mirror of the strengths and weaknesses of the culture from which it arises. But there is some observational evidence available which, though admittedly unrigorous, suggests that the frequency of existential sickness actually exceeds the prevalence of that theme in art.

For years now psychotherapists have noted, in public and private, that there has been a wholesale, dramatic shift in the symptomatology of their patients. At the turn of the century, hysteria seems to have been the most frequent disorder, with a shift taking place in the twenties and thirties in the direction of obsessive-compulsive symptomatology. But by the time the Second World War was ending, existential sickness was swamping the others. While once the psychotherapist could expect some physical expression of a psychological problem or some guilt-laden preoccupation with sexual and aggressive impulses, now he was faced with a surprisingly sophisticated, if desperate, questioning of the value of being alive. The questions to which the patients had no answers flooded out: If there is no God, then aren't values arbitrary? Why make plans if death ends everything and could happen any time? Why work and save money for a future? Why spend half your life going to school? Is there any point in concerning yourself with what others think? Why obey laws? Isn't love an illusion, if our sexuality is like that of animals? Why try to accomplish anything, if a society that one cannot control molds everything we think and do? Are emotions important and trustworthy guides if they merely reflect ways we felt toward our parents years ago that are stuck in the unconscious mind? Why try to be popular? Why marry? Why raise a family? Why endure any deprivation? Why do anything? Why care? Why feel? Why think?

Most persons with existential sickness who seek the services of a psychotherapist do so when the disorder is not very far along, when the episodes of depression and despair are still fairly frequent. The questions mentioned come out of these emotions. That they are questions without answers indicates the meaninglessness, apathy, and aimlessness lurking behind the depression and despair. If the person is helped by psychotherapy, he may sink no further into vegetativeness. But for every person helped in the early stages of existential sickness there must be many who are not. Evidence of them is difficult to amass, as they are chronicled on no surveys. Some may even continue to hold a job for a time, especially if nothing particularly creative or difficult is expected of them. Others may sink so deep into indifference and aimlessness that unless they find some way to withdraw from obligations to society, they will be institutionalized. Probably many hobos and recluses are suffering existential sickness.

If existential sufferers are institutionalized, they are likely to be forced into nosological frameworks based on a medical model, leading to erroneous diagnoses as simple schizophrenics or psychotic depressives. The category simple schizophrenia is generally recognized now to be an ill-defined conglomerate. If there is any underlying consistency of meaning, it concerns a vegetative, withdrawn state in which nothing seems to matter and the person can no longer care for himself. This, of course, could as easily be called existential sickness. Though somewhat less vague, the category psychotic depression also presents difficulties. Some persons so diagnosed show vegetativeness rather than the active suffering of depression. But it is generally assumed that anyone who is vegetative *must* be depressed. It would seem more straightforward and less interpretative to label such sufferers existentially sick. Whether or not we give up the categories of simple schizophrenia and psychotic depression entirely, I would encourage you to recognize that some proportion of the persons so diagnosed might be more appropriately considered existentially ill.

Please note the trend of what I am saying. Currently, the most frequent symptoms brought to the psychotherapist's office seem to be those of meaninglessness, apathy, and aimlessness. And clearly more people are seeking psychotherapy than ever before. Add to this group of existential sufferers some proportion of the forgotten souls, inside and outside of our mental hospitals, who have sunk to marginal social status. I would remind you that the largest number of hospital beds go to the mentally ill and that the number of social dropouts seems higher now than ever before. Add to that multitude many persons who though superficially meeting their obligations to society are just going through the motions, their convictions rotted by the encroachments of meaninglessness. All in all, it adds up to quite a host.

But the accounting does not even stop here. Thus far, I have considered only the hard-core, vegetative form of existential sickness. To complete the tally, we should include two sorts of person whose difficulties stem from underlying existential pathology, but whose manner of expressing this may be a bit deceptive. Perhaps their existential sickness is in an early stage or somehow arrested at a point short of vegetativeness. Time and experience will help us unravel these mysteries. For the moment, I will simply consider the two types as variants of the existential sickness.

The first variant is *nihilism*, or the actively practiced attempt to discredit the meaningfulness of everything purporting to have meaning. Whereas the vegetative person lives his sense of meaninglessness in apathy and aimlessness, the nihilist shows some direction and energy. But his direction is that of disproving meaning, and his energy is based on despair and the angry pleasure involved in succeeding in destruction. Nothing is sacred or safe from this advocate of doom. He will be quick to point out that love is not altruistic but selfish, how philanthropy is a way of expiating guilt, that children are vicious rather than innocent, how leaders are vain and power-mad rather than inspired by a grand vision, and how work is not productive but rather a thin veneer of civilization hiding the monster in us all. Nothing is what it seems for the nihilist, as long as what it seems is meaningful. His aim is to reduce everything to such a sorry state that there is little reason to go on. Indeed, he goes on solely for the acute sense of absurdity to be obtained from the destruction of meaning. I do not mean to imply that all attempts at analysis are nihilistic. Detailed scrutiny of phenomena and apparent meanings can be very valuable when they are engaged in with an open mind and a view toward determining what the true meaning is. But when the tools of analysis are misused to demonstrate an already made assumption of the meaninglessness of life, then we are dealing with nihilism.

So many nihilists are there these days that the state is not fully recognized as a disorder, and may even appear to be a quite sophisticated attitude. Take, for example, the expression of nihilism in Camus's *The Myth of Sisyphus*. The thesis of this work is that man is by his nature a creature who seeks after meaning, but existence is by its nature an arbitrary and therefore meaningless series of events. There is no grand design, no master plan, however much we wish to impose such notions on life. God is dead, and in his absence the only inevitability is death. As death is unpredictable, man's penchant for seeing meaning in his life is doomed to frustration. He can plan all he likes, but death will come when he least expects it and render valueless all he has attempted.

According to Camus, the only way that man can rise above this bitter paradox is to become aware of it, to realize that although he seeks meaning life is really meaningless. The resulting sense of absurdity is considered the highest possible achievement of man. In an impassioned justification of nihilism, Camus (1955) exclaims, "I cherish my nights of despair" [p. 87]. However attractive may be Camus's feverish, brittle intensity, however much he may be considering problems we all share, I encourage you to recognize that there are certainly alternatives to his conclusion. Indeed, the Roman stoic Horace also believed that death was the only inevitability in life and that its unpredictability was a terrible fact. But he reached the conclusion opposite to Camus's on the best conduct of life. Where Camus became strident, Horace became placid. Where Camus devalued man's attempts to find meaning, Horace embraced them as even more important in the light of imminent death. For Horace, the unpredictability of death only freed man from the necessity of predicting meaning on absolutes. He felt that each man could well cherish the meanings he found in or gave to things in life without being intimidated by the short-lived nature of these meanings. The only way in which the inevitability of death needed to be taken into account was as a reminder to take one's humble, day-to-day meanings seriously and aim for satisfaction within one's own lifetime.

In a superficially similar way, Camus advocated living in the moment. But in contrast to Horace's peaceful emphasis on cherishing one's friends, family, fine foods, aesthetic delights, and even moral purity, Camus advocated cramming in as many experiences as possible, without evaluating or preferring them differentially. For Camus, no value judgments among experiences are really justified because decisions of that sort denote meaningfulness, which is irrelevant to life. He advocates aimlessness, develops arguments justifying meaninglessness, and revels in the ensuing despair! Why I consider his position a variant of existential sickness should be clear.

In art, the film *Last Year at Marienbad* is a similar expression of nihilism. It was quite common for serious and interested students of the cinema to return to see this film again and again, hoping to puzzle out its meaning. And each time they came away frustrated, having tried out hypothesis after hypothesis, such as "It's a dream"; "She is really in a mental hospital"; "The match game is the key to it all"; "It is about a husband and wife"; "A spy ring is involved." No hypothesis really worked, though the seemingly meaningful episodes within the film continually provoked the search for an overall meaning. In my opinion, there was no overall meaning to be found and the film was intended to frustrate any such search, toward the end of demonstrating the futility of believing in meaning in any usual sense. Scene followed scene in apparently aimless fashion, no one seemed to decide anything, and the emotions were generally bland. How pleased the film maker must have been at the frustration, anger, and eventual passivity of his audience.

The other variant of existential sickness might be called *crusadism*, by which I mean the incessant need to seek out and follow dramatic and important causes. I suspect I will have even more difficulty than with nihilism in convincing you that crusadism is a disorder, for those who follow causes undoubtedly do some, even considerable, social good. First I should make clear that I do not intend to include in crusadism *any* espousal of a cause, under any circumstances. Nor do I mean to condemn zeal for social change. Rather, I am pointing to the kind of person who must follow causes, any causes, regardless of their content, in order that he keep one step ahead of meaninglessness, apathy, and aimlessness. As soon as one cause is fulfilled, he must find another quickly so as not to fall apart existentially. Whatever social good comes of the efforts of such a person does not change the fact that his commitment to causes is a desperate attempt to avoid the more vegetative form of existential sickness. Crusaders are caught up by the vitality, drama, and group cohesiveness inherent in causes and movements, with the actual content and goals pursued being less important. This exposes the vulnerability of crusaders to meaninglessness—the commitments they make are not based on the substance of a cause so much as on its accouterments.

Anyone who has spent time observing social action movements knows that there is always a hard core of people who show up time after time at virtually any and all movements, however disparate their goals. These hard-core activists are almost invariably crusaders, who cannot experience a sense of meaning unless it is accompanied by the drama and rhetoric of a movement. There is something badly askew here. Social action movements, with their emphasis on confrontation politics, perhaps even to the point of civil disobedience and outright militancy, are certainly by their nature dramatic and exciting. But they are also dangerous and disruptive of any sort of everyday life. Should participation in a movement not therefore arouse fear, frustration, and impatience to return to one's more usual pursuits? But such considerations will only arise if the more usual pursuits seem meaningful, important, engaging, and emotionally satisfying. And if life's usual pursuits are as worthwhile as this, one will not be so quick to drop them at the slightest hint of a cause to be followed and a movement to join. Civil disobedience and confrontation politics would again become the last resorts they were intended to be, and as which they are most effective in promoting social change.

I have discussed three forms of existential sickness. In crusadism, the person desperately pursues meaning in the form of big, dramatic causes strongly believed in by others for fear that he will otherwise sink into meaninglessness. In nihilism, the person takes a desperate sense of meaning, based on paradox and absurdity, in tearing down apparent, conventional, and appropriate meanings, which otherwise would not be able to elicit his commitment. In the vegetative form, the person is no longer employing even these desperate attempts to maintain a sense of meaning, having sunk deeply into indifference, apathy, and aimlessness. It is tempting to order these three forms of existential sickness on a continuum, with crusadism showing the least, nihilism next, and the vegetative state the most disorder. The last state is clearly psychological death, and nihilism is close to this because it deals in a negative form of meaning. In contrast, the crusader is still attempting to cling to a positive form of meaning, however extreme and superficial it may be.

The Core of Personality

Existential sickness is aptly summarized as the failure to find a viable, consistent sense of meaning that can apply in everyday life.

In order to understand how this sickness comes about, we must know about the peripheral personality type that is premorbid to it and the manner in which this premorbidity defines a vulnerability to stress. Further clarification will be added by also considering the personality type that is ideal in the sense of being invulnerable to stress. But both personality types will share the same core, or human nature. It is to the core that I propose to turn first, putting special emphasis on the aspects of it that define the search for meaning inherent in man.

I assume that in man's nature there are *biological, social,* and *psychological* needs (Maddi, 1967). The biological needs reflect metabolic requirements, and their continual frustration leads to intense suffering and even physical death. Included here are such well-known needs as that for food, water, air, and elimination. In the most straightforward definition of these metabolic prerequisites, there is little necessity for taste and sophistication. Cooked meat tastes better and is more digestible than raw meat, but in the absence of the wherewithal to cook, raw meat will undoubtedly be eaten. Foul air may burn the nostrils and cause nausea, but it will be breathed with alacrity if there is no alternative. Similarly water will be consumed. Although it may be much nicer and more hygienic to eliminate in a modern toilet, the pants will be fouled sooner than the biological organism damaged. The part of us that is biologically motivated acts straightforwardly in terms of obtaining the goals that are consistent with physical survival, nothing more and nothing less. Decorum is something developed out of other than biological needs. And though it is perhaps somewhat less obvious, so too are taste and subtlety matters arising from other than biological necessity.

In proposing social needs, one cannot point to anything so dramatic as physical death as the outcome of prolonged deprivation. Nonetheless, it is quite apparent that the absence of interaction with others is a potent source of frustration and suffering. I would list as social needs at least those for communication and for contact. It seems to me that these needs are most straightforwardly met by engaging in a wide range of interactions with people. Talking to service personnel, colleagues, acquaintances, friends; dating; going to and having parties, dinners, and lunch meetings are ways to communicate and have contact. Even simply watching people go by or having them around as background will work, as is attested by the ubiquitous sidewalk cafe in Europe. In order to know the potency of social needs, one has only to remember times of relative isolation, like being in a strange town. At such times, one may even catch oneself smiling at perfect strangers on the street. If isolation continues for too long or is too complete, one becomes distinctly uncomfortable, anxious, and lonely. One is no longer sure of who one is.

Although loneliness is admittedly not as dramatic or final as physical death, perhaps it is not irrelevant, in trying to stress the potency of social needs, to point out that a large proportion of suicides occur following a period of time in which there has been little social contact (Stengel, 1965). The current research on sensory and social isolation is also relevant (see Fiske, 1961; Zubek, 1969). As such isolation is prolonged, subjects become increasingly uncomfortable, catch at any available source of stimulation (even if it is banal, such as routine instructions played over a loud speaker), and may even become disoriented and experience pseudohallucinatory states.

But it might be disputed that social needs are inherent, unlearned parts of man's nature. Is it not possible that isolation studies produce their dramatic effects because they employ as subjects persons who have already grown up in our society, therefore believing in the importance of social contact? What is needed here is similar experimentation using infants, who one could presume have not yet been greatly influenced by culture. Fortunately, such research does exist (Harlow, 1953; Harlow, 1962), and its results are clear. When primates are deprived of physical and social stimulation from birth, they develop into severely limited adults. As adults, they are unusually frightened of others, unable to cope with the normal experiences of life, and cannot even copulate. And at the human level, there have for many years been observational studies (Ribble, 1941; Spitz, 1945, 1946) which indicate that infants reared without mothering are generally retarded in physical and social development, even to the point of being abnormally vulnerable to physical disease and death. Putting all these findings together, there seems to be considerable evidence to support the contention that social needs are inherent and not merely learned.

In discussing social need satisfaction, I focused upon the simplest, most straightforward way, which is to increase the number and variety of people and social experiences. But another way to meet these needs is to work in depth toward increasing the richness of some few intense relationships. The way involves *intimacy* and *love*, in that you come to feel that some other person or persons are very important to you and you to them. You do not wish to keep your mutual experience just on the surface, preferring instead to go progressively deeper, creating new levels of experience all the while.

You will recall that I made the distinction between the simplest, most straightforward expression of biological needs and some more tasteful, subtle form of them and that I considered the difference to be based on nonbiological aspects of man's motivational nature. I believe something similar with regard to social needs. The difference between the simplest forms of communication and contact and the more intense forms called intimacy and love are produced by other than social motivations.

My contention is that psychological needs provide the push toward taste and subtlety in the biological domain and intimacy and love in the social domain. By psychological needs I mean capabilities, even requirements, of mind as opposed to body or groups. These needs have been described in various ways, but they seem well summarized by referring to the push *to symbolize, to imagine*, and *to judge*. Symbolization is the mental act of generalizing from specific experiences so that you establish categories of things and events. A symbol is something that exists in the mind, that has no material or tangible aspects. Once you realize that words are symbols, it becomes clear that symbolization is a uniquely human and ubiquitous function of mind.

Another function of mind is imagination, or the process of developing ideas and sequences of ideas that resemble possible experiences in the world, but have no actuality outside of the mind. It goes without saying that one cannot imagine much without having symbolized previously. Also, it is almost impossible to construe examples of imagination without realizing that in imagining one is trying out possibilities for subsequent action. It is sometimes believed that imagination is a substitute for action rather than a preparation for it. Surely there is some gratification to be obtained by dreaming about something, and this gratification may reassure you somewhat. But is seems to me that when satisfying and exciting fantasies are not carried out in some form, it is because the fantasizer fears either that he will be punished or that he will prove unworthy of his fantasy. It is the fear that stifles the action. Without the fear, there would be a natural, easy flow from fantasy into action. For that matter, even when fear stifles action, recurring fantasies have a way of creeping into one's actions, willy-nilly, when least expected. So the adolescent boy who fantasizes making love to a beautiful classmate finds that he begins to think about her, experience her, and interact with her in more intimate fashion, even though he is frightened to death of a sexual confrontation. But the subtle changes that take place in his actual interactions with her express well the manner in which imagination is a preparation for action. Perhaps she has similar fantasies of him, which lead her to avoid him without any apparent reason, while at the same time she subtly encourages him. Let them be alone to- gether in some unexpectedly secure circumstances, or let another possible sexual partner loom up to cause jealousy, and the love and attraction they prepared for in their fantasy may find sudden if frightening expression. Similar circumstances befalling two young people who had not fantasized about each other in such fashion might not have had any effect on action at all. What I am saying is that the function of imagination as a preparation for action is so potent and natural that even fear of consequences cannot demolish it completely.

The mental faculty of judgment involves any sort of evaluation, whether it be moral or preferential. In order to judge, one must compare experiences or experiential possibilities along some abstract dimension of value or preference. A major function of judgment is to act as a check on the validity of imagination. Imagination suggests a course of action, and judgment permits determination of whether the ensuing experience was pleasant or acceptable. Judgment can also be used, of course, to evaluate experience which does not come through the act of imagination but is imposed by the outside world.

What I am saying is that the person symbolizes, imagines, and judges because he needs to do so. The goal, or object, of these three processes differs. The goal of symbolization is *recognition*, in that a symbol permits you to determine the class of things to which an experience belongs. So when you see a small, fragile baby carriage, you recognize that it is a toy because you have symbolized a class of objects resembling bigger, more functional things but having no function other than imitation. The goal of imagination is *change*, for the action message included in fantasies invariably refers to something different from present actualities. This is true even when the fantasies involve some cherished remembrance because the implication is that the present should be changed into the past. Finally, the goal of judgment is *values* and *preferences*. Values indicate, of course, what is good and what is bad, being the stuff of morality. But preferences make no ethical pronouncements, being limited to what is liked and disliked. In an overall sense, the goal or object of all three psychological needs together is increased *meaning*. To recognize something is clearly to invest it with more meaning than something might have that goes unrecognized. To work toward change is to try to increase the meaningfulness of experience by rendering it more stimulating, less boring. And to order experience in terms of considerations of value and preference is to render it more meaningful by setting it in a personally relevant context.

By conceptualizing the needs for symbolization, imagination, and judgment in this fashion, I have assumed that the search for meaning is inherent in man. My main argument in support of this position is that the expression of these three needs is so ubiquitous. One cannot conceive of a human, unless he is severely maimed, who does not symbolize, imagine, and judge virtually all the time. Something so ubiquitous would be difficult to explain through learning, though the specific content of symbols, fantasies, values, and preferences would undoubtedly express particular learning experiences. It must certainly be admitted that the argument of ubiquity is less dramatic than the physical pain and loneliness that can be marshaled as evidence for the inherent nature of biological and social needs. But I encourage you not to be swayed by drama alone, for the evidence of ubiquity is quite extensive. Psycholinguistic research (Osgood, 1962) has shown that every one of the many societies and culture areas studied employed judgments in attempting to understand and order experience. Thanks to the painstaking recordings of anthropologists, there is evidence that imagination is fully as ubiquitous as judgment. There is no society without a mythology, and myths are nothing more than the shared imaginings of a group of people. Insofar as it would be impossible to judge and make myths without employing symbols, then the evidence mentioned above must extend to the ubiquity of the symbolizing function as well.

There is little known about the possibly dire effects of depriving the person of the ability to symbolize, imagine, and judge, because such deprivation is extremely difficult to achieve. Perhaps something approximating such deprivation in the imaginative realm has recently become possible through research on dreams (Dement, 1960; Kubie, 1962). In this research, subjects are awakened just at the point when they begin a dream. Then they are permitted to go to sleep again, only to be awakened when they begin to dream again. Normally, there is a fairly long period of time between falling asleep and the onset of the rapid eyeball movements signaling dreaming. But under dream deprivation, subjects get to the point at which they begin dreaming virtually as soon as they fall asleep again. There are also many indications of discomfort and pain in the waking state at having been deprived of dreaming. As long as you are willing to accept dreaming as an instance of imagination, there would seem to be evidence that man possesses an inherent need to imagine.

One can also mount a fairly substantial evolutionary argument for the existence of inherent psychological needs in man. From an evolutionary standpoint, man was aided in surviving the numerous pressures upon him, given the frailness of his body, by having evolved a brain and central nervous system of marvelous scope and flexibility. His big advantage was to be able to receive vast amounts of information and process it in many ways, such as classifying it, evaluating it, and comparing it to memories and fantasies. In this fashion, a rich basis for effective and useful action was achieved. Through his marvelous brain, man became preeminent among the creatures. But once this brain was evolved, it could hardly lie fallow. The very functions that led to its survival are the things it is designed to do. It is inconceivable that the human brain would not engage in symbolization, imagination, and judgment as a natural, inherent aspect of its functioning. And more than two billion years of evolution stand behind that statement.

Once it has been assumed that man's nature is composed of biological, social, and psychological needs, it is logical to decide that what is best is for all three sets of needs to be expressed fully in living. Only by expressing them all will a person be able to avoid the accumulation of frustration and other dire consequences attendant upon need deprivation. But when one or more of the three sets of needs are stifled, or defended against, the result is a lopsided personality—too biological or too social or too psychological— undermined and limited by the fact that it insufficiently expresses all that is in man's nature.

The key to whether man's nature, or core of personality, will be richly or imperfectly expressed in living is development. Ideal development is that set of circumstances which permit and encourage exploration of biological, social, and psychological possibilities, culminating in a peripheral personality which should be considered ideal because the three possibilities are actualized in it. Deviant development is that set of possibilities which render one or more of these possibilities anxiety-provoking and therefore the subject of defensive processes. The result is a peripheral personality that is premorbid, or vulnerable to the disruptive effects of stress, because the underlying true nature is not fully expressed.

Conformism as Premorbidity

I should like to propose that the peripheral personality that is premorbid for existential sickness is best conceptualized as *conformism*. Conformism can be understood as a personality type in which psychological needs are a source of anxiety and have been defended against. This means that the conformist makes minimal, or stereotyped, use of symbolization, imagination, and judgment in living, relying instead on the most simple, unsubtle forms of biological and social needs.

This tendency toward biological and social reductionism is clearly seen in the self-definition and world view of the conformist. He defines himself as *nothing more than a player of social roles and an embodiment of creature needs* (Maddi, 1967). The difficulty is not that man is not these two things, but that what he is in addition to them finds little representation in the conformist's sense of identity.

Considering yourself to be an embodiment of biological needs hardly sets you apart from other species. Neither does the view of yourself as a player of social roles, for most subhuman species have social differentiation of at least a rudimentary sort. And there is little in either of these two components of identity that permits much sense of difference between individual men, except in the trivial sense that the particular social roles played this moment may be different for me than for you and the biological needs that I have right now may happen to be different from those you have. But tomorrow, or an hour from now, the situation may change, and we may not have even that small basis for distinguishing ourselves from one another.

Consider social reductionism further. If you view yourself as a player of social roles, you are in effect accepting the idea that the social system is a terribly potent force in living. You do not see society as a collection of individuals who can influence and change their common life decisions by exchange of opinion and other techniques whereby people convince each other. Rather, society appears to be institutions and laws that transcend individuals and have a life of their own. This inclines you to the belief that the current content and form of the social system is its necessary and unchangeable nature and that individuals have no choice but to conform to its pressures. In the long run, conforming to social system pressures even comes to appear morally worthwhile. This takes the form of the conviction that it is the social system, as currently constituted, that protects everyone against chaos, and that therefore we all ought to do our share to support its institutions, however restricting they may be. The way to give this support is to play adequately the social roles that are given to you as a responsibility of citizenship.

There are parallel implications of biological reductionism. If you define yourself as little more than an embodiment of creature needs, you obviously come to believe that such needs as those for food and water are terribly important and real forces in living. Physical survival seems unquestionably of paramount importance, and hence, the degree to which biological needs are satisfied is taken as the hallmark of adequate living. It becomes difficult to imagine justifying deprivation of these needs under any circumstances. Any alternative to direct, immediate, and constant expression of these needs, if an alternative could even be construed as possible, would be unwise because it would constitute a violation of all that is important.

The person who engages in both biological and social reductionism must necessarily feel powerless in the face of social pressures from outside, and powerless in the face of biological pressures from inside. Biological needs and social roles seem like givens, like causal factors independent of his puny power to influence. He would never seriously reject a social role or change it. He would never think to question just how important physical survival is anyway. Soon he will become his social roles and biological needs—there being no longer any act of consciousness worth speaking of to mark the fact that his identity is not the only one possible. There will be little basis for raising abstract questions of the nature of existence.

This is not to say that once the person becomes his social roles and biological needs he never again experiences conflict. Indeed, he frequently experiences the conflict inherent in the likelihood that social roles and biological needs will lead in different, if not incompatible, directions. This potentiality for conflict arises from the fact that while social roles become institutionalized along the lines of what is socially acceptable, biological needs are defined in terms of animalistic urges, without regard to propriety. The only self-consciousness the conformist ever feels consistently has to do with his inability to satisfy both aspects of his identity with the same set of actions. He will try to assuage biological and social pressures at different times, or in different places, keeping possible incompatibilities from the eyes of others and from direct confrontation in his own awareness. His life will be fragmentary, disunified, a pastiche of bits and pieces.

As I have said, the main problems of the conformist's identity are that it is very concrete, fragmented, and conflictual. But his difficulties do not stop here. The generalization of his identity into a world view potentiates his limitations on a grand scale. This world view is based on *pragmatism* and *materialism*. The pragmatism comes primarily from viewing not only oneself but everyone as having to play the assigned social roles. The only relevant question becomes how good the people are in implementing these roles. A person is good if he plays his roles well, and bad if he does not.

How often one hears that the world is the way it is, so one might as well be practical about it. This is an essentially pragmatic view and issues from the belief that society is superordinate to man and is, therefore, unchangeable and all-powerful.

Materialism comes primarily from the belief that not only you, but others as well, are no more than embodiments of biological needs. If a person believes this enough then the goods that are the objects of the needs will be coveted as possessions. Also coveted will be the things and processes instrumental to obtaining the objects of the needs. In short, the pursuit of material things is elevated to the status of a natural process. How often one hears that narrow self-interest is the only justifiable motivating force besides the socially determined avoidance of guilt. This statement sums up the implications of conformism inherent in biological reductionism as a world view.

The world view and identity of the conformist conjoin so that his relationships to other people are contractual rather than intimate. If you and everyone else are considered bound by certain rules of social interaction and in need of certain material goods for satisfaction and survival, relationships will tend to be based on the economic grounds of who is getting what from whom when and for how much. The conformist will not be willing to just let an interaction go in whatever direction that develops, nor will he be willing to continue or terminate it on the basis of how interesting or stimulating it is. Rather, he will want it structured in advance, and it will have to be clear all along what is in it for him in terms of social status or material advance. And once he gets what he wants, there will be no further reason for contact. Bonds of affection, loyalty, camaraderie, and love will not tend to develop in any full-blown sense of those terms. The conformist's relations will tend to be cold-blooded.

He will usually not have friends in any proper sense of that word, but rather only associates. He may even call these associates friends, unwittingly trivializing that concept rather than face his own superficiality, but it is an implicit contract nonetheless that will define the relationship. Let a "friend" who has been useful in business cease to be so, and there will be no further reason for contact or affection. Let a wife no longer further his emphasis on

pragmatism and materialism, and he will mysteriously cease to feel
love for her. The affection for the friend and love for the wife were
from the first trivial forms of those emotions based on a contractual
sense of who is doing what for whom. All along, the conformist will
have had little real sense of involvement with them, knowing and
understanding them only in terms of their relevance to his social
role playing and biological need gratification. When he repudiates
them, he will display remarkably little sense of who they are and
what they want. Nor will he experience much remorse, unless
replacing their contractual obligations to him is difficult. Even then,
he will not be missing them—whatever he may say—but rather
what they formerly provided for him.

By way of summary, it would be well to try to get into the
conformist's skin for a moment. He worries about such things as
whether he is considered by others to be conscientious, a nice
person, admirable. He wonders whether people can guess the animal
lusts within him and if he can satisfy these lusts without interfering
too much with social role playing. Since his relationships with others
are defined in terms of limited, specific goals of an external nature, his
social life will be rather structured and superficial. The absence from
these contractual relationships of intimacy, commitment, and spontaneity leads to a nagging sense of loneliness and disappointment.

However unappetizing this description seems, I encourage you
not to think of conformity as a sickness in itself, but rather as a
predisposition to sickness of an existential sort. Conformity is simply
too common and livable to be considered frank sickness, though it is
a state with its own characteristic sufferings and limitations. The
conformist is still too much enmeshed in the problems of living, still
too much concerned with having a successful life to be considered
grossly psychopathological. Indeed, the life of the conformist may
go on in a rather empty, though superficially adequate, way for a
long time. He may even be reasonably successful in objective terms,
keeping his vague dissatisfactions and anxieties to himself. But if he
encounters stress of the right content and intensity, his adjustment
will crack and he will be precipitated into existential sickness.

In speaking of precipitating stress, I do not mean the things that
merely make the person worry. The threat of social censure or
biological deprivation is a potent source of concern for the conform-

ist, but it does not cause a breakdown into existential sickness because there is no disconfirmation of his self-definition and world view. What will produce breakdown are stresses that force recognition of the conformist's overly concrete, fragmentary, conflictual, superficial life. The most effective stresses in this regard are those that directly undermine a belief in the importance of social role playing and mindless pursuit of biological satisfaction (Maddi, 1967).

One obvious stress is the threat of imminent death. When one treats physical survival as paramount in importance, one acts as if he will not die. Then the threat of imminent death, especially if sudden or occurring in youth, can be an undermining shock. If the threat actually culminates in death, the conformist will die "the death of Ivan Ilych," in the great novella by Tolstoi. Ilych knows he is dying of a horrible disorder, and this colors all his perceptions and judgments. Most of the visitors to his bedside are business associates who, he comes to realize, are only performing what they experience as a distasteful obligation of their social role. Then he realizes that the same thing is true of his own family. None of these people is deeply touched by his drift toward death, for theirs is a contractual rather than intimate relationship to him. And even more horrible, he realizes the appropriateness of their behavior because he too has thought of and experienced them only in contractual, superficial terms. The triviality and superficiality of their materialism and social conformity—and his own—are thrown into sharp relief by the threat of death. He becomes acutely aware of his wasted life and can tell himself nothing that will permit a peaceful death. He realizes that he has always felt deprived of intimacy, love, spontaneity, and enthusiasm. By renouncing himself and the people around him, he is finally able to feel truly human and alive just at the time when he dies physically. This story is didactically and literarily powerful because this is a tragic way to die. What bankruptcy it is when it is death that must free us from the impoverishing shackles of social conformity and biological need gratification!

If the conformist faced with imminent death should actually recover, he is likely to experience existential sickness. If the threat of death disconfirms your self-definition, then you have none to work with; and in an adult, this leads to meaninglessness, apathy, and aimlessness. Before he dies, Ilych is certainly an example of this.

The other obvious stress that can precipitate existential sickness is gross disruption of the social order, through such things as war, conquest, and economic depression, leading to disintegration of social roles and even of the institutionalized mechanisms for satisfying biological needs. Such catastrophe has two effects on the conformist. First, it makes it difficult to continue to obtain the usual rewards for playing social roles and expressing biological needs. Secondly, and more importantly, disruption of the social order demonstrates the relativity of society to someone who has been treating it as absolute reality. The conformist is left with a disconfirmed self-definition and world view and has little basis for avoiding meaninglessness, apathy, and aimlessness. Thinking along very similar lines, Durkheim (1951) saw social upheaval, or anomie, as a factor increasing suicide rates.

The final stress is difficult to describe because it is less dramatic than the others. Not only is this stress less dramatic, but it is usually an accumulation of events rather than something that need happen only once. And yet, this final stress is probably the most usual precipitating factor in existential sickness. The stress I mean is *the repeated confrontation with the limitations on deep and comprehensive experiencing produced by conformity*. These confrontations usually come about through other people's insistence on pointing out the conformist's existential failures. The aggressive action of other people is more or less necessary because the conformist usually avoids self-confrontation. But let there be a close relative who is suffering because of the the person's conformism, and confrontations will be forced.

A good example of this kind of stress and its effects is found in Arthur Miller's *After the Fall*. During the first two-thirds of the play, Quentin discovers that his is what I would call the conformist's self-definition. The discovery is a terribly painful process. It begins when his first wife, working up the courage for a separation and divorce, tries, after a long period of docility, to force him to recognize the limitations in their relationship and her deep dissatisfaction with him. In listening to his own attempts to answer her charges and in considering her attacks, he begins to recognize that his has been little more than a contractual commitment to her. He has been merely conforming to social roles in being husband and father. Under her scrutiny, he begins to recognize his superficial sexuality as well. He feels at fault for his limitations, but can do little about them, instead asking pathetically for understanding. His wife is also important in forcing recognition that his offer to defend his old law professor in court is not out of deep affection, or intimacy, or even loyalty, but rather out of an attempt to convince people that he does have feelings for this man. Frightened and distraught by what he is learning about himself, Quentin finally begins to envy his wife for her ability to experience deeply and face the truth.

After the breakup of his first marriage, Quentin moves impulsively into a second. His second wife, Maggie, idealizes him, and he feels reassured about himself, though he has not really changed. It is only after they have been married for some time that Quentin begins to appreciate Maggie's extraordinary neediness and lack of differentiation as a person. Her adulation of him can no longer serve to reassure him, and to make matters worse, he has new evidence of his superficiality in his inability to reach her in any significant way. He must stand by and let her commit suicide, having decided that the most he can do is save his own life. Whatever depth of personality in a husband could have saved her, he simply did not have.

After Maggie's death, Quentin spends two years or so in a state of meaninglessness, apathy, and aimlessness. He does not work, he does not relate to people, he merely drifts. This period is clearly one of existential sickness, and can be seen as precipitated by the disconfirmation of his self-definition and world view through forced recognition of the limitations produced by his social and biological conformity.

Individualism as the Ideal Personality

In turning to the ideal peripheral personality, you will recall that it should show vigorous expression not only of biological and social needs but psychological needs as well. This personality type is properly called *individualistic*, especially by contrast with the type which suppresses psychological needs. After all, of the three sets of needs, it is the psychological which is most uniquely human. All subhuman species have biological requirements for survival and satisfaction, and these requirements are generally acted upon in a straightforward and simple manner. Most subhuman species have patterned, rigid social relationships, aptly described as role playing. Only in man is it reasonable to consider psychological needs to be of much importance. And once psychological needs are expressed along with the others, the person will be pursuing biological and social satisfactions with a tendency to symbolize his experience, imagine alternatives, and judge the value of what ensues. The biological and social satisfactions obtained will not be the common, predictable ones, but will show a flair, something unusual or especially vivid.

The individualist's self-definition is *someone with a mental life through which he can understand and influence his social and biological experiences and urges.* Although he recognizes and accepts social and biological pressures, he does not feel powerless in the face of them and experiences considerable room to maneuver in the process of finding just the right life for himself. He believes that he is capable of choice and has freedom, though he is not so naive as to think that there are no constraints upon him, no necessities. But his stance is one which questions whether things that seem constraints and necessities really are recalcitrant to being influenced. And when he finds some bedrock necessity—such as the death of a loved one or imposed confinement in prison—he is prepared even then to investigate what little measure of choice may remain to him.

Understandably, the world view of the individualist matches his self-definition. He does not view society as a given, as unchangeable, as something governed by laws superordinate to man. Nor does he view man as just another species in the animal kingdom, with little that is unique except vanity perhaps. Rather, he views *society as the creation of men, properly in their service, and believes man to be unique among living things because of his extraordinary mental powers which make it possible for him to be master of his own fate.* Certainly the individualist will be realistic enough to recognize that social systems are not always responsive to their publics, and that men often act as if they believe themselves not to be different from the apes. But he will consider such social systems and such men to be less than ideal, to have fallen short of what it is within man's power to achieve. The value of this judgment is that it provides the individualist with a format for action. He may decide to withdraw from such inhuman societies and men. Alternatively, he may try to convince the men that they are wrong and influence the social system through political action. What is important is that his world view will set a standard for social systems and men that is fully consistent with the standards that he holds for himself.

It should be recognized that I call this ideal personality type the individualist not because he has a steely aloofness and indifference to others, in the style of the nineteenth-century inner-directed man. He is an individualist only because his thoughts and actions are relatively uncommon and expressive of the psychological needs. Actually, he will relate to others more deeply than the conformist, substituting *intimacy* for contract. When he encounters the common tendency to relate contractually, he will try to break through this superficiality by talking about it directly. Once he does this, he may well find people encouraged through his lead to share their feelings of loneliness and unfulfillment with him; and the road to subtle, complex social relations has already been found. Although common experiences and sentiments are certainly fertile ground for intimate relating, differences need not be considered anathema. Indeed, the individualist finds the differences between himself and others to be interesting and provocative rather than threatening. This makes it possible for him to explore his own uniqueness through vigorous expression of symbolization, imagination, and judgment, without any necessity of this process separating him from others. He will be particularly able to understand and appreciate the very special qualities marking another's individuality, because his own is so strong and important.

When the individualist is bothered by the commonly encountered penchant for unreflective biological responding, he can choose to explore other forms of expression. For example, instead of merely eating food, he can make hunger the basis for more comprehensive satisfaction by cooking especially tasty dishes or by eating in the company of people with whom he feels intimate. And the same with sex. He can make sexual expression a subtle, complex, changing thing, indulged in with people toward whom he feels intimate and affectionate on other than simply sexual grounds. In principle, the individualist is so complex and integrated that he can continue a single sexual relationship for a lifetime, without any appreciable diminution of passion and commitment. For him, sexuality is not a disembodied biological urge, but rather a multifaceted expression of intimacy.

Certainly the individualist will act unconventionally with some frequency. Some critics of my position would argue that it amounts to advocating the unleashing of monsters on the world. What is to stop a person from murdering or robbing if he feels so free to put his imagination into operation? Psychologists like Rogers (1961) would answer by contending that there is nothing basic to the organism that will lead in the direction of such monstrosities. He would believe that only an imagination already perverted by psychopathogenic social pressures would lead the person in the direction of terrible transgressions toward his fellow men. I have considerable sympathy for this position, but would add to it the notion that judgment is a maturing supplement to imagination. Your imagination might even include the bases for catastrophic action, perhaps at a time when someone has hurt you badly, and still you might not act on the fantasies if judgment provided some balance. I sincerely believe that although the individualist may well make mistakes in life, he will not be a monster simply because he does not conform to the most obvious social pressures.

It should be remembered that Ralph Waldo Emerson's (1940) conclusion that "whosoever would be a man must be a nonconformist" [p. 148] is echoed by many of the world's finest thinkers. If a critic responds claiming that this is the sort of thinking that permits such abominations as Hitler and Charles Manson, I would suggest that these were badly twisted men who showed less imagination than repetitive, compulsive preoccupations, and less judgment than megalomaniacal overconfidence. It is only by losing the usual standards of what is meant by imagination and judgment that Hitler, Manson, and the individualist can be discussed in the same breath. But a secondary argument could be made that the position I am taking makes it at least possible for some twisted person like Hitler to gain dangerous power because those around him believe enough in imagination and judgment as guides to living that they may not see in time that he is only a pseudoexample of the individualist. Here we see a very weak argument. Indeed, it is much more likely that people who define themselves as social role players and embodiments of biological needs will not recognize or be able to stop a man like Hitler. It is to the point that Hannah Arendt (1964) subtitled her treatise on the final solution to the "Jewish problem" *A Report on the Banality of Evil*. To judge from reports, the rank and file Germans were simply conforming to rules and orders when they gassed people!

This highlights an important feature of individuality, as I have construed it. Some of the discussion may have suggested that the individualist is effete, without the discipline and persistence for hard work. This is far from true. Do not be misled by the emphasis on subtlety, taste, intimacy, and love. More than anyone else, the individualist will have standards, know what he wants, and be willing and able to pursue his desires with rigor and self-reliance. He can even perform unpleasant tasks gracefully if they are definitely related to reaching the desired goals.

Another consequence of relying upon imagination and judgment as guides to action is that the life of the individualist will be a frequently changing, unfolding thing. New possibilities will be constantly developing, though the reliance on judgment does ensure that the process of change will not be without pattern or continuity. Because of the unfolding nature of his life, the individualist will have little occasion to feel boredom or disappointment over missed opportunities. Rather, he will feel emotions deeply and be enthusiastic and committed. But his life will not be quite that rosy. When you are in a continual process of change, you cannot predict outcomes. *Ontological anxiety* (May, 1958), or what is sometimes called *doubt* concerning existence (Frankl, 1955), is a necessary concomitant of individualism. When you stop to think about it, it is quite understandable that someone who is his own standard of meaning will be unsure and anxious at times when he is changing.

Looked at in this way, doubt is actually a sign of health rather than illness. Powerful expression to this view is given by Frankl (1955, p. 30) when he says:

> Challenging the meaning of life can . . . never be taken as a manifestation of morbidity or abnormality; it is rather the truest expression of the state of being human, the mark of the most human nature in man. For we

can easily imagine highly developed animals or insects—say bees or ants—which in many aspects of their social organization are actually superior to man. But we can never imagine any such creature raising the question of the meaning of its own existence, and thus challenging that existence. It is reserved for man alone to find his very existence questionable, to experience the whole dubiousness of being. More than such faculties as power of speech, conceptual thinking, or walking erect, this factor of doubting the significance of his own existence is what sets man apart from animal.

What remains to be mentioned is that the individualist will not be vulnerable to the stresses that have an undermining effect on the conformist. If the individualist actually comes to the point of death, he will be much more graceful than Ivan Ilych. Death for the individualist will be no more than a very unfortunate interruption of an intense and gratifying life process. I contend that someone who is living well will more easily face death than someone who senses that he has not even lived at all. When faced with the threat of death, the individualist will experience little of the therapeutic effect emphasized in the pessimistic strain of existential theorizing (e.g., Sartre, 1956). You simply do not need the threat of death to remind you to take life seriously and live in the immediate moment if you are already doing so.

As to social upheaval, it is certainly common to assume that it leads to various dire consequences, such as suicide. But it is also likely that times of social upheaval involve intense creativity. While some people are committing suicide, others are using to good advantage the freedom achieved by the breakdown of repressive social institutions. We should remember, for example, that the Renaissance was a time of extraordinary social upheaval and political instability (Maddi, 1965). While the suicide rate may have been high, so too was creativity. That the flooding of creativity may have been due to the great prevalence of individualists, for whom freedom from social constraint was helpful, is suggested by the following quotation from the *Oration on the Dignity of Man* by Pico della Mirandola (1956, p. 17):

Neither heavenly nor earthly, neither mortal nor immortal have we created thee, so that thou mightest be free according to thy own will and honor, to be thy own creator and builder. To thee alone we gave growth and development depending on thy own free will. Thou bearest in thee the germs of a universal life.

Such writing was common in those days when it was man who was extolled rather than God, the social system, or the animal kingdom.

Finally, there is the matter of an accumulated sense that your life is a failure in terms of commitment and depth of experience. Actually, I am speechless here. It is simply incomprehensible that a person with an individualist's orientation to life would ever be in the position of experiencing the painful course of self-revelation leading to existential sickness seen in Arthur Miller's Quentin.

IDEAL AND NONIDEAL DEVELOPMENT

Although I must be brief, I do want to include a word about development. The ideal developmental situation does not obstruct but actively encourages the vigorous expression of all three sets of needs. In this regard, it is valuable for the child to experience what Rogers (1959) calls unconditional positive regard from the significant people in his life. This ensures that the child is appreciated as a distinct human being. With such appreciation, he comes to value himself and is able to act without fear and inhibition. But unconditional positive regard is not enough because it does not lend much direction to development. The child must grow up around people who value symbolization, imagination, and judgment and support the child when he shows evidence of these processes. This will include teaching him by word and deed that doubt—the natural concomitant of psychological expression—is not to be avoided, no matter how painful it may be. An important way of doing this is to be truly interested in and appreciative of the child's individuality so that he feels it was worth enduring doubt long enough to realize the admirable outcome of self-reliance. In addition, the child's range of experience must be broad, so that the generalizing function of symbolization and the ordering function of judgment will have raw material with which to work. A broad range of experience may also fire the imagination.

It is also crucial that the significant people in the youngster's life recognize the importance of social and biological functioning as well, so that they can encourage him in such expression. Their encouragement, however, should not be in the service of accepting social roles and animalistic urges, so much as in the conviction that social and biological living is what you make it, and, in the final analysis, these two sides of man are not so separate from each other and from the life of the mind.

From this statement, it is easy to see what would be nonideal development leading to conformism. All that is necessary is to grow up around people who value only some aspects of you; who believe in social roles and biological needs as the defining pressures of life; and who are afraid of active symbolization, imagination, and judgment. Let these significant people act on their views in interaction with the child, and he will become a conformist.

SOME RELEVANT RESEARCH

Although my intent here is mainly theoretical, I would like to point to some research themes relevant to conformism and individualism. But at the outset, I should address a ready criticism. Much of the research in which conformity is measured on some performance task suggests that conforming tendencies are situation specific (e.g., Hollander & Willis, 1967). This could be taken as evidence that no conformist personality type exists. But such a conclusion seems premature, however mystifying the performance results may be. There is, after all, a considerable body of research suggesting that indeed the tendency to conform may be quite general. I refer to the research employing questionnaire measures of socially desirable responding and internal versus external locus of control.

Crowne and Marlowe (1960) have reported an extensive attempt at construct validation for their carefully developed Social Desirability Scale (M–C SDS). On the face of it, the tendency to respond in a socially desirable direction should express conformity and an emphasis on social role playing. By and large, the empirical findings bear this out. In an extensive research program (Crowne & Marlowe, 1964) it was determined that persons scoring high, compared to low, in socially desirable responding show greater attitude change after delivering an appeal for an attitude they did not originally endorse (thereby resolving cognitive dissonance); express higher need for affiliation; and terminate psychotherapy sooner (perhaps out of unwillingness to face themselves). In addition, the higher the M–C SDS score, the greater the tendency to give common word associations and fewer, more concrete responses on the TAT, Rorschach, and sentence completion tests. In their fantasy productions, high M–C SDS scorers are especially rejecting of people, but tend to underestimate the extent to which their friends really reject them. The highest thresholds in a perceptual task requiring the recognition of obscene words belong to these high social-desirability scorers.

There is also a group of findings concerning socially desirable responding and performance of simple laboratory tasks. Subjects high on the M–C SDS generally perform better on the pursuit rotor (Strickland & Jenkins, 1964) and do more skillfully a motor steadiness task (Strickland, 1965) and other simple motor tasks (Willington & Strickland, 1965). Although the results may indicate superior motor ability in these subjects, it seems more likely that we are observing the heightened attentiveness produced by a wish to appear socially desirable. Consistent with this interpretation is the finding (Crowne & Marlowe, 1964) that subjects high in M–C SDS are less likely to rate a monotonous spool-packing task as dull.

In general, the picture emerging is of a personality type characterized by intense interest in appearing attentive, consistent, competent, and acceptable, in the context of conformity, and showing superficial interest in, but lack of deep commitment to, others and a general unwillingness to face these facts. The implications of defensiveness are supported by Conn and Crowne (1964), who found that high M–C SDS scorers selected euphoria as an alternative to the expression of anger in a manner suggestive of reaction formation. Similarly, Fishman (1965) found that subjects high in M–C SDS expressed less verbal aggression toward the experimenter when he imposed nonarbitrary frustration (whereas arbitrary frustration did not differentiate high from low M–C SDS scorers). Apparently, the person high in socially desirable responding can only express anger when he can give himself justification (or rationalization) for it.

Any information concerning the relationship of M–C SDS to psychopathology should be of interest, as I have contended that conformism is the premorbid state for existential sickness. Even though the M–C SDS was specifically designed to be independent of frank psychopathology, there is some research indicating that this is not so. Katkin (1964) reports the correlations between the M–C SDS and the MMPI scales commonly used to assess psychopathological trends. Eight of the ten correlations reached significance, raising the possibility that conformity predisposes toward sickness. That the strongest correlation was between the M–C SDS and the Schizophrenia Scale is noteworthy, as I have contended that many persons diagnosed schizophrenic are actually suffering from existential sickness.

A few years back, Rotter (1954) proposed that an important characteristic of personality is whether the locus of control over reinforcement (or goals) is perceived as internal or external. There is by now a commonly used measure of this characteristic called the Internal-External Control Scale (I-E Scale) with adequate psychometric properties (Phares, 1957; James, 1957; Rotter, Seeman, & Liverant, 1962). As I intimated earlier, conforming persons and individualists ought to believe in external and internal control, respectively. The construct validation of the I-E Scale bears this out.

First of all, there appears to be a mild but dependable tendency for people who feel externally controlled to respond in a socially desirable fashion (Lichtman & Julian, 1964; Strickland & Rodwan, 1963; Crowne & Liverant, 1963; Seeman, 1963). Such a relationship increases the plausibility of a conforming personality type.

There are several studies showing differences in learning as a function of internal versus external locus of control. Seeman & Evans (1962) reported that among hospitalized tuberculosis patients, those believing in external control had obtained less objective knowledge about their own conditions than those believing in internal control. This finding was not attributable to socioeconomic or hospital-experience variables. Controlling for intelligence and the novelty of stimulus materials presented for learning, Seeman (1963) demonstrated that prison inmates scoring low in externality were superior to those scoring high in retention of information presented to them concerning procedures related to achieving parole successfully. As might be expected, it has also been shown that subjects high in externality tend to be acquiescent, both when acquiescence is measured by questionnaire (Odell, 1959) and in Asch-type performance situations (Crowne & Liverant, 1963).

Consistent with the implications of self-reliance in the results mentioned above are studies comparing various socially significant groupings of people as to the internal or external nature of their beliefs concerning control. Battle & Rotter (1963) found that lower-class blacks were significantly more external than lower-class whites or middle-class blacks and whites. Using adult subjects, Lefcourt & Ladwig (1965, 1966) reported higher rates of belief in external control among black than among white prison inmates. In a third ethnic-group investigation, Graves (1961) adapted the I-E Scale for high school students and found whites to be most internal, followed by Spanish-Americans, and then American Indians. Concerning males enrolled in a southern black college, Gore & Rotter (1963) found that subjects scoring most internal signed statements expressing the greatest amount of interest in social action concerning civil rights. That these statements did not represent empty commitments is shown by Strickland (1965), who found that actual black activists have a stronger belief in their own power than do blacks who do not take part in the civil rights movement. Similar results were obtained by Coleman, Campbell, Hobson, McPartland, Mood, Weinfeld, and York (1966) in their study of 645,000 pupils in grades 3, 6, 9, and 12 in 4,000 American public schools. The extent to which pupils felt they had some control over their own destiny showed a stronger relationship to achievement than all of the traditional "school" factors together.

In all of the ethnic studies, groups whose social position is lowly either by class or race tend to score higher in the external control direction. And to judge from the already reported attitudinal and action correlates of the belief in external control, it is easy to see why disadvantage because of class or race tends to perpetuate itself. Supporting the dire implication of the ethnic studies are the findings of Cromwell, Rosenthal, Shakow, and Kahn (1961) to the effect that schizophrenics have a stronger belief in external control than do normals. If, as I have contended earlier, some proportion of people diagnosed schizophrenic are actually suffering from existential sickness, then this result lends some support to the contention that conformity is the premorbid state for this sickness.

The research reviewed thus far has concerned the aspect of conformity emphasizing social reductionism in the definition of life.

Unfortunately, there is a dearth of research concerning biological reductionism. As part of another study, Paul Costa and I collected some information concerning this phenomenon that is presented here merely in the spirit of exploration. We devised a Biological Reductionism Scale (BR Scale) that, after piloting and psychometric analysis, consists of 10 items. As to reliability, the scale has an Alpha of .75. Examples of items are "Man's ability to think makes him different in kind, not just degree, from the other animals" and "Sexuality in man is more an expression of affection than a biological need."

Scores on the BR Scale were obtained from a sample of male and female college students numbering 60. Also obtained on these subjects were scores on measures of imagination, originality, interest in variety, stimulus-seeking, judgment, divergent thinking, and internal versus external locus of control. With the exception of the BR Scale, the other measures are already in the literature. Although this simplified our task at the outset, it complicated the attempt to clarify the meaning of the results, for the measures often turned out on empirical analysis to be something slightly different than expected. In any event, the results do show promise.

We surmised that the BR Scale would correlate positively with the I-E Scale on the grounds that one form of reductionism ought to occur generally with the other. The correlation was not significant, but further analysis of the internal consistency of the I-E Scale showed that on our sample at least there are two distinct components involved. One component contains items concerning the person's beliefs about his ability to influence the events of his personal life (e.g., "People's misfortunes result from the mistakes they make"), whereas the other component deals with the control over more distant social systems or politic events (e.g., "By taking an active part in political and social affairs the people can control world events"). Treating these two components separately led to the uncovering of a correlation of .24 ($p < .03$) between the social system component of the I-E Scale and the BR Scale. This lends support to the contention that someone who sees himself as an embodiment of biological needs will also consider social role playing of importance.

The BR Scale also showed a correlation of -0.26 ($p < .02$)

with a composite measure of imagination composed of the Plot Titles, Symbol Production, and Remote Consequences Tests from the divergent thinking battery (Guilford, 1967) and the Novelty of Productions Score derived from TAT stories (Maddi, Propst, & Feldinger, 1965). Further, there was a correlation of $-.23$ ($p < .04$) between the BR Scale and a composite of the three need-for-variety-measures scored from TAT stories (Maddi et al., 1965). Finally, the BR Scale and a measure of stimulus seeking (Zuckerman, Kolin, Price, & Zoob, 1964) showed a correlation of $-.24$ ($p < .03$). The general implication of these findings is that persons who define themselves as embodiments of biological needs tend not to be imaginative, original, or interested in novelty or stimulus-seeking. This suggests that biological reductionism is properly considered an aspect of conformism.

Also relevant is research on the personalities of creative persons, assuming that creativity is generally accepted as evidence of a fruitful, committed, valuable life. Of the recent creativity studies, that of MacKinnon (1962, 1965) is especially careful and comprehensive. In this study, there were clear personality differences between creative and noncreative architects. One of the most overwhelmingly clear findings of this study is that the creative architects are more transcendent than the control group. The creative architects describe themselves as being rather uninterested in conventional socializing, unconcerned with their acceptance by others, unusual and idiosyncratic in their habits and beliefs, and more concerned with quality than acceptability or output in their work. Although they consider themselves able to be intimate with friends, they care little for social amenities. In addition, they do not seem overly concerned by their self-preoccupation and disdain for the social system. Lest you doubt whether these self-descriptions bear any relationship to the way other people see these creative architects, let me assure you that they do. MacKinnon's staff of psychologists found the creative architects to be, on the basis of personal contact with them over a period of some days, much as they described themselves. The creative architects were less predictable, repetitive, and conforming, though more imaginative, intense, and original, than were the control architects. Corroboration of the transcendent qualities mentioned thus far was also obtained from the life histories of the creative architects. All in all, they were not adapting to social institutions so much as changing them or else functioning outside of them.

The research reviewed here just scratches the surface of what is needed in order to conduct an empirical evaluation of the theorizing I have presented. Of special interest would be study of whether (1) persons who define their lives in humanistic terms really are superior in imagination, symbolization, and judgment, (2) conformists do indeed tend to become existentially ill when they break down, and (3) individualists or conformists tend to have developmental histories appropriate to their states.

Some Contemporary Social Concerns

Thus far, I have concerned myself almost exclusively with phenomena of individual lives or of relations among two or at most a few people. Now I would like to sketch some of the implications of my position to some group and social system phenomena of current note. At the outset, you should recall that the world view of the individualist leads him to consider it best when society and government are truly integrations of the individuals they contain. This means that he expects the social institutions and especially the laws of his society to be strictly representative of the public involved. Hence, forms of government which are not well suited to quick and sensitive response to their publics, such as monarchies, dictatorships, and oligarchies, are not really consistent with the individualist's expectations. For that matter, neither are forms of government of an excessively communistic nature ideal from the individualist's viewpoint, because even though they are beholden to their publics, they tend in their extreme emphasis on common good to stifle individualism. Some form of democratic government comes closest to expressing the individualist's world view.

But the mere existence of a democratic form of government hardly ensures that the individualist will be satisfied, for there may be a wide gap between the idealized form of a government and the way it actually works. When a democratic society becomes very large and industrialized, the public is likely to become passive politically because the level of technical competence needed to make policy decisions is great and the formulation of policy is participated in by so many officials that responsibility for decisions becomes diffuse. And once the public becomes passive, the possibility that officials and governmental institutions will be unrepresentative is high, even though the society is technically democratic.

If such unrepresentativeness occurs, the individualist will use his powers of symbolization, imagination, and judgment to oppose the system in an attempt to produce social change in the direction of greater representativeness. As governments and social institutions are by their nature protective of the status quo, and unrepresentative examples of them are even more so, it would not be especially surprising to see individualists having to mount extraordinary efforts to produce change. Such efforts might well include civil disobedience and confrontation politics. But even in these extreme measures, it will be possible to discern the operation of judgment. In other words, the extremity of the measure will be determined by what is necessary to produce the needed social change, nothing more and nothing less. In contrast, the conformist will either succumb to the unrepresentative government, clinging to the idea of his country right or wrong, or try to act like the individualist in a kind of pseudo-protest. This pseudoprotest will actually be a new conformity, and as such will show stereotypy rather than differentiation, imitation rather than imagination, and naive optimism rather than judgment. With this brief outline, I would like to proceed to an equally brief consideration of black and white protest in this country.

No one who has seriously investigated the matter disputes that our society has denied to blacks the economic and political security and opportunity that would have ensured resources necessary for an adequate life. Our government and institutions have been un-representative of the blacks, and they are certainly justified in protest aimed at changing this debilitating situation. But the paradoxical effect of unrepresentative government is that the longer it exists the more it erodes the basis for protest on the part of those not repre-sented. This is because it is individualists who are capable of mount-ing effective protest, and the security and opportunity that must be minimally present to encourage this kind of personality are scarce among oppressed peoples. Material deprivation has been of such long standing for blacks, and the usual paths of upward mobility have been so effectively blocked, that blacks actually began to believe in the myth of their own inferiority, thereby sinking even further into impotency and despair. There was widespread acquiescence to white oppression, and that is, after all, nothing but conformism.

The hallmark of black conformity is, of course, the Uncle Tom phenomenon. Though this is happily decreasing, feelings of inferiority unfortunately persist in less obvious forms. Even so gifted and articulate a person as James Baldwin had to admit, in *Notes of a Native Son* (1955), that though he hated and feared whites, "This did not mean that I loved black people; on the contrary, I despised them, possibly because they had failed to produce Rembrandt" (p. 35). But to paint like Rembrandt, or want to, is to conform to white standards. A great many modern blacks still carry the seeds of a sense of inferiority. This means that the few blacks who have managed to emerge with something approaching the individualist's personality must lead vigorously and shoulder a massive job of reeducation.

Ideological protest, the stuff of speeches, books, and teaching, is especially useful in reeducation attempts. Such protest seems justified to me, regardless of how inflammatory it may seem, as long as it is geared toward helping the black overcome a sense of inferiority and forcing the white to recognize the content and degree of his oppression of the black. From Frederick Douglass to Eldridge Cleaver to Leroi Jones, there is a direct line of ideological protest which starts by berating the whites for excluding the blacks and ends by insisting that it is the whites who now need the blacks in order to infuse our dying culture with vitality. Also relevant are the campaigns, waged in churches, schools, and meeting halls, to convince blacks that "black is beautiful." This involves concentrating on the possibilities of black physiognomy and mentality rather than adopting white aesthetic standards. In all this, it seems to me that great strides are being made. Indeed, the white is even beginning to adopt black standards rather than the other way around.

Nowhere are the beginnings of self-confidence more apparent than in the black's unwillingness to be integrated. From the black viewpoint, the white interest in integration is no more than a newer, subtler way of staying on top. To assimilate the black into the existing social structure is to make him like a white, and there is little individuality in this, no matter what the increase in standard of living. Blacks want to be separate in order to explore and realize their own special capabilities for living. Once black individuality is secure, it will be time enough to work out some mutually defined basis for integration. Until then, there is little for the white community to fear, and much to respect, in the black's aloofness from a precipitous integration.

Ideological protest is obviously important, but there must also be economic and political protest if much social change is to ensue. I need not chronicle the dramatic impact that Martin Luther King's nonviolent protest had on our social institutions and government. The strikes, marches, demonstrations, boycotts, mass meetings, and acts of civil disobedience had the dual effect of humiliating and frightening enough whites to prepare the way for reforms and inspiring blacks to believe in their own power. Though it is common now to feel disappointment over nonviolent protest, it should not be forgotten that some reforms did take place as a result of it. Blacks did secure more access to sound educations, voting rights, and public utilities. The current demonstrations and strikes at universities and construction sites are a direct continuation of nonviolent protest, and it seems to me that those two social units are making relevant changes. The increasing tendency of blacks to organize politically so that they either vote for black candidates or obtain economic and political benefits for backing white candidates should be seen as a form of political protest. Needless to say, the emergence of black mayors and legislators is indicative that political protest is beginning to have an effect.

I think it worth considering that the violent, militant aspects of black protest actually represent a new form of conformism. After all, to enact violence when you are a small minority which is relatively disorganized and powerless is suicidal, as Mohammed Ali has recently said. A weak minority can only hope to produce social change by increasing the guilt of an indifferent majority and by provoking mild fear over the possibility of violence. Actual violence, however, decreases guilt by arousing moral indignation and engenders a sufficiently intense fear that retaliation is likely. If violence is engaged in by a minority in hopes of producing social change, then there is at least a failure in judgment involved, suggesting that conformism rather than individualism is involved. But another possibility is that the violence does not, strictly speaking, have the intent of social change, expressing instead a profound rejection of the social system bordering on anarchism, which is nihilism potentiated to the social level. You will recall that nihilism was considered a frank form of existential sickness. Consistent with this is the likelihood that black violence is an overcompensatory attempt to get even with the white for years of oppression through one grand and powerful act. In the black violence that has taken place in our cities, the fantasy—and sometimes the actual plan—has been to burn everything down and to kill the oppressing whites. What is actually accomplished, though more modest, is still grand. Soaring fires are set; police and troops are held at bay; fear is instilled in all white hearts; and the radical black emerges unafraid and manly, though outnumbered, outgunned, and doomed. No Uncle Tom he. He may actually lose the battle on the streets, but he wins back his manhood. In that the sense of inferiority is at the heart of overcompensatory behaviors, we see once again the seeds of conformity.

In attempting to understand current white protest, it is useful to recognize that there are different facets of it. There is, for example, sympathy protest, which involves supporting blacks in their drive for freedom from oppression. Protest of this sort puts the enlightened people among the advantaged of a society in the position of attempting to improve conditions for the disadvantaged. It seems to me that an individualist could engage in such protest, in the sense that he requires the social system to be responsive enough to be representative of its entire public, not just some segment of it to which he belongs. But sympathy protest would not be engaged in lightly by an individualist. Actually, social protest generally would not be the preferred activity for an individualist, because it virtually requires subverting personal wishes and goals for the good of the cause. In a way, an individualist would have to function as if he were a conformist in order to join in effective protest. He would surely know he was not a conformist, but acting like one would be painful anyway. Only if he viewed society as seriously unrepresentative would he accept this interference with his individuality. And his commitment to protest would last only as long as it was needed to produce social change. In sympathy protest, this general attitude would be even more salient because the problems of society would not directly effect the protester. It seems to me that any greater commitment to sympathy protest on the part of advantaged whites raises the suspicion either of a subtle conformity, perhaps to peer-group pressures, or of crusadism, as discussed earlier. Blacks seem to have an implicit understanding of this, being mystified as to why whites would want to help them so energetically and altruistically.

A significant proportion of white protest aims at ending the Vietnam war. This war certainly affects whites directly, and it does seem as if a sizable proportion of our public does not believe the war issues form a national threat sufficient to justify carnage in the name of heroic defense. These facts would certainly provide a basis for protest on the part of individualists, to whom it would seem as if the government is recalcitrant to being influenced in less extreme ways.

Sympathy protest and war protest are part and parcel in whites of a more general dissatisfaction with the conditions of life, that is most properly called humanistic protest. White youngsters especially seem no longer willing to live in a society that uses violence and mur-der to get its way and relies on pragmatism and materialism in everyday transactions, all while more lofty ideals are espoused. Clearly, the individualist could participate in such protest, for its stated aims are quite consistent with his world view.

By now, social science research (e.g., Smith, 1968) has shown that the white humanistic protester tends to come from an upper-middle-class background, complete with educated and capable parents who are politically effective and have taught their offspring likewise. These protesters are not rebelling against their parents so much as identifying with them. But it would be a mistake to con-clude that these activistic whites are merely neurotic complainers, unable to accept their favored position in society. More to the point is the recognition that as more and more budding individualists are poured out of their advantaged homes into the broader society, the proportion of the public impatient with and frustrated by social institutions and governmental structures expressing pragmatism and materialism increases as well. That their home experience suited these youngsters for lives of individuality and intimacy rather than pragmatism and materialism is an interesting commentary. Admittedly, pragmatism and materialism are valuable orientations when a society is emerging from a preindustrial into an industrial phase. The persons in such a society need some personality basis for working hard, hoarding resources, being competitive, and avoiding the time-consuming snares of intimacy and self-exploration. But once the society transcends its industrial phase and becomes affluent, pragmatism and materialism are no longer appropriate orientations because there is little more improvement in the quality of life that can be brought about by increases in productivity and money. An affluent society frees its members to improve their lives through indulgence of their own processes of symbolization, imagination, and judgment, leading in the direction of subtlety, taste, intimacy, and love.

In our society, an individualist might well engage in humanistic protest. This does not mean, however, that all participants in such protest are genuinely individualistic. After all, not all parents who can provide economic affluence and social security for their youngsters also stimulate in them the vigorous expressions of symbolization, imagination, and judgment that would make them individualistic. Such psychologically disadvantaged youngsters carry within them the basis of a new conformity. They are caught in a dilemma wherein pragmatism, materialism, and competitiveness are no longer useful as values or action-formats but there is little to replace them. The inability to develop values and action-formats emphasizing exploration of self and others is a function of not having been encouraged toward individualism. Such youngsters are bogged down in symptoms of incipient existential sickness: chronic boredom; skepticism concerning all values and ideas; and a longing to feel some tangible, concrete, immediate sense of meaning in life. It is likely that they will mouth the rhetoric of humanistic protest and simulate its actions because that is better than doing nothing and because of peer-group pressure. They will often suffer from crusadism, displaying an enormous emptiness in their own lives and commitments, however strident their protestations.

I would like to conclude this consideration of social phenomena with a word about the Hippie life. Once again, there are aspects here of both individuality and conformism, and it is important to discriminate between them. In essence, the Hippie phenomenon attempts to replace ambition, competitiveness, pragmatism, and materialism with communal, cooperative ways of life in which a person is valued for "doing his own thing." These emphases on intimacy and love based on appreciation of the differences among people are very close to what I have been calling individualism. It seems to me that the Hippie phenomenon is a kind of societally generated experiment in individualistic, humanistic living that well attests to the degree to which our society has entered a postindustrial, affluent phase.

But the Hippie movement has not been entirely successful. One of the difficulties is that many new conformists are attracted to it. These persons are excessively burdened by vulnerability to boredom, antiintellectualism, and a longing for simple, dictated meaning. One destructive outcome is to precipitate, in some instances, an interest in cultish, authoritarian, mystical religions. In other cases, a destructive outcome has been drug abuse.

In subscribing to authoritarian religions and leaders, youngsters are reverting to a meaning orientation in which what is important is determined externally. This is clearly a form of conformity. In using drugs, one can arrive at a stimulating, committed, uncompetitive life the easy way. But a drug culture is a pseudohumanistic one, because the expressions of social intimacy and individual exploration are artificially produced and excessively passive. The individualist actively and artfully uses his wits in the process of exploring himself and others, and in shedding the competitiveness and isolation of a former orientation. One exercises no latent capabilities and changes little when instant intimacy and individuality are obtained through biochemical alterations, however satisfying they may be in the short run. Apparently there are many members of the early drug movement in this country, including Richard Alpert, who now agree with this position.

Concluding Remarks

I have tried to cover too much ground for there to be any neat way to summarize and conclude. Indeed, I am painfully aware of the brevity and generality with which I have treated some of the topics in this paper. My main aim, however, has been to present an overview of my position, some sense of what its essential features are, and the range of phenomena to which it is relevant. Considering topics in greater depth and tying together loose ends will have to wait until subsequent occasions, I am afraid.

Basically, I have considered the inherent tendency in man to search for meaning through exercising symbolization, imagination, and judgment. Although all men possess this motivational tendency, the events of development determine which of two broad meaning-orientations or personality types will actually occur. Although the types have been presented as mutually exclusive, it is probable that actual persons possess qualities of both in varying degrees. In individuality, the person supplies his own meaning, being self-reliant and changing throughout his life, sometimes burdened by doubt, but generally feeling powerful and in control of his fate. Individuality is construed as the ideal state of personality. In conformity, the person accepts the meaning imposed upon him by a society and a body that he has come to believe are absolutes which require that he serve them without any possibility of choice. Such a person is vulnerable to stresses which can disconfirm this meaning-orientation. If the stresses occur, he may well be precipitated in existential sickness, whether in the form of crusadism, nihilism, or vegetativeness. These states all share an underlying sense of meaninglessness, apathy, and aimlessness, though their expressions may differ. I have also suggested some social and individual phenomena to which my position is relevant. In addition, I have pointed to some relevant research. But it is clear that much painstaking empirical endeavor is necessary in order to determine the adequacy of what has been said.

I have engaged in a very macroscopic, broad kind of theorizing. As an approach it has not been popular in psychology of late. But I have always felt that such theorizing really should be done by at least some psychologists, though I admit to a little surprise and amusement at finding myself doing it. Hopefully, once the broad outlines of the positions are clear, it will be possible to concentrate on particular parts in greater depth, thereby rendering the whole more convincing and useful.

REFERENCES

Arendt, H. *Eichman in Jerusalem: A report on the banality of evil.* New York: Viking Press, 1964.

Baldwin, J. *Notes of a native son*. Boston: Beacon Press, 1955.

Battle, E., & Rotter, J. B. Children's feelings of personal control as related to social class and ethnic group. *Journal of Personality*, 1963, **31**, 482–490.

Camus, A. *The myth of Sisyphus and other essays*. (Trans. by J. O'Brien.) New York: Knopf, 1955.

Coleman, J. S., Campbell, E. Q., Hobson, C. J., McPartland, J., Mood, A. M., Weinfeld, F. D., & York, R. L. *Equality of educational opportunity*. Washington, D.C.: U.S. Office of Education, 1966.

Conn, L. K., & Crowne, D. P. Instigation to aggression, emotional arousal and defensive emulation. *Journal of Personality*, 1964, **32**, 163–179.

Cromwell, R., Rosenthal, D., Shakow, D., & Khan, T. Reaction time, locus of control, choice behavior and descriptions of parental behavior in schizophrenic and normal subjects. *Journal of Personality*, 1961, **29**, 363–380.

Crowne, D. P., & Liverant, S. Conformity under varying conditions of personal commitment. *Journal of Abnormal and Social Psychology*, 1963, **66**, 547–555.

Crowne, D. P., & Marlowe, D. A new scale of social desirability independent of psychopathology. *Journal of Consulting Psychology*, 1960, **24**, 349–354.

Crowne, D. P., & Marlowe, D. *The approval motive: Studies in evaluative dependence*. New York: Wiley, 1964.

Dement, W. The effect of dream deprivation. *Science*, 1960, **131**, 1705–1707.

Durkheim, E. *Suicide*. Glencoe, Ill.: Free Press, 1951.

Emerson, R. W. Selected Writings of . . . . B. Atkinson (Ed.). New York: Modern Library, 1940.

Fishman, C. G. Need for approval and the expression of aggression under varying conditions of frustration. *Journal of Personality and Social Psychology*, 1965, **2**, 809–816.

Fiske, D. W. Effects of monotonous and restricted stimulation. In D. W. Fiske & S. R. Maddi (Eds.), *Functions of varied experience*. Homewood, Ill.: Dorsey Press, 1961.

Frankl, V. *The doctor and the soul*. (Trans. by R. Winston & C. Winston.) New York: Knopf, 1955.

Gore, P. M., & Rotter, J. B. A personality correlate of social action. *Journal of Personality*, 1963, **31**, 58–64.

Graves, T. D. Time perspective and the deferred gratification pattern in a tri-ethnic community. Tri-Ethnic Research Project, Research Report No. 5. Boulder: University of Colorado Institute of Behavioral Science, 1961.

Guilford, J. P. *The nature of human intelligence*. New York: McGraw-Hill, 1967.

Harlow, H. F. Mice, monkeys, men and motives. *Psychological Review*, 1953, **60**, 23–32.

Harlow, H. F. The heterosexual affectional system in monkeys. *American Psychologist*, 1962, **17**, 1–9.

Hollander, E. P., & Willis, R. H. Some current issues in the psychology of conformity and nonconformity. *Psychological Bulletin*, 1967, **68**, 62–76.

James, W. Internal versus external control of reinforcement as a basic variable in learning theory. Unpublished doctoral dissertation, Ohio State University, 1957.

Katkin, E. S. The Marlowe-Crowne social desirability scale: Independent of psychopathology? *Psychological Reports*, 1964, **15**, 703–706.

Kubie, L. The concept of dream deprivation: A critical analysis. *Psychosomatic Medicine*, 1962, **24**, 62–65.

Lefcourt, H. M., & Ladwig, G. W. The effect of reference group upon Negroes' task performance in a biracial competitive game. *Journal of Personality and Social Psychology*, 1965, **1**, 668–671.

Lefcourt, H. M., & Ladwig, G. W. Alienation in Negro and white reformatory inmates. *Journal of Social Psychology*, 1966, **68**, 153–157.

Lichtman, C. M., & Julian, J. W. Internal vs. external control of reinforcement as a determinant of preferred strategy on a behavioral task. Paper read at Midwestern Psychological Association, St. Louis, 1964.

MacKinnon, D. W. The nature and nurture of creative talent. *American Psychologist*, 1962, **17**, 484–495.

MacKinnon, D. W. Personality and the realization of creative potential. *American Psychologist*, 1965, **20**, 273–281.

Maddi, S. R. Motivational aspects of creativity. *Journal of Personality*, 1965, **33**, 330–347.

Maddi, S. R. The existential neurosis. *Journal of Abnormal Psychology*, 1967, **72**, 311–325.

Maddi, S. R. *Personality theories: A comparative analysis.* Homewood, Ill.: Dorsey Press, 1968.

Maddi, S. R., Propst, B. S., & Feldinger, I. Three expressions of the need for variety. *Journal of Personality*, 1965, **33**, 82–98.

May, R., Angel, E., & Ellenberger, H. F. (Eds.) *Existence.* New York: Basic Books, 1958.

Odell, M. Personality correlates of independence and conformity. Unpublished master's thesis, Ohio State University, 1959.

Osgood, C. Studies on the generality of affective meaning systems. *American Psychologist*, 1962, **17**, 10–28.

Phares, E. J. Expectancy changes in skill and chance situations. *Journal of Abnormal and Social Psychology*, 1957, **54**, 339–342.

Pico della Mirandola. *Oration on the dignity of man.* (Trans. by A. R. Caponigri.) Chicago: Gateway Press, 1956.

Ribble, M. Disorganizing factors in infant personality. *American Journal of Psychiatry*, 1941, **98**, 459–463.

Rogers, C. R. A theory of therapy, personality, and interpersonal relationships, as developed in the client-centered framework. In S. Koch (Ed.), *Psychology: A study of a science.* Vol. 3. New York: McGraw-Hill, 1959.

Rogers, C. R. *On becoming a person.* Boston: Houghton-Mifflin, 1961.

Rotter, J. B. *Social learning and clinical psychology.* Englewood Cliffs, N.J.: Prentice-Hall, 1954.

Rotter, J. B., Seeman, M., & Liverant, S. Internal versus external control of reinforcements: A major variable in behavior theory. In N. F. Washburne (Ed.), *Decisions, values, and groups.* Vol. 2. London: Pergamon Press, 1962.

186   *Nebraska Symposium on Motivation, 1970*

Sartre, J. P. *Being and nothingness.* (Trans. by H. Barnes.) New York: Philosophical Library, 1956.

Seeman, M. Alienation and social learning in a reformatory. *American Journal of Sociology,* 1963, **69,** 270–284.

Smith, M. B. *Social psychology and human values.* Chicago: Aldine Press, 1968.

Spitz, R. A. Hospitalism. In *The psychoanalytic study of the child.* Vol. 1. New York: International Universities Press, 1945.

Spitz, R. A. Hospitalism: A follow-up report. In *The psychoanalytic study of the child.* Vol. 2. New York: International Universities Press, 1946.

Stengel, K. *Suicide and attempted suicide.* Baltimore: Penguin Books, 1965.

Strickland, B. R. Need approach and motor steadiness under positive and negative approval conditions. *Perceptual and Motor Skills,* 1965, **29,** 667–668.

Strickland, B. R., & Jenkins, O. Simple motor performance under positive and negative approval motivation. *Perceptual and Motor Skills,* 1965, **19,** 599–605.

Strickland, B. R., & Rodwan, A. S. The relationship of certain personality variables to decision making in perception. Paper read at Midwestern Psychological Association, Chicago, 1963.

Willington, A. M., & Strickland, B. R. Need for approval and simple motor performance. *Perceptual and Motor Skills,* 1965, 1965, **21,** 879–884.

Zubek, J. P. *Sensory deprivation: Fifteen years of research.* New York: Appleton-Century-Crofts, 1969.

Zuckerman, M., Kolin, E. A., Price, L., & Zoob, I. Development of a sensation-seeking scale. *Journal of Consulting Psychology,* 1964, **28,** 477–482.

Hypnosis, Motivation, and the Ecological Validity of the Psychological Experiment[1]

MARTIN T. ORNE[2]

Institute of the Pennsylvania Hospital and University of Pennsylvania

INTRODUCTION

It is the hope of understanding the sources of human behavior that has always been the basis of psychology. Regardless of whether attention momentarily turned to other species, to simpler mechanisms, or to apparently remote mathematical concerns, the ultimate object of interest has always been man. The very scientists who objectified psychology and examined simple processes of behavior in animals revealed an intense and abiding concern for improving the human condition. Pavlov, for example, devoted many years to the study of psychiatric treatment techniques; Watson invented the first behavior therapy for phobias; Hull helped found the Department of Behavioral Science at Yale which merged anthropology, psychiatry, and psychology; and Skinner wrote *Walden II*.

1. The research from our laboratory which is reported on in this paper was supported in part by Contract #DA–49–193–MD–2647 from the U.S. Army Medical Research and Development Command, Grant #AF–AFOSR–707–67 from the Air Force Office of Scientific Research, Contract #Nonr 4731(00) from the Office of Naval Research, and by a grant from the Institute for Experimental Psychiatry.

2. I would like to express appreciation to my colleagues, Harvey D. Cohen, Kenneth R. Graham, and David A. Paskewitz, for helpful comments in the preparation of this paper. I am particularly grateful to A. Gordon Hammer, Frederick J. Evans, Emily C. Orne, and David Rosenhan for their detailed criticisms and many incisive suggestions. Appreciation is also due Karen Ostergren for her editorial comments.

Some kinds of research can be carried out only with animals, but other questions which address themselves to human experience and complex human behavior can be asked only by studying human subjects. Not surprisingly, then, psychology's focus of interest has inevitably returned to man. In this discussion we will not be dealing with animal research. This paper will concern itself solely with experimental studies of human behavior and experience. Experimental studies of human behavior typically have considerable face validity. Generalizations from laboratory findings appear to have intuitive merit so that both the investigator and his scientific public are inclined to make the inferential leap to domains of behavior and experience beyond the laboratory. Such a leap is a complicated one, often not warranted on the basis of current evidence.

Consider the physical sciences. Assuming that conditions are kept constant, phenomena observed in the laboratory will tend to obtain outside the laboratory environs, but even here, under some circumstances, as Heisenberg has pointed out in atomic physics, the procedures involved in observing an event may so distort it as to make prediction impossible. This type of difficulty is a far more serious issue in psychology. Human behavior and experience may be distressingly modified when subjects are aware that they are being studied. The subject's participation in the psychological experiment may have significant motivational and perceptual consequences that can alter his behavior sufficiently to make inference to other contexts hazardous and, under some circumstances, misleading.

In most instances the purpose of carrying out an experimental study is the hope of answering significant questions about enduring human attributes, motivations, and behaviors. However, the psychological experiment is, by its very nature, what Garfinkel (1967) has called episodic. This means that it is regarded by everyone concerned as isolated from the rest of an individual's experience. It is implicitly understood that at the conclusion of the experiment the episode will be concluded and the individual will be basically unchanged. Fears expressed, actions undertaken, emotions felt in the context of an experiment are experienced as specific to that situation and intended not to carry over beyond it. In this regard it is analogous to other episodic events such as playing a game or having a good cry in response to a sad movie. Yet we hope to use observations obtained in episodic situations to draw meaningful inferences about enduring motivations of individuals as they manifest themselves in nonepisodic contexts.

It is possible that some mental processes are more validly scrutinized in the laboratory than others. Sleep, for example, though perhaps modified somewhat by the situation, will, on the whole, be the same process within the laboratory as outside of it; but the tendency to rouse in response to stimuli is likely to be affected, and the content of dream reports even more so.

Hypnosis, with its potential for bringing about a meaningful dyadic relationship in a remarkably short time and permitting apparently profound modifications of a subject's experience, would appear particularly amenable to laboratory research. Here, hopefully, is a sufficiently robust phenomenon such that its effects ought to swamp any differences the experimental situation may introduce. Yet our experiences in studying hypnotic phenomena have served to focus attention on the peculiar nature of the psychological experiment. I do not think it is a mere coincidence that observations on the nature of the psychological experiment grew out of studies of hypnosis. Hypnosis is a caricature of a meaningful dyadic relationship and, as such, emphasizes and throws into relief components that, while present in a wide range of other situations, would not as easily be recognized elsewhere.

In this paper I intend to discuss some of our attempts to understand hypnosis and the implications of our studies for the understanding of the special nature of the experimental situation. I will, then, outline a number of procedures I have called quasi controls that are designed to help the investigator evaluate the potential impact of the experimental situation itself on the data that are obtained. I will also briefly illustrate the use of these methods in other areas of research. Moreover, I will try to discuss the particular problems and limitations of quasi controls and the difference between these and conventional controls.

Once the implications of the subject's recognition that he is the object of study are recognized, it becomes tempting to explain away rather than to try to understand broad areas of research findings. It seems appropriate that hypnosis, which first uniquely demonstrated these problems, should also provide an unusually compelling example of the limitations of the explanatory power of these ideas. For these reasons I have reviewed the evidence for and against the view that much of hypnosis can be understood by an exclusively motivational analysis. Thus, it has been widely accepted that the hypnotized subject has an increased motivation to please the hypnotist, a view that I myself formerly strongly supported (Orne, 1959b). This concept makes such sufficient intuitive sense that it had not been previously challenged, nor had it been tested empirically. When subjected to scrutiny, however, it becomes clear that it cannot account for the behavior of hypnotized individuals. Finally, I hope to outline constructive implications for psychological research that may be drawn from this work and the directions to which they point in future studies of human behavior and experience.

The Nature of Hypnosis

Hypnosis is unquestionably a fascinating phenomenon, yet sooner or later most investigators become troubled by aspects of it that are not immediately apparent. With considerable distress they learn that their first-hand observations of hypnotic behavior seem not to be consistent with descriptions in the literature. Even more troubling, the more one reads the literature, the more confused the published picture becomes. It soon becomes evident that when the material is reviewed historically, very different behaviors have characterized hypnosis at different times.

Mesmer, for example, is considered the "father of modern hypnosis" (Binet & Féré, 1888; Boring, 1950), yet the behavior that occurred during his treatments does not at all resemble what is seen today. In his clinic, individuals would sit around an oaken tub filled with magnets, holding on to metal rods (to conduct the magnetic fluid). The surroundings were impressively carpeted and draped, music was played in the background, incense burned—all designed to heighten expectation. Eventually, Mesmer, in magician's robes, would come down and, without uttering a word, lay his hands on one patient and then another. Patients would, one by one, appear to have a seizure, a hysteric fit, from which they went to sleep, only to awaken minutes or hours later without symptoms.

We do not see hysteric seizures followed by sleep as part of hypnosis today. Nor is hypnosis pursued nonverbally today. Rather today we speak to our patients and they respond peacefully, as it were, and without hysterics. Similar discordances between descriptions of behavior generally recognized to be hypnosis today and those of an earlier period can be found in the work of Coué (1922), not to mention Charcot (1886), who, for instance, indicates that if the top of the subject's head is rubbed he will pass from the stage of sleep to the stage of somnambulism.

It seemed to me important to determine how a phenomenon which everyone agrees is the same may be characterized by such variant behaviors. On the basis of White's (1941) theoretical framework, an experiment was developed to test the hypothesis that subjects in hypnosis behave in whatever manner they believe characteristic of hypnotized individuals (Orne, 1959b). For this purpose it was desirable to find an item of behavior that had not previously been associated with hypnosis and yet might seem plausible to the average college undergraduate. Such an item, by the way, was difficult to come by in view of the broad range of behaviors that, at one time or another, have been attributed to hypnosis. After some search, however, I came up with catalepsy of the dominant hand.[3] While catalepsy itself is believed by some authorities to be an invariant accompaniment of hypnosis, when it occurs it always occurs in the entire body—both hands, both feet, even the trunk. It had never been reported to occur in one hand while the other remained flaccid. Nevertheless, catalepsy of the dominant hand might sound plausibly scientific to an undergraduate psychology student, vaguely reminding him of learning about crossed hemispheres, stuttering, etc.

Two matched sections of a large college class were given a lecture on the nature of hypnosis which included a demonstration. Three "volunteers" were selected from the class and hypnotized. (Unbeknownst to the group, these individuals had been previously hypnotized and given a posthypnotic suggestion that the next time they entered hypnosis they would manifest catalepsy of the dominant hand.) Hypnosis was induced with the volunteers, and the

3. Catalepsy is the phenomenon usually associated with catatonia—a waxen flexibility where any limb will remain in the position in which it is placed.

classic hypnotic phenomena were then demonstrated. Casually catalepsy was tested and, in passing, it was mentioned that catalepsy of the dominant hand was a typical hypnotic behavior. Two of the subjects happened to be right-handed and one left-handed, illustrating the point. In all other respects the lecture was accurate and the subjects were actually deeply hypnotized. The parallel class received the identical lecture and demonstration with the same three subjects. The only difference was that catalepsy was not tested and not commented upon.

Approximately one month later subjects from both classes were invited to come to the laboratory to participate in an experiment. When they were hypnotized we observed a new characteristic of the hypnotic trance—catalepsy of the dominant hand—associated exclusively, of course, with attending the appropriate lecture!

This experiment, trivial from one point of view, has, nevertheless, broad implications. It would appear that in hypnosis we are dealing with a chameleon. In other words, the subject's hypnotic behavior is influenced by whatever behaviors he believes to be characteristic of being hypnotized.

Today there seems to be considerable consistency in hypnotic behavior. I once asked a large number of individuals at random to describe hypnosis, and found that, despite initial disclaimers to the contrary, they invariably were able to describe the behaviors displayed by hypnotized people. The general views about the phenomenon can apparently be traced back to the descriptions given by Thomas Mann (1931) in *Mario and the Magician* and by George Du Maurier (1895) in *Trilby*. Although, of course, not everyone has read these two particular works, an incredibly large number of fictionalized accounts take their inspiration from them. We have been unable to find adults in our culture who do not have at least a rudimentary acquaintance with the kind of behavior which characterizes hypnosis.

The subject's prior knowledge about hypnosis is, of course, only one part of his knowledge of what constitutes appropriate behavior. Cues from the hypnotist, on an ongoing basis, also serve to define how a subject should behave. For this reason it is almost impossible to determine what precisely constitute the core phenomena of hypnosis. Working with children did not avoid the problem.

since even some six-year-olds appeared to have a reasonably accurate concept of what constitutes hypnotic behavior.

It seemed another way around this problem would be to ask anthropologists to work with a native population. One might reasonably assume that African Bushmen would not have read the slick magazines or been influenced by movies or television. These individuals would be truly naive. It sounded encouraging when a former student described hypnotized Bushmen as behaving very similarly to college undergraduates he had seen in hypnosis. The encouragement was short-lived, however, when it became clear what had occurred. The hypnotist, working through an interpreter, had proceeded to induce hypnosis. How was he to know, however, whether an individual was hypnotized? In order to recognize the state and report on it in some detail, he had very carefully, but without awareness, shaped the behavior until it resembled that with which he was familiar. This behavior pattern rapidly then became stable and reliably associated with hypnosis. In other words, while natives had not heard of hypnosis, the hypnotist had, and he then induced the kind of behavior with which he was familiar. Of course these observations can tell little about what the intrinsic behavioral characteristics of hypnosis are.

It should be noted that the hypnotist was proceeding in a rigorously empirical fashion to study hypnosis by hypnotizing naive subjects and observing their responses. He was able to note the differences in their behavior in hypnosis and outside of hypnosis. Unfortunately, the observed behavior was a function more of his preconceptions than of hypnosis. For example, had the hypnotist believed that catalepsy was an invariant accompaniment of hypnosis (a view, in fact, currently held by several outstanding clinicians), he would have been able to report that, in his experience, this is true not only with American subjects but even with naive natives. Thus we seem to be dealing with a phenomenon whose behavioral manifestations include whatever the hypnotist or the subject believes them to be. Two hypnotists with differing views can go out into the real world and validate their views by careful experiments without necessarily being aware that the behavior of their subjects mirrors their own preconceptions. It is not surprising, then, that the literature of this field has been characterized by an inability to replicate and acrimonious disputes about the inaccuracies of other people's research.

Demand Characteristics in Hypnotic Research

When I became aware of the extent to which subjects' expectations and subtle cues from the hypnotist may affect the behavior of the hypnotized individual, there seemed to be no reason to assume that this would hold only for the general behavior which characterizes hypnosis; it should also affect those specific behaviors that are considered data in an experimental context using hypnosis. Subjects should respond not only to specific verbal suggestions but also to the context in which these suggestions are made. The behavior that is expected and desired of them in an experiment would, of course, be communicated only partially by the specific suggestions; it would also be communicated by subtle cues which the subject might have gathered about the experiment beforehand, cues given by the experimenter in the course of the study, and, perhaps most importantly, by the experimental procedure itself. The sum total of these cues which would communicate the purpose of the research, the hypothesis that the investigator hoped to demonstrate, the kind of behavior he expected to find, I termed the demand characteristics of the experimental situation.

I was first impressed with the effect of such variables while carrying out pilot work to elucidate the nature of hypnotic age regression. Controversy has long existed about the extent to which hypermnesia can reliably be induced by age regression. In previous work I had observed that in addition to increased memory one also finds increased confabulation (Orne, 1951). This observation had earlier been made by Stalnaker and Riddle (1932). It seemed reasonable to use the well-known Carmichael, Hogan, and Walter (1932) effect in serial recall as a means of studying this process. In their classic study it had been shown that labeling ambiguous figures would, with serial recall, yield a progressive change in reproductions in accordance with the labels. Thus the subject would be shown the original labeled ambiguous figures and then asked to draw six serial reproductions of these figures; he would then be age-regressed back to the time when he observed the original picture, and told to copy his hallucination. This should establish a clear mnemonic drift in the direction of the label and away from the original figure. It would then be possible to discover whether age regression led to increased accuracy of recall or, instead, to increased confabulation.

The seven drawings could be randomized and then given to "blind" judges with the instruction to order them in the sequence in which they were made. Accuracy of recall would cause judges to place the seventh picture (the copy of the hallucination) early in the series, whereas an absence of increased memory or an increase in confabulation would leave the picture in seventh place, perhaps even cause judges to ask if some drawings were missing.

One subject showed the Carmichael, Hogan, and Walter effect to a striking degree. Thus when he reproduced an ambiguous picture that had been labeled "canoe," he was not satisfied to add pointed canoelike tips, but by the second time had added a paddle, and by the third and fourth drawings he had managed to fill in someone sitting and paddling, with his girl friend sitting in the bow, eventually adding a guitar, picnic basket, and other things which seemed to belong to the scene. Somehow the effect was working too well, and on a hunch the subject was told, "That's fine but now I want you to draw the design as you originally saw it." Very agreeably he accurately reproduced the original picture. When asked why he had elaborated the drawings so dramatically he explained that if the label said canoe, this would clearly be what was wanted, and if he was asked to reproduce it several times at half-hour intervals, naturally he would be expected to improve the resemblance to a canoe. Why else would he be asked to do this?

The subject's observation was extremely instructive. Incidentally, I have been unable to replicate the Carmichael, Hogan, Walter study despite several efforts to do so, and wonder about the extent to which similar factors may have determined the original results.

Subsequently, becoming more interested in this kind of effect, I replicated the Ashley, Harper, and Runyon (1951) study which had been planned to reconcile a controversy about the effect of economic status in children on perceiving coin size. At the time there was considerable controversy about the Bruner-Goodman effect (1947), which was that poor children perceive coins as larger than do rich children. This effect, while repeatedly replicated in some laboratories, could not be found by others. Ashley, Harper, and Runyon had argued that the difficulty in showing a clear effect was the interindividual variability and what ideally would be desirable were perfectly matched subjects who differed only in the extent to which they perceived themselves to be rich or poor. Further, they argued, this could readily be obtained by hypnosis. Thus, the same subject could be tested in his normal state and in hypnotically induced rich and poor states. One would thereby have perfectly matched "groups" of subjects, differing only in the extent to which they believed themselves to be rich or poor. Using this technique, Ashley, Harper, and Runyon obtained data clearly supporting the Bruner-Goodman hypothesis.

A pilot study for the replication was carried out with a few subjects (Orne, 1959b) and it was clear that Ashley, Harper, and Runyon described a powerful effect indeed. In brief, the experimental procedure was to hypnotize the subject and obtain his coin size estimates, then to induce amnesia for the individual's past life and to provide him with a different life history. With the "poor" suggestion he was told that he came from a large family, that life had been hard on him, that while he managed to get by, there was never quite enough to eat, and that he had had to work extremely hard from an early age contributing to the family; it was possible for him to go on in school only by obtaining complete scholarships, and even then he worked extra to try to send whatever money he could home, and so on. When these suggestions were given, the subject's whole behavior changed. He became extremely intense in his efforts, seeming to care a great deal about the procedure, and when asked to make estimates by matching the size of a light spot of variable diameter to that of particular coins he would grossly overestimate. Again amnesia was induced for this experience and a new life history was provided, indicating that the student had come from a very wealthy family, that he could remember in his childhood how the chauffeur would take him to school in the Rolls, that he had lived in a big house, that his friends had envied him, that he had gone to the best schools and belonged to the best clubs, that he was somewhat annoyed because his monthly allowance had been cut to $2,000, which was barely enough to squeeze by on, and so forth. With these instructions the subject behaved very differently, slouching and leaning back in the chair, showing a certain amount of contempt for the situation, apparently not caring about what he was doing, while judging the size of the coins considerably more accurately, with perhaps a slight tendency to underestimate.

There was one additional procedure which had been carried out by Ashley, Harper, and Runyon, which was to give each subject a metal slug four times with statements that it was made of lead, silver, gold, and platinum, respectively, and then to ask for size estimates for those identically sized disks. Again a lawful change in estimates of the disk size was shown, particularly under the poor condition, depending upon the value of the presumed composition of the disc.

When subjects were awakened and memory was induced for the experience, they were asked what the experiment was about. Typically they said they didn't know, weren't sure, and so forth. When pressed, without having been given cues as to what was expected, they suddenly began to explain that they supposed that I expected money to mean more to them if they were poor than when they were rich and that, therefore, it ought to seem bigger in the poor condition, whereas a rich boy would most likely see it as smaller.

It should be emphasized that nothing which had been said, as such, would have communicated why the experiment was being done. The suggestion per se would not have helped. However, the procedure itself was a dead giveaway. From the point of view of the subjects, they were being asked to make coin size estimates three times, the only difference being suggestions concerning the extent to which they saw themselves as rich or poor. If this was not sufficient to get the idea across, there was the matter of being given identically sized disks and asked to make coin size estimates, after being informed that the disks were composed of different metals. Certainly if the experimenter went to the trouble of telling them what these disks were made of, he anticipated differences in their responses, and the only parameter that was available for such differences to occur was that of perceived size. Therefore, it was the procedure rather than anything which the subjects were told that communicated the experimenter's expectations.

One subject, however, had a different idea. He came to an alternative, plausible hypothesis, which was that the poor students would work harder and be more accurate in their estimates, whereas rich students would not care and their estimates would therefore go all over the lot. When the data were subsequently examined, it turned out that the subjects who formulated the Bruner-Goodman hypothesis yielded data which fully supported this hypothesis. The only aberrant subject was the one with the different hypothesis, and in his case the estimates made while poor were more accurate and showed less variability than those he made while rich. These data indicated that it would be vital to take into account the subject's perception of what was expected—what I called the demand characteristics of the experiment—in order to understand his behavior.

In a more systematic way another group of subjects was run in the Ashley, Harper, and Runyon design and careful post-inquiries were carried out. These inquiries were judged by independent judges, and a high degree of association could again be demonstrated between the perceived hypothesis of the experiment and the subject's performance.

It should be emphasized that the effect which demand characteristics have on behavior in such a situation ought not to be conceptualized as voluntary compliance with what the subject believes is expected of him. While this may in some instances occur, the more typical situation is one in which the individual's experience is changed by the situation. Thus Mesmer's patients did not voluntarily choose to behave as if they had a hysteric seizure; rather such a seizure resulted from the pressures of the total situation. If an appropriate interview could have been carried out with Mesmer's patients, it is likely one would have elicited the information that a seizure of this kind characteristically "happens" in the course of treatment.

Unfortunately, it was not possible with a procedure of this kind to determine whether subjects were actually responding to the demand characteristics of the situation or whether they were responding in line with the original hypothesis and subsequently, by reflecting upon their responses, deducing what had been expected. Accordingly, I wanted to devise a technique to explore what subjects might be perceiving in the situation without, however, first giving them the opportunity of responding in hypnosis. It could not then be argued that the subject's response was predicated on the subjective experience of being poor or rich.

It was crucial in running a comparison group of this kind that it be exposed to the identical set of cues provided for the hypnotic group, since I had observed that hypnotists characteristically treated hypnotized subjects differently from waking individuals. One way to try to solve this problem was to ask subjects to simulate. But the literature was very explicit in indicating that subjects are unable to simulate successfully, and when I first applied the procedure it became clear that this was true. Thus, when I asked a subject to simulate hypnosis he would begin somewhat reluctantly and, after a few minutes, look at me somewhat sheepishly, smile, and ask, "Am I doing all right?" He might then proceed to simulate a few more moments, only to interrupt again or in some other way clearly indicate his ambiguous status. It would have been obvious to any discerning layman that these subjects were not hypnotized.

On reflection, however, it became clear why this was the case. Subjects knew that I knew they were simulating. They were being asked to carry out an essentially impossible task, namely, to simulate hypnosis knowing full well that I was aware of their actual status. There was no way in which they could "win."

A relatively minor variation of this procedure altered the situation in significant ways. In it, one of my associates instructed the subject, who had repeatedly been unable to enter hypnosis despite wishing to do so, as follows: "Your task today will be somewhat different. You are going to try to fool Dr. Orne and make him think you are actually going into deep hypnosis. He knows that he will be working with highly hypnotizable individuals who are able to enter deep trance but that some subjects will try to simulate. He will not know which is which, however. I can't tell you how to do this task. Do the best you can based on whatever knowledge you have of hypnosis. However, if Dr. Orne catches on to the fact that you are simulating he will stop the experiment immediately. So don't think you have given yourself away, for as long as he continues with the experiment, you will have been successful in fooling him. This is a difficult task but we have found some intelligent subjects are able to do it successfully. Good luck!" Given this simple instruction, untrained, unhypnotizable individuals proved capable of behaving in ways which were exceedingly difficult to distinguish from the behavior of deeply hypnotized subjects. Without special test procedures experienced hypnotists were unable to discriminate these individuals at better than chance levels.[4]

The simulating subjects provided a way of evaluating in behavioral terms the kind of demand characteristics implicit in the experimental situation. We now had a group of subjects who were maximally responsive to the demand characteristics. When the Ashley, Harper, Runyon experiment was repeated with highly hypnotizable and simulating subjects run blind, we observed identical results in both groups.

It should be emphasized that the failure to find differences between subjects in the Ashley, Harper, Runyon design who are deeply hypnotized and those who are simulating tells us absolutely nothing about the Bruner-Goodman effect. It merely indicates that a highly plausible alternative hypothesis exists to explain the Ashley, Harper, Runyon finding: namely, that the response is a

4. In a number of studies testing the behavior of subjects in response to painful stimuli (Shor, 1962), to suggested emotions (Damaser, Shor, & Orne, 1963), to memory and retroactive inhibition (Fisher, 1960), to age regression (O'Connell, Shor, & Orne, in press), to suggested self-destructive or antisocial behavior (Orne, & Evans, 1965), and to a wide range of other situations, we were unable to demonstrate any differences between hypnotized and simulating subjects. Because of the remarkable ability of simulating subjects to mimic the behavior of hypnotized individuals, some colleagues argued that no real differences existed. We have never accepted this view. Not only does the simulating subject disclaim feeling any of the subjective events that his behavior would normally reflect, but he is able to describe in detail why and how he decided to behave as he did. Hypnotized individuals, on the other hand, insist on the subjective reality of what has happened. When a hallucination is suggested, as of a picture of the hypnotist on the wall, subjects, hypnotized or simulating, will point to where the picture is "seen." When later asked why they decided it was there rather than somewhere else, simulators readily explain their reasons, whereas the previously hypnotized subject has difficulty comprehending the question. He will merely assert that that is where it was. Typically it is not possible for him to go beyond this assertion regardless of the circumstances under which he is asked—by the hypnotist, by another investigator, a research assistant, or a friend. Other phenomena, such as those I have termed trance logic (Orne, 1959b), can often be demonstrated with hypnotized individuals but not with simulators. It certainly ought not to surprise us that, given radically different instructional sets, different processes will be active within the two groups of subjects despite the remarkable ability of one group to mimic the behavior of the other. More recently, we have been able to devise experimental situations where these differences are demonstrated behaviorally. Some of them will be discussed later.

function of the demand characteristics of the situation rather than the direct effect of the hypnotic suggestion to be "poor" or "rich."

Compliance as an Inadequate Explanatory Mechanism

With the recognition that many findings about hypnosis can be explained by the subject's response to the demand characteristics of the situation, it is inevitable that attempts should be made to explain the entirety of the phenomenon on the basis of such mechanisms. In an early attempt to conceptualize hypnosis (Orne, 1959b) I built upon the formulations of Hull (1933), White (1941), and Sarbin (1950) and proposed that hypnosis is characterized by (1) a desire on the part of the subject to play the role of the hypnotized subject, (2) an increase in suggestibility which was translated as an increase in motivation to conform to the wishes of the hypnotist, and (3) a less well defined aspect which I regarded as the essence of hypnosis, in the context of which increased motivation to please and a tendency to play the role of the hypnotized subject could be seen as epiphenomena. In order to understand the essential characteristics of hypnosis it would, of course, be necessary to determine how much of the phenomenon could be explained in terms of role playing and an increased motivation of the subject to please the hypnotist.

The close similarity between an increased motivation of the subject to please the hypnotist and a conceptualization such as an increased responsivity to the demand characteristics of the situation is not accidental. I assumed that the increased motivation to please the hypnotist was an intrinsic attribute of hypnosis. Perhaps because the formulation intuitively seemed sound or because it was congruent with the Zeitgeist, it was not challenged despite the absence of empirical evaluation. Indeed, it was perhaps inevitable that others would conclude that, because simulating subjects could mimic much of the behavior of the hypnotized individual, one could explain away the actual phenomenon. Not only has there been a tendency to assume that all hypnotic phenomena can be understood in terms of demand characteristics, but also demand characteristic effects have erroneously been equated with compliance.

Relatively recently, influenced by the work of London and Fuhrer (1961) and Rosenhan and London (1963a), I have begun to examine empirical evidence bearing on the hypothesis that hypnosis increases the subject's motivation to please the hypnotist. It seems appropriate to review this work in the context of this paper, partly because it deals directly with motivational issues, but even more so because it clearly demonstrates the danger of explaining away rather than understanding a phenomenon. Certainly it shows that an uncritical—and, in my view, inappropriate—use of the concept of demand characteristics cannot adequately account for a complex phenomenon such as hypnosis.

There are three ways in which the concept of motivation to please the hypnotist or to comply with his wishes has been used to account for hypnotic phenomena: first, by way of the view that an individual who has been hypnotized by an experimenter is then more motivated to follow his instructions than if he had not been hypnotized; second, by way of the view that the tendency for an individual to enter hypnosis in the laboratory is merely a specific example of the general tendency to comply with requests of the experimenter (in other words, those individuals who enter hypnosis during an induction procedure are the very ones who initially already had a greater motivation to please the experimenter than those who do not respond in this way); and, finally, by way of the view that posthypnotic phenomena do not represent a special class of events but can simply be understood in terms of the subject's continued intense wish to please the hypnotist.

The Effect of Inducing Hypnosis on the Subject's Wish to Please the Hypnotist

On the basic question of whether the induction of hypnosis increases the motivation of the subject to comply with the wishes of the hypnotist it is difficult to obtain clear-cut findings. The widely held conviction that this is true is based on casual observations that hypnotized subjects seem to do whatever is requested of them. For this reason I normally begin my lectures to students by asking one individual to remove his right shoe, another to take off his necktie, still another to give me his wallet, and still another to exchange his coat with his neighbor. After obtaining compliance with a number of utterly ridiculous requests of this kind, I ask the students whether they have been hypnotized, and upon receiving a negative answer, I am able to point out that if they had previously gone through an induction process and had been asked to carry out the identical actions, observers would have said, "See, this demonstrates how a hypnotized individual is controlled by the hypnotist." Obviously this kind of control was already inherent in the student-teacher relationship; however, because the full amount of control one person might exert over another is normally neither exercised nor measured, it appears that hypnosis causes a significant increment in compliance. In a variety of ways we have tried to find behaviors which subjects would *not* carry out in the context of an experimental situation. We have been unable to do so. Thus, it has not been possible to demonstrate a unique increment in control due to hypnosis. (It was in the context of this question that the experiments in serial addition which will be referred to later were carried out.)

It is possible to phrase the question concerning the hypnotic subject's endurance thus: Will an individual in hypnosis perform a difficult task longer than he will out of hypnosis? Several studies have shown increased performance during hypnosis if one does not specially motivate the waking state (see Hull, 1933). Here the question of appropriate controls is exceedingly complex. This problem was traditionally phrased in terms of whether it is possible for hypnosis to cause an individual to transcend his normal volitional capabilities. Several studies have shown that it is relatively easy with appropriate motivation for nonhypnotized subjects to exceed their previous hypnotic performance (Orne, 1953; Barber & Calverley, 1964; Levitt & Brady, 1964). There can be no doubt that under these conditions the kinds of instructions used during hypnosis are quite different from those used in the waking state or for a control group. Furthermore, if subjects think that the experimenter is attempting to demonstrate increased performance during hypnosis they may easily provide him with supporting data, not by increasing their hypnotic performance but by decreasing their waking performance (see, for example, Zamansky, Scharf, & Brightbill, 1964).

One ingenious solution, eliminating differences in instructions, has been used in the study by London and Fuhrer (1961). These workers used identical hypnotic procedures for very good and very poor hypnotic subjects, both groups having been convincingly told that their hypnotic performance was adequate for the purposes of the experiment. With a variety of physical tasks the authors report the startling finding that unsusceptible subjects showed a significantly greater increment in performance in response to hypnotic instructions than good hypnotic subjects. Certainly these findings do not support the general belief that hypnosis increases the motivation of the hypnotized individual to carry out whatever kinds of tasks are suggested. Evans and Orne (1965) have replicated these studies and, while their data did not reach significance, they showed trends in the direction reported previously. In any case, the results, again, do not support the view that there is an increase in performance with hypnosis.

As a subsidiary question in this section we may also ask whether hypnosis, without any specific posthypnotic suggestions, has the effect of enhancing a subject's wish to please the hypnotist *after* the trance is terminated. This is of particular interest to clinicians, for it has often been said that the induction of hypnosis alters the relationship between doctor and patient in such a way that the patient becomes more prone to accept, uncritically, requests by the doctor and, in some ways, becomes more dependent upon him.

We have carried out a study which bears upon this question. It makes use of a postcard-sending procedure that has also been employed in other studies to be reported later in this paper. It is therefore first of all necessary to describe this experimental procedure. (This technique was tested and then utilized to study posthypnotic behavior by Esther Damaser [1964] in our laboratory.)

The Effect of Laboratory Instructions on Behavior over a Period of Weeks

A technique was needed which would measure the extent to which individuals would persist in carrying out requests without any further reinforcement beyond knowing that their behavior was of interest and importance to the research study, and without knowing or understanding how that behavior would be used. We decided upon a task which would yield data over as long a period as desired and which would not necessitate the subject's returning to the laboratory or being given any feedback whatsoever (Orne, 1963). Particularly well suited to these criteria is the request to mail one postcard each day to a post office box. The subject can be given any desired number of cards and appropriate instructions. The receipt of the subject's card provides quantifiable, objective data about the effectiveness of instructions in inducing individuals to carry out a trivial but tedious daily task.

The first study, concerned mainly with evaluating the procedure, was designed to investigate whether or not a single experimental manipulation would visibly affect the rate of postcard sending, or whether individual variability was so great that the task would prove to be useless for experimental purposes. We postulated that the primary variable involved would be the manner in which the task was defined rather than monetary reward as such; in particular, that if subjects agreed to perform the task and were paid in advance for so doing, *noncompliance would evoke guilt.*

Thirty-four subjects solicited through student employment services were randomly assigned to four groups.[5] All subjects were given a paper-and-pencil test and then one interview. During this interview they were told that another part of the experiment involved their doing something every day for eight weeks, that this something could be done at home and that it didn't take much time. The subjects were asked if they would like to participate in this part of the experiment. Three subjects refused, saying that they had enough to do without burdening themselves further; all the other subjects agreed to do this "something." Subjects were told that the reason for getting their commitment before explaining the task was that we did not wish them to discuss the experiment, and we felt it less likely that subjects who were actually taking part in the study would discuss it. After the subject had agreed to do this undefined something every day for eight weeks, he was given 56 preaddressed postcards and instructed to mail one every day.

Experimental groups differed as follows:

Group A. Subjects were paid $2.50 and were told that this sum represented payment for the entire experiment.

Group B. Subjects were paid $8.10 and were told that this sum represented payment for the entire experiment.

Group C. Subjects were paid $2.50 and were told that this sum was payment for participation in the paper-and-pencil test.

5. Two subjects were eliminated from the study because they had been told about it by another subject. Thus the initial N was actually 36.

They were further told that they would be paid 10¢ for every postcard that they mailed, and that they would be paid this sum after the eight weeks had passed. They were told that they would be paid for only one postcard each day during the 56 days.
Group D. Subjects were paid $2.50 and told that this sum represented payment for participation in the paper-and pencil test. They were then also paid 10¢ per postcard and told that they were being paid in advance because we were confident that they would mail all of the postcards. Thus each of these subjects was given a total of $8.10, the same as Groups B and C, but of course the significance of this money differed for the three groups.

In analyzing the data, the number of postcards sent was corrected in such a fashion that subjects could get credit for only one postcard each day. As predicted, Group D performed differently from the other three groups in having a higher mean and a smaller variance ($F = 8.243$; $.01 < p < .02$). None of the other three groups differed significantly from each other either in their means or in their variances.

TABLE 1

PRELIMINARY POSTCARD STUDY

Group	N	Mean	Variance
A (paid $2.50)	7	33.86	134.14
B (paid $8.10)	9	29.11	186.36
C (paid $2.50 and 10¢ per postcard)	8	32.38	189.70
D (paid $2.50 and 10¢ per postcard in advance)	7	38.43	19.62

TESTS OF HOMOGENEITY OF VARIANCE

Group	F ratio	Significance
A vs. B	1.39	NS
A vs. C	1.41	NS
B vs. C	1.02	NS
A vs. D	6.84	$p < .05$
B vs. D	9.50	$p < .01$
C vs. D	9.67	$p < .01$
(A + B + C) vs. D	8.243	$p < .02$

TEST OF MEAN DIFFERENCE

Group	t[a]	Significance
(A + B + C) vs. D	2.22	$p < .05$

[a] The t test took into account the heterogeneity of variance. A Mann-Whitney U test also yielded the same result.

This finding, incidentally, confirmed our belief that subjects' motivation to undertake experimental tasks is not essentially a function of payment within the range of rewards usually given in laboratory research. However, the importance of the finding here is that it demonstrates that postcard sending over time is a behavioral task sensitive enough to be used as a measure of motivation.

The Effect of Hypnosis on Responses to Subsequent Requests

We are now prepared to return to the study (Orne, 1963) concerned with the effects of hypnotic trance on the subsequent relationship between the participants. It utilized 53 volunteer subjects for hypnotic research who were given 100 postcards with the request to mail one daily, much in the same fashion as previously described. If the successful induction of hypnosis does somehow make the experimenter more important to the subject, then the request to send postcards should be more effective with subjects who responded by going into hypnosis than with those subjects who failed to do so.

The 53 volunteer subjects were first administered an abbreviated version of the group adaptation (Shor & E. Orne, 1962) of the Stanford Hypnotic Susceptibility Scale, Form A (Weitzenhoffer & Hilgard, 1959). Subsequently they were individually given a modification of a preliminary version of the Stanford Hypnotic Susceptibility Scale, Form C (Weitzenhoffer & Hilgard, 1962), adapted to permit the administration of perceptual items and allowing an 11-point scale of hypnotic depth to be used. At the conclusion of the hypnotic part, subjects were asked by the same hypnotist-experimenter, in the same fashion as in the previous experiment, whether they would be willing to participate in something else. One subject did not agree to participate in the postcard tasks. All others were given 100 self-addressed postcards. The correlation was computed between postcard sending and hypnotizability.[6] It was found to be −.11, obviously insignificant, and in a direction opposite to that required by the "compliance hypothesis." We feel compelled to conclude that the assumption of stronger compliance motivation on the part of successfully hypnotized subjects is not justified.

6. The subjects in this study were run by Jeremy Cobb at Brandeis University.

The Relationship between the Subject's Willingness to Please the Experimenter prior to Hypnosis and His Subsequent Response to Hypnotic Suggestions

Over the years we have worked with a large number of subjects. For methodological reasons we have been interested in the extremes of the distribution—the highly susceptible and largely insusceptible individuals. One would expect that if good subjects are particularly motivated to please the experimenter they would be more reliable in keeping appointments and arriving punctually. Yet Emily Orne noticed in several studies which used insusceptible subjects and very good somnambulists that the insusceptible individuals were consistently more reliable and punctual. This was true despite the fact that everyone in the laboratory is exceedingly careful to treat subjects with consideration and to communicate our appreciation for their participation. This is particularly true with highly hypnotizable individuals, since they represent a relatively small proportion of the population and are essential for the research. (In studies which require subjects to come back more than once, the attrition rate of good somnambulists is especially striking.) For some time we have been studying arrival times in the laboratory. Evans and Emily Orne have been able to show consistent significant negative correlations between punctuality and the ability to respond to hypnosis. (These correlations also hold particularly well for later sessions.)

We have also done a pilot study with a small number of subjects ($N = 17$) evaluating the relationship between postcard sending and hypnotizability when the request is made before the question of hypnosis is raised with the subject. With a small sample of this kind no significant trends emerged. If there is a trend, it is unlikely to be of any significant magnitude. Neither of these results justifies the assumption that a stronger motivation to comply is characteristic of individuals who subsequently show that they are able to enter hypnosis.

The data most relevant to the relationship between effort and hypnotizability, where hypnotizability was measured afterward, were obtained by Rosenhan and London (1963a), investigating the baseline performance of subjects on physical endurance as measured by a hand dynamometer and weight holding, before the possibility that the subjects were to be hypnotized was mentioned. Significant differences between susceptible and insusceptible subjects emerged, indicating a superior performance on the part of the insusceptible subjects. To the extent that we may assume no difference in physical capacity correlated with hypnotizability, these data suggest that subjects who prove to be good hypnotic subjects before the induction of hypnosis are, if anything, less motivated to follow the instructions of the experimenter than individuals who subsequently show themselves to be insusceptible. In a subsequent paper, the same authors (Rosenhan & London, 1963b) found an opposite trend in baseline responses related to the learning of nonsense material and suggest that baseline differences may be task specific. While further work is required on this issue, the indications are that those who become good somnambulists are not characterized by the general tendency to be highly motivated to carry out instructions.

Some data are available concerning baseline performances of subjects who know that hypnotic experiments will be conducted. Under these circumstances London and Fuhrer (1961) report that insusceptible subjects performed better on a variety of performance tasks. Shor (1959), during an experiment which required subjects to choose the highest level of electric shock that they would be able to tolerate, found good hypnotic subjects stopping at a considerably lower level of intensity than insusceptible subjects. Care must be taken in the interpretation of these kinds of data, however, as Zamansky, Scharf, and Brightbill (1964) have demonstrated that the relatively poor baseline performance of good hypnotic subjects may be a function of their wish at some level to have their hypnosis performance appear particularly dramatic.

POSTHYPNOTIC PHENOMENA

If one wishes to explain hypnosis as simply a function of the subject's wish to please the hypnotist, posthypnotic suggestion is of particular interest. It is the phenomenon which is usually associated with the notion of increased behavioral compliance on the part of the subject and, more than any other, implies an increased control over the individual's behavior. Yet here too, as we shall see, data do not support such an explanation.

Two studies were performed by Hull's group (1933) to measure the persistence of posthypnotic behavior. Kellogg (1929) suggested to subjects that they would, while reading a book of sonnets, breathe twice as fast as usual on even-numbered pages and twice as slowly as usual on odd-numbered pages. Subjects were tested immediately after waking, on the following day, and then at intervals of one to two weeks and, in some cases, at longer intervals of up to 99 days. A control group of subjects was not hypnotized but given the same instructions. Kellogg's conclusions were as follows:

> The performance of the waking control subjects shows no loss in the power of the suggestion with time. In all cases, at the last time of testing, nine or ten weeks after the instructions were given, the response is greater than at the first test. The performances of the trance subjects, on the other hand, show a loss in the force of suggestion with time, the ratio obtained at the last test being in all cases lower than at the first waking test. [p. 507]

Because Kellogg's experiment involved practice effects from repetition of the response, Patten (1930) investigated the persistence of posthypnotic suggestion over time, using each subject only once. They were instructed to press their right forefinger down when the names of animals appeared while they were looking for words which repeated themselves on the list revolving on a memory drum. Subjects were tested at time intervals varying from 0 to 33 days after the posthypnotic suggestion had been given. A waking control group was employed which was given the same instructions. The conclusions Patten draws are:

> The magnitude of the response of the amnesic subjects decreases with time. The magnitude of the response of the conscious subjects decreases somewhat with time. . . . The reactions of the amnesic subjects are not as large nor as persistent as those of the conscious control subjects and they exhibit a somewhat faster decrement with time. [p. 325]

Damaser (1964) in our laboratory conducted a study of post-hypnotic behavior utilizing the sending of postcards, which is a task rather well suited to an investigation of this phenomenon. It was felt important to control for possible personality and treatment differences between good and poor hypnotic subjects. For this reason a somewhat different design from that of the earlier study was used. From a large number of subjects, a group of very good hypnotic subjects and a group of subjects who were able to achieve only medium hypnotic depth were selected. After the decision was made that a subject was adequate for the deep group, he was randomly assigned to one of three categories. The first group was given a posthypnotic suggestion in hypnosis that they would send one postcard each day, and they then were awakened with suggestions of amnesia. The second group was given the identical posthypnotic suggestion and then awakened with amnesia, but in the waking state was also requested to send one postcard each day. The third group was deeply hypnotized but not given any posthypnotic suggestion except amnesia; however, after being awakened each subject was asked to send a postcard every day. Thus of the three groups, one had "posthypnotic suggestion alone," the second had "posthypnotic suggestion plus a waking request," while the third had "waking request alone." These groups had been carefully equated for hypnotizability and had been exposed to the same amount of inter-action, both hypnotic and waking, with the experimenter. The same design was carried through with the medium hypnotic group; here, however, the amnesia instructions for posthypnotic behavior were not given. The results are shown in Table 2.

TABLE 2
POSTHYPNOTIC SUGGESTION STUDY
Corrected number of postcards from day 1 through day 69

	Deep Hypnotic Group		Medium Hypnotic Group	
Posthypnotic suggestion only	A		A′	
	4		9	
	19		5	
	60	Mean, 24.0	4	Mean, 17.00
	32		3	
	5		64	
Waking request only	B		B′	
			57	
	32		66	
	60		52	
	42	Mean, 36.50	60	Mean, 57.50
	12		44	
			66	
Posthypnotic suggestion and waking request	C		C′	
	45		43	
	25		68	
	23	Mean, 35.75	1	Mean, 46.50
	50		61	
			60	

Because of technical difficulties the sample sizes are too small to draw definitive conclusions. However, it will be noted that the deep and the medium "posthypnotic suggestion alone" groups sent considerably fewer cards than the other two groups. This finding is consistent with those reported by Kellogg (1929) and Patten (1930).

It must be pointed out that great care is needed in interpreting the observation that a simple request appears to elicit behavior from laboratory subjects more reliably over a longer period of time than a posthypnotic suggestion. From the point of view of the subject the task may be entirely different. Thus, the individual who has been given a posthypnotic suggestion tends to perceive his role in the experiment as complying as long as he feels compelled to do so; some subjects even interpret their role as trying to resist the suggestion. Characteristically, subjects do not feel it appropriate to push themselves to carry out suggestions, as they would perceive this to be cheating. This makes sense if the subject correctly appraises the purpose of the experiment as an attempt to measure the response to a posthypnotic suggestion. On the other hand, a subject complying with a waking request who has committed himself to the task views it as his obligation to carry it out as long as he possibly can. We should, therefore, not be surprised by the fact that the latter group of individuals carry out behaviors more consistently and over a longer period. It is for this reason that Damaser (1964) included the group which combined waking request and posthypnotic suggestion. We had hoped somehow to potentiate the waking request by means of posthypnotic suggestion. While results based on such small samples are presently equivocal, they do not point in that direction. If anything, posthypnotic suggestion interfered with the waking request, though the differences are not statistically significant.

Because of the different ways in which subjects interpret a waking request and posthypnotic suggestion, it is difficult to design an experiment with appropriate controls. Perhaps we need to be satisfied with recognizing that posthypnotic suggestion is a different phenomenon from the waking request. Certainly the consistently poorer performance of good hypnotic subjects should convince those of our colleagues who deny the existence of posthypnotic suggestion that what happens is at any rate different from simple compliance. And it should caution those of us who would assume that hypnosis is a uniquely effective tool for the control of behavior.

However, from our present viewpoint another aspect of the data is perhaps more relevant. If we assume that hypnosis increases the motivation of the individual, certainly postcard sending in response to a waking request should be more frequent by good hypnotic subjects than by medium hypnotic subjects. However, if we examine our data on this, we find that the medium subjects sent considerably more postcards than the deep subjects—a difference which would reach significance had it been predicted. Thus, here again we are compelled to dismiss the simple formulation that hypnotic phenomena are invariably associated with high motivation on the part of the good hypnotic subject.

Does the Subject Carry Out a Posthypnotic Suggestion in Response to Interpersonal Needs or to Intrapsychic Needs?

Two recent studies were designed to help clarify the mechanism of posthypnotic behavior and tend to show that the response cannot be explained in terms of pleasing the hypnotist. In one study by Nace and Orne (1970) it was reasoned that an overt response to a posthypnotic suggestion requires that the need to carry out the behavior be sufficiently strong to result in action; however, there may be forces opposing this action. If one considers those subjects who fail to respond to a posthypnotic suggestion, in at least some a strong residual action tendency must exist which is nearly sufficient to lead to overt behavior. In an appropriate situation, the effects of such an action tendency should be demonstrable.

Subjects were seen in three experimental sessions in the laboratory. All the experimental rooms contained pencil boxes with a standard variety of different-colored pencils. On each occasion subjects were given one of the Stanford Hypnotic Susceptibility Scales (Weitzenhoffer & Hilgard, 1959, 1962) and were required to carry out other tasks, including filling out questionnaires and receipt forms for payment. The latter activities provided opportunities for unobtrusive observation of choice of writing instrument, four times in the first session, three in the second, and two in the third. In the third session, Form C of the Stanford Hypnotic Susceptibility Scale (Weitzenhoffer & Hilgard, 1962) was used, but to it the following posthypnotic suggestion item was added: "When you wake up and I take off my glasses you will feel a compelling desire to play with the blue pencil." After the trance the posthypnotic suggestion was tested, and the subject's experiences during the session were discussed with him without any particular reference to the posthypnotic suggestion. The experimenter then indicated to the subject that before finishing, it was necessary for him to fill out another questionnaire, asked him to make himself comfortable behind the desk, and left the room. Later the secretary observed which writing instrument was chosen to sign the receipt. Thus, in the third session both opportunities for observation of choice of writing instrument came after the cue for the carrying out of the posthypnotic suggestion.

The question was whether subjects who had received the post-hypnotic suggestion but had not carried it out would now tend to choose the blue pencil for filling out the questionnaire. The task required the subjects to use some writing implement, and therefore provided them an opportunity to discharge, in the absence of the hypnotist, an action tendency that had previously been insufficiently strong to be expressed in behavior. The results, set out in Tables 3 and 4, were strikingly lawful. The very best hypnotic subjects, of course, carried out the posthypnotic suggestion. The essentially unsusceptible individuals did not carry out the posthypnotic suggestion, nor did they tend especially to use the blue pencil in filling out the questionnaire. However, those individuals who responded to a good many of the hypnotic items but did not enter a very deep trance were the ones who subsequently used the blue pencil for the

TABLE 3

CHOICES OF WRITING INSTRUMENTS EXPRESSED AS PERCENTAGES
OF TOTAL CHOICES PER SESSION

Writing Instrument	Session 1	Session 2	Session 3
Blue pencil	1.44	2.00	23.36
Combined red, green, and char- treuse pencils	12.92	18.67	10.28
Yellow pencil	33.49	27.33	22.43
Own pencil	33.49	22.00	16.82
Pen	18.66	30.00	27.10

NOTE: Altogether 50 subjects were involved. They made 209 choices in session 1, 150 choices in session 2, and 107 choices in session 3. In a few instances, then, a subject chose more than one instrument in a single period of observation.

A very conservative use of χ^2, which takes into account all the dependencies in the data, shows that the increase in the use of the blue pencil is significant at the .001 level.

TABLE 4
HYPNOTIZABILITY PERFORMANCES OF SUBJECTS CLASSIFIED ON THE
BASIS OF RESPONSE TO POSTHYPNOTIC SUGGESTION

Response to P.H.S.	SHSS:A		SHSS:B		SHSS:C	
	X	S.D.	X	S.D.	X	S.D.
Did *not* carry out p.h.s. and did *not* use blue pencil ($N = 18$)	5.94	3.14	7.17	2.39	5.83	2.65
Did *not* carry out p.h.s., but *did* use blue pencil ($N = 8$)	7.13	3.52	8.38	1.65	7.75	2.33
Carried out p.h.s. ($N = 18$)	8.50	2.47	9.78	2.22	8.56	1.27

NOTE: Data from subjects ($N = 6$) who used a blue pencil before the posthypnotic suggestion was given are excluded from this analysis.

questionnaire. These data strongly support the view that a posthypnotic suggestion which is not carried out will, in some subjects, nonetheless lead to an action tendency which, under appropriate circumstances, will manifest itself in overt behavior. The use of the blue pencil in filling out the questionnaire can be seen as a relatively easy posthypnotic test item. Of relevance to our discussion here is that the use of the blue pencil occurred not in the presence but in the absence of the experimenter, apparently serving an intrapsychic need, perhaps being analogous to a Zeigarnik effect (1927). It would seem that the posthypnotic suggestion certainly increased the likelihood of the use of the blue pencil, but that this effect was not the same thing as an increased tendency to please the hypnotist.

Using a very different approach, Orne, Sheehan, and Evans (1968) investigated the effect of a posthypnotic suggestion on behavior occurring outside the experimental context. Fisher (1954), in a now classic study, hypnotized subjects and gave them the posthypnotic suggestion that whenever they heard the word "psychology" they would scratch the right ear. On their awakening, he tested the suggestion and found they responded. Shortly thereafter one of his colleagues entered the room, and a "bull session" ensued, implicitly terminating the experiment. During this session the word "psychology" came up, and 9 of the 12 subjects failed to respond. When the colleague eventually left, Fisher turned to the subjects in such a way as to imply that the experiment was still in progress, and used the word "psychology" conspicuously, thereby eliciting the suggested ear scratching in all subjects. These findings have supported the view that posthypnotic behavior can best be understood as the result of the subject's providing what the hypnotist desires of him. There are two issues subtly intertwined in this experiment, however: (1) whether the subject will carry out a posthypnotic suggestion outside the experimental context if he is not specifically required to do so, and (2) whether the subject's interpretation of an ambiguous suggestion can subsequently be modified by the hypnotist.

Consider the suggestion: "Whenever you hear the word 'psychology' you will scratch your right ear." It would seem extremely unlikely that the suggestion was intended or taken to mean that henceforth and for the rest of his life the subject was to respond by scratching his right ear whenever he heard the word. Rather, most subjects would correctly interpret it to mean "As long as this experiment continues, you will scratch your right ear whenever you hear the word 'psychology.'" If subjects interpreted it in this fashion, their behavior was merely an appropriate reflection of how they perceived an ambiguous instruction, and would have no bearing upon the more basic issue of whether an unambiguous posthypnotic suggestion would be carried out outside an experimental setting.

It is to this latter issue that the Orne, Sheehan, and Evans (1968) study was addressed. Subjects, whose hypnotizability had carefully been established in earlier sessions, were solicited for an experiment which involved two sessions on succeeding days. This requirement was discussed with them prior to their coming to the laboratory. On the first day they were given a series of personality tests and deep hypnosis was induced. At that time they were given the posthypnotic suggestion that for the next 48 hours whenever they heard the word "experiment" they would run their hand over their head. It should be noted that this suggestion has a specific time limit which is legitimized by the fact that the individual will be returning to the laboratory on the succeeding day. The session was completed, the subject sent home. The next day when he came to the laboratory and the investigator came to pick him up in the waiting room, as they walked down the corridor the latter remarked casually, "I appreciate your making today's 'experiment.'" This, however, was not the crucial test. Subjects are reimbursed for their experimental participation in the main office, which is some distance from the experimental suite, but through which they must pass in order to come and go. This is a routine procedure to which subjects had earlier become accustomed. As the secretary paid the subject on the first day, in a perfunctory fashion she asked him to sign the payment receipt for the "experiment." The next day when the subject arrived in the waiting room, he was met by the receptionist, who asked whether he was there for the psychological or the physiological "experiment." These, then, were the crucial tests outside the experimental context.

A crucial issue bearing on the interpretation of the findings was whether the secretary and receptionist were indeed perceived to be outside the experimental setting or whether the subject recognized them to be really agents of the experimenter. For these reasons, a special group of quasi controls simulating hypnosis was also run. The hypnotist was blind to the actual status of the subjects. By virtue of their instructions, simulating subjects (a comparison group which we will discuss at greater length later) are particularly prone to be suspicious of the experimental situation. As a result, they provided a very hard test of whether the hypnotic subjects perceived what happened in the main office and the waiting room as part of the experiment or not.

The results were clear. Deeply hypnotized subjects characteristically responded to the posthypnotic suggestion outside the experimental context, whereas simulators characteristically did not. The greater tendency to respond outside the experiment on the part of the deeply hypnotized subject was matched by an equally interesting difference within the experimental situation. Thus, simulators responded more consistently to the posthypnotic suggestion when the word "experiment" was used by the hypnotist than deeply hypnotized subjects, who occasionally seemed unaware of the use of the word when it was sufficiently well embedded in the context.

These findings indicate that the posthypnotic phenomenon cannot be explained by a strong motivation on the part of the hypnotized subject to please the hypnotist. Rather, the posthypnotic suggestion appears to set up a temporary compulsion for the subject to respond independently of whether the hypnotist is present or even aware of the response.

INCONSISTENT NONEXPERIMENTAL OBSERVATIONS

Throughout this discussion we have examined data selected because they raise questions about the assumption that hypnosis necessarily increases the motivation of subjects to carry out the request of the hypnotist. The most relevant area where one would find evidence to support this view is the clinical situation. It is the impression of all therapists with whom I have discussed the matter that the induction of hypnosis during treatment seems to intensify the transference relationship and thereby more rapidly makes the therapist a significant figure for the patient. Gill and Brenman (1959) have discussed this issue at length in their classic text.

Equally relevant are the clinical data on the removal of symptoms. These data, in fact, provide the only clear-cut situations where individuals can be shown to undertake behavior in response to a request in hypnosis, which they appear unwilling or unable to undertake on the basis of a waking request. Unfortunately, truly controlled data are lacking, and a study is needed to investigate in a rigorous fashion the extent to which the induction of hypnosis facilitates symptom removal. One observation has often been made, namely, that the success of therapeutic suggestions does not depend upon the depth of hypnosis (as traditionally measured) achieved by the patient. Thus, sometimes individuals who would, by a laboratory definition, be considered unsusceptible show a dramatic therapeutic response. This point is interesting in the light of London and Fuhrer's (1961) findings that hypnotic procedures affect the performance of individuals who appear unsusceptible to hypnosis as measured by standard tests.

Another type of evidence, best exemplified by Pattie's (1935) paper on uniocular blindness, shows that some subjects will go to incredible lengths to succeed in following a suggestion. Thus, one of his subjects spent hours in the library learning about optics in order to be able to maintain the appearance of uniocular blindness. Similarly, subjects will, in response to a suggested burn, produce localized scratch marks and will, if given the opportunity, often actually burn themselves surreptitiously with a cigarette, thus raising a blister. It would be possible to go on in this way indefinitely, listing anecdotal data which suggest the intensity with which some subjects attempt to meet the demands placed upon them by a hypnotic suggestion. Indeed, it is this kind of evidence which causes us to assume so easily that an increase in motivation is a concomitant of hypnosis.

There are, however, differences between the clinical situation and the experimental one. In the former, suggestions are given that have intense personal reference, whereas in the latter the tasks are obviously peripheral to the interests of the subject. Further, most anecdotal evidence, such as that presented by Pattie, is based upon work with subjects with whom the experimenter has had prolonged and intense contact. These situations, though in a laboratory context, approximate clinical situations. Perhaps it will be necessary to distinguish between what happens as the result of largely impersonal induction of hypnosis in the laboratory and the phenomenon we see in clinical practice based on a highly meaningful, intensely personal relationship. In the laboratory little or no contact with the experimenter is necessary for the induction of hypnosis. Even a tape recording is fully adequate as an induction stimulus. Hypnosis takes place largely as a function of factors (such as attitude, aptitude, personality, etc.) which the subject brings to the experiment. This is, of course, quite distinct from the situation in clinical practice, where there usually exists a significant personal relationship, as well as the patient's expectations of help. It is quite possible that there is an interaction between the induction of the hypnotic phenomenon, its effect on the motivation of the individual, and these two types of settings.

To recapitulate briefly, the main points that have been made so far are:

1. Using human beings as subjects in the context of episodic relationships (in hypnotic studies and other psychological experiments) is a complex matter. Generalizing from episodic laboratory behavior to everyday life is hazardous.

2. This became particularly apparent in our early studies on hypnosis which indicated (a) that the very heterogeneous behavioral events associated with hypnosis may all be viewed as behaviors that meet "the expectations of the hypnotist," and (b) that the effects of demand characteristics can determine the

kinds of data that are obtained in studying mental processes, where hypnosis is used as a means to induce those processes.

3. The whole question of the interaction of the motives of experimental subjects with their changing perceptions of the total experimental context needs to be scrutinized.

4. This kind of examination of the hypnotic situation reveals that the phenomena cannot, in fact, be fully explained in terms of strong or increased motivation to comply with the demands of the hypnotist, though, no doubt, some compliance occurs in the course of interpersonal relations such as therapy or in experimental situations where compliance is inevitably maximized.

We shall now turn to a closer look at the operation of demand characteristics in experimental situations other than hypnosis.

THE EXPERIMENTAL SITUATION AS A SPECIAL FORM OF INTERACTION

Our model for experiments comes from the physical sciences. There, in order to establish the effect of a particular independent variable, one compares objects exposed to a particular value of the variable with control objects which are not, all other conditions being held constant. When the object of study becomes an active, sentient human being, his awareness of the process of study may interact with the parameters under study. This is obvious in hypnotic research, but the problem is present in varying degrees in all behavioral research involving man.

THE MOTIVATION OF THE EXPERIMENTAL SUBJECT

Far from being passive responders, as assumed by the conceptual model of the traditional experiment, subjects are active participants in a very special form of social psychological interaction which we call the psychological experiment. A subject does not miraculously arrive in the experimenter's laboratory, but he is brought there by specific incentives. He is somehow solicited. Even if participation is made obligatory in the context of a course, a modicum of cooperation must in some way be involved, and more often than not we are dealing with individuals who have had the option of participating and have volunteered. While we tend to use financial rewards to secure subject participation in our research, the level of monetary reward usually involved is hardly sufficient to compensate the individual for his time, much less for the tedium, discomfort, or even pain that may be involved. With the exception of the occasional "professional subject," payment (within the range of monetary reward usually employed) appears secondary.

Elsewhere (Orne 1959a, 1962, 1970), I have emphasized that a great many subjects volunteer to participate in research in the hope of helping science, contributing to human welfare, and so forth. Certainly there is also a wide range of other motives that bring the subject to the laboratory. These include not only curiosity and an interest in learning about experiments but also, not infrequently, hopes of obtaining some form of personal help by participating. Whatever brings the subject, it is my conviction that he soon acquires a stake in the research. Seeing that he is already there and already participating, he is likely to want his participation to be useful. While no doubt subjects are concerned about what psychologists think of them and how they evaluate them—a motive that has been singled out, emphasized recently by Milton Rosenberg (1969), and termed "evaluation apprehension"—I have been equally impressed by the extent of the subject's concern to have his data be useful to the investigator. For example, in a psychophysiological study, equipment failure can in no way be construed as reflecting upon the subject's capabilities, yet it is invariably resented. In one way or another subjects tend to experience great concern about the success of the study as a whole and hope that their performances will contribute to it.

In the context of research subjects are willing to tolerate discomfort and even pain, so long as it seems relevant and necessary to the research task at hand. However, this tolerance is limited to discomfort that is perceived as essential for the research. For example, subjects will accept with relatively little annoyance repeated venipunctures in order to permit the investigator to draw several blood samples at different times in the course of an investigation. However, they greatly resent being stuck twice in an experiment requiring a single venipuncture because the investigator is unable to find the vein the first time. Whereas in the former case the discomfort associated with blood samples being taken was necessary for the purpose of the experiment, in the latter instance the additional discomfort of the second puncture is related to the experimenter's ineptitude rather than the needs of the research.

From the subject's point of view, the only way in which his participation can have real meaning is for the experiment to be important and successful. The greater the investment of time, effort, and discomfort on the part of the subject, the more he is compelled to care about its outcome and assume that it is important. Anyone who has carried out research where human subjects are exposed to considerable stress in the course of an experiment but are otherwise treated with consideration (and where the situation is so arranged that no subject perceives himself to have failed in the situation) can attest to the importance his subjects ascribe to the research. In fact, the more stress and discomfort there is associated with the study, the more likely it will be for the subject to think of the research as vitally important. It should not surprise us that the more investment the individual makes, the more he will be committed to assume his efforts are not in vain.

It is consistent with this that we have found it quite impossible to design an experiment which the subjects perceive as meaningless. For example, some years ago we tried to create a meaningless experiment. The subject was placed in a room with a pile of several thousand pages of serial additions in front of him. Each page took about 10 minutes to complete. The experimenter told him to begin working and after completing the first sheet to go on to the next and so forth, and to work as accurately and as rapidly as he could. He then asked for the subject's watch and left him with the words, "Just keep working; I will be back eventually." We found it necessary to stop subjects, since after several hours they came out merely to go to the bathroom and wanted to return to the room to continue their work.

When it became clear that this task was not seen as meaningless, it was modified and subjects were given the same pile of papers for serial addition, together with a pile of several hundred instruction cards. They were told to complete a sheet of paper and then to pick up the top card, which would tell them how to proceed. They were again asked for their watches by the investigator, who told them to just keep following the instructions, and promised to return eventually. After the subject completed the first sheet he picked up the top card, which read: "Tear up the sheet you have just completed into a minimum of 32 pieces and throw it into the wastebasket. Then go on to the next sheet and work as accurately and rapidly as you can. Once you have completed the next sheet, pick up the next card, which will give you instructions as to what to do next." All the cards were identical.

Again subjects persisted in working on this task for hours. We reasoned that perhaps they thought that sooner or later they would run across a card which would be different and tell them that they had somehow won, so we added yet another variation. This time the subjects were again placed in the room and given a stack of papers to work on. However, instead of a stack of instruction cards, there were now merely three instruction cards. They were told, as before, to pick up the top card for their instructions, which would be self-explanatory. Their watches were taken from them and they were told that the investigator would eventually return. This time the card said: "Tear up the page you have just completed into a minimum of 32 pieces and throw it in the wastebasket. Go on to the next page and continue to work as accurately and rapidly as you can. Place this card on the bottom of the pile. When you have completed the page, pick up the card at the top of the pile and follow its instructions." Under these circumstances the subjects knew by the time they had completed the third sheet that there were no surprises. All cards would be the same. Yet they continued to work at a high rate with remarkably few errors.

We then reasoned that because there was a one-way screen in the room, subjects suspected they were being watched. We eliminated the one-way screen. By mounting a microphone in the table, we were able to monitor the scratching of the pencil on the sheets of paper and thereby obtain an accurate measure of rate. We also marked the back of the pages with invisible ink and were therefore also able, by random sampling even from small pieces, to obtain an adequate measure of accuracy. The results were not appreciably different from those of the earlier studies. The interesting part of the research, however, was the fact that not a single subject doubted that we were somehow able, in ways he was unable to discern, to obtain an accurate record of his performance. No subject assumed that the experiment was meaningless. Indeed, they found it interesting and were convinced that there was some very important reason why the study was being carried out. Some subjects explained it as a frustration-tolerance task, some thought it was an ingenious way to determine the amount of inner-directedness, and others advanced various different hypotheses. The fact was that all subjects appropriately imputed meaning to the experiment, though the specific hypotheses were idiosyncratic. Parenthetically, this and similar work suggest that a James-Lange type of notion may apply to the recognition of meaning in a life situation. The meaning may not, contrary to widely held current beliefs, reside out in the environment but rather may be in large measure a function of involvement in a task. Once effort is invested, the individual will find meaning.

The extent to which a subject invests in the outcome of the experiment will, of course, be a function of many factors. Thus if he has to go to some trouble to volunteer and the experiment is tedious or stressful, the investment will tend to be higher. If the experiment involves little effort and participation makes no demands, he may care less about its outcome. He may even be inclined to see if he can throw sand into the wheels of progress. The subject's perceptions of the real situation will also be a factor. To the extent that the experimenter seems competent, it will be easier for the subject to cling to the notion that the experiment has a significant purpose. To the extent that the experimenter seems confused, unprofessional, or lackadaisical, the subject may well come to believe that the experimenter himself is merely satisfying some course requirement. To the extent, however, that the subject is involved in the study and is committed to its outcome, he will want it to work.

How Demand Characteristics Function

The remarkable tendency of some subjects to help an investigator by validating an implicitly communicated hypothesis forcibly drew my attention to one aspect of the potential importance of demand characteristics. Certainly if subjects could show such extreme compliance, an investigator must concern himself with how the individual perceives what the investigator seeks to prove. However, I soon realized that in most situations conscious compliance of subjects was a rare phenomenon. The kind of behavior I observed when trying to replicate the Carmichael, Hogan, and Walter (1932) experiment involved the subject's deliberate falsification of his actual memory to produce memories that he thought I hoped to see. However, except in rare instances, subjects conceive their role in the experiment as having to be honest in reporting their actual experiences, and therefore, willful distortions of this kind are rare. As I have pointed out elsewhere, subtle cues which are not fully recognized by the subjects are more likely to alter their behavior than obvious ones. The latter tend to obtrude themselves upon the individual's awareness and demand a response which would be tantamount to falsifying data wittingly in order to please the experimenter. This tends to be recognized as a kind of cheating, which would negate the value of the experiment. (A similar effect was observed by Rosenthal [1963] when he tried to pay subjects more for producing good, that is, biased, data; under these circumstances he noted less bias.)

It was never my impression, except in rare cases, that the mechanisms by which demand characteristics affect subjects' behavior were those of willful or conscious compliance, though it would appear that I have not been sufficiently explicit about this point. I see the subject's behavior and experience modified in subtle and complex ways by the operational implementation of the experimental task. Much as a green light on the road communicates directly the appropriate behavior to a driver, and just as a chair in a waiting room calls forth "be seated" behavior, so the experimenter's intentions and hypotheses are communicated through his operations. From the subject's point of view, these operations serve to define the appropriate behavior, the "right" behavior, the way one acts. The subject is not being compliant in any useful sense of that word. Rather, he is behaving in ways that, unthinkingly, he perceives as correct and appropriate.

Consider the experiment on unilateral catalepsy (Orne, 1959b). The experimental manipulation caused subjects to believe that unilateral catalepsy was characteristic of the behavior of hypnotized individuals. Later, when they were hypnotized, they manifested this item of behavior because, as far as they were concerned, it was part of being hypnotized. They validated the hypothesis of the experimenter—not explicitly to please him but simply because that was hypnosis from their point of view!

With increasing awareness of the part that subtle cues may play in experimental situations, I have tended to expand the concept to include all aspects of the individual's motivated perception of the experimental situation. It has become increasingly clear that the experimental situation for the subject depends upon what he perceives to be the relevant variables. These may or may not correspond to what the experimenter intended. Thus subjects who vary in sophistication, when run in identical experimental procedures, may be participating in what, from their points of view, *are entirely different experiments!* Unless it is possible for the investigator to ascertain in detail how the subject perceives the situation, it is impossible for him to know whether a given set of stimuli or a particular manipulation has produced the intended effect. An approach of this kind recognizes the need to study, in an experiment, the effects of specifiable conditions on human behavior; but it also recognizes that the conditions must be specified not only as they are seen by the investigator but also as they are seen by the subject. How the conditions are seen by the subject will, however, depend upon a myriad of subtle cues, many of which are rarely if ever reported when the experiment is published.

The concept of demand characteristics derives from the work of Lewin (1929), the term being a literal translation of *Aufforderungs-charakter*, usually referred to as a valence in the English literature. It shares the ambiguity of the Lewinian concept concerning its locus. It is an attribute of the experimental situation while at the same time it is the consequence of the subject's perception of the organization of the experimental situation. Its elucidation in any instance requires not only a knowledge of the cues objectively present in the experimental situation but also an understanding of the subject's perception of the situation.[7]

7. Demand characteristics and the subject's reaction to them are, of course, not the only subtle and human factors which may affect the results of an experiment. Experimenter-bias effects which have been studied in such an elegant fashion

The Cues Which Help Determine the Demand Characteristics of the Experimental Situation

The sum total of cues which communicate the purposes and intent of the experiment, particularly regarding those aspects about which the subject is not informed (or believes himself not to have been informed) constitutes the demand characteristics. What the subject actually perceives is a function of his attention, motivation, and his interpretation of the cues based on his prior knowledge, experience, suspiciousness, and such other factors as his intelligence.

The subject's perception of the experiment will, of course, depend in large part upon the instructions. These will be believed, however, only to the extent that they are congruent with the scuttlebutt concerning the research, the behavior of the experimenter, and the experimental procedure itself. The congruence among these different sets of cues will in large part determine the plausibility of the instructions. This is, of course, particularly true of deception research. Unfortunately, subjects have learned to distrust psychologists, and for this reason the experimental procedure often serves as a more compelling set of cues than the instructions. Here, as in other aspects of our experience, actions speak louder than words (see, for example, Silverman, Shulman, & Wiesenthal, 1970; Stricker, Messick, & Jackson, 1967).

Very significant information, which is generally ignored and rarely reported by investigators, comes to the subject from the manner in which he is solicited, the place in which the experiment is conducted, the person of the experimenter, and his mien and dress. One very potent source of cues that is rarely controlled but which may dramatically affect the subject's perception is the secretary or

by Rosenthal (1966) may frequently be confounding variables. These effects depend in large part on the experimenter outcome expectations. They can become significant determinants of data by causing subtle but systematic differences in (1) the treatment of subjects, (2) the selection of cases, (3) the observation of data, (4) the recording of data, and (5) the systematic analysis of data. To the extent that bias effects cause subtle changes in the way the experimenter treats different groups they may alter the demand characteristics for those groups. In some studies, therefore, demand characteristics may be one of the important ways in which experimenter bias can be mediated. Conceptually, however, the two processes are very different. Experimenter effects are rooted in the motives of the experimenter, while demand characteristic effects depend upon the perception of the subject.

research assistant with whom the subject speaks in order to arrange an appointment. It is essential to talk to the subject in order to arrange an appointment, and some form of reaction to questions, which are almost inevitable, must be made. Monitoring telephone conversations of this kind is an eye-opening experience. The general instruction "Don't tell the subject anything about the experiment" is well-nigh impossible to follow. Even if the research assistant strives not to answer the questions, the degree of discomfort with which she refuses to answer certain questions is in and of itself a communication. More likely than not, however, a good deal of information is transmitted to the subject as a quid pro quo in the process of having him accommodate to the schedule of appointments. If an investigator really tries to control this source of random variation, then he must spell out in detail the kind of answers that are appropriate for any conceivable question that might be asked. Fortunately, these tend to be reasonably finite and, provided the experimenter makes himself available to whoever does the scheduling in the early part of the study, he can get to know the kind of information that is communicated in this fashion.

A similar caution, of course, should apply to anyone other than the investigator who meets the subject, though, of course, he himself will need to think through that information may legitimately be communicated. Even experienced investigators will often be unaware of the highly variable amount of information that they make available to their subjects in informal contact before the beginning of the study.

One final source of information that is rarely controlled but is extremely important in many studies is the technician. Especially in psychophysiological studies where electrodes must be attached to the subject, the technician or the investigator (if he combines the roles) must interact with the subject over a considerable period of time. Silence is extremely oppressive and almost impossible to maintain. Questions about the experiment are all but inevitable, and considerable care is required if one hopes to have a fairly standard amount of information communicated.

The importance of the secretary and the technician as sources of cues is seen to be particularly striking once it is recognized that the subject appropriately can trust information from these sources far more than that coming from the investigator. He recognizes that these individuals are less likely to try to misrepresent the purpose of an experiment, and he is inclined to believe that they will have no reason to withhold or alter information whereas the investigator may well feel compelled to do so as part of the experiment.

The Rules of the Game

Most volunteer subjects participating in a psychological experiment recognize it as an elaborate ritual with rules that are reasonably well understood by them as well as by most experimenters. For example, subjects recognize that once they agree to participate in a psychological experiment they cannot be told the precise purpose of the study, since this may influence their behavior. They realize full well that it may be necessary for the investigator to deceive them as part of the experiment. It is this widespread recognition that is often particularly troublesome and that results in the type of comment made to me by a subject that "psychologists always lie." This awareness has implications for deception studies which make them troublesome, not only because of the moral problems but because of methodological issues to which we will return later.

It is this recognition of the rules of the game of the experiment which prevents the subject from being overly compliant in the sense of willfully falsifying data. The rules subsume the episodic nature of the experiment. One consequence of this is the willingness of subjects to take abuse in the course of an experiment. Some studies expose subjects to situations that make even the listener feel uncomfortable. One would expect subjects in such situations to become angry and hostile. Peculiarly enough, I know of no instance where a subject became sufficiently outraged to assault an investigator—though at times one feels such behavior might have been justified. Complaints about treatment are very unusual and even direct verbal chastisement of an investigator is rare. Furthermore, subjects assume that during the course of psychological experiments adequate precautions for their safety and welfare are taken. They recognize the constraints of reality upon the investigator and the consequences that would result if any irreversible serious harm were caused in the course of the investigation.

Agreement to participate in an experiment involves a far more complex social contract than is generally appreciated. The nature of this contract will at times become a recognizable determinant of the subject's behavior.

THE POSTEXPERIMENTAL INTERVIEW

Even a postexperimental inquiry, designed inter alia to check on demand characteristics, will not be free of those same demand characteristics. As I have indicated, subjects tend to be concerned that their data be useful to the investigator; thus they may feel that if they concede awareness of aspects of the study about which they were not informed (such as a deception), they would compromise the utility of their findings. For such reasons, even when the investigator asks what the study was about he may well be told "I don't know" or given some similar noncommittal answer.

Unfortunately, the needs of the investigator in this tend to parallel those of the subject: he is no more anxious to learn that the subject has seen through his deception than the subject is to tell him. Certainly, having to discard the data from a particular subject—particularly if he has yielded the right kind of data—is less than desirable. He, even more than the subject, has a stake in the outcome of the research. The peculiar interdigitation of the needs of the experimenter and the subject tends to result in what may best be described as a "pact of ignorance" (Orne, 1962)—an unspoken agreement between investigator and subject that they shall not look too deeply into the subject's awareness of the situation.

The above considerations suggest that it is essential that a postexperimental interview be conducted in a manner analogous to a clinical interview. The experimenter must elicit the subject's perception of the experiment. Often this is sought by asking the following questions: What is the experiment about? What do you feel the experiment is trying to demonstrate? What do you think is my hypothesis in the experiment? How do you think you performed in the experiment? How do you think others performed in the experiment? Have you any comment which may help to clarify things not apparent in the experimental situation? To ask questions of this kind by way of a questionnaire at the end of an experiment very rarely succeeds in eliciting a clear picture of what the subject thought about the experiment. He is most likely to respond in a way that will protect the integrity of the experimental performance.

On the other hand, in an interview it is possible for the investigator to convey that the experiment is truly over and that he now wants to understand how the subject perceived the situation. In other words, he changes the role relationship between subject and experimenter. In many ways during a postexperimental interview the setting can be one where the subject becomes a coinvestigator, collaborating with the experimenter to help him understand what was really happening. In the context of such an interview it is possible to push the subject to elaborate his perceptions of the situation without providing him any substantive information. It will not be possible, of course, to determine the extent to which the subject's insights into the experimental procedure actually played a role in his performance during the experiment. His understanding may well have emerged only during his reflection on the situation with the experimenter.

As useful as postexperimental inquiry information may be, it is subject to major limitations. Not only is it difficult to prevent subtle biases from intruding, but also it is impossible to be certain how the insights that are elicited have affected prior behavior. One thing is certain—experimenters being human, it is far easier to conduct exhaustive inquiries designed to elicit a subject's true perception of the situation during pilot research, before the investigator has a major investment in the particular experimental design, than it is during the actual study itself.

The inquiry procedure is a technique which obviously can be carried out only with human subjects. In one sense it may legitimately be considered a control procedure in that it helps to clarify the meaning of the data observed during the experiment. In another sense, however, it is a very special kind of control, quite dissimilar from the usual sort. Instead of employing a group of subjects who are not exposed to the experimental variable under study to help clarify its effect, it utilizes the active cognitive processes of the subject, which normally confound the data, as a means to clarify them.

THE CONCEPT OF QUASI CONTROLS

The purpose of an interview after an experiment is to help the investigator understand how the subject perceived the specific stimuli so that he is better able to interpret the behavioral data. With the major emphasis on behavior that has characterized psychology, at least until very recently, it has been fashionable to deny the relevance of such information. This should not be taken to mean, however, that the behavior has not been interpreted. Quite the contrary! Conventionally the investigator has operationally defined concepts such as stress, incentive, frustration, and so forth in terms of some manipulable experimental condition and then gone on to study the consequent behavior in order to make inferences about the basic psychological processes under investigation. In other words, instead of determining from the subject how he perceived the situation in order to interpret his behavior, the investigator has decided for the subject what the situation was supposed to mean, and, assuming that he was correct in his interpretation, has drawn inferences from the behavior. In many instances this procedure works because, intuitively putting himself in the subject's place, the investigator correctly surmises how the subject perceives the situation. We might say that this experimental model has functioned because the investigator has unwittingly taken advantage of information about what may have been going on in the subject's experience; he may have even talked to subjects to find out, even though he probably writes about the experiment as if it had been carried out quite independently of such information.

A particularly dramatic example of this kind was seen when Richard Solomon and his associates (Turner & Solomon, 1962) began to study traumatic avoidance conditioning with human subjects. Subjects were given a warning signal 10 seconds before a very painful 15-second shock was delivered to the ankle. A variety of manipulanda were employed. If the subjects moved the manipulandum appropriately while being shocked they could terminate the shock. If the appropriate response was given after the warning signal and before the shock was delivered, they could avoid it entirely. These procedures are closely analogous to the shuttlebox avoidance conditioning paradigm used with dogs.

Subjects were run by Lucy Turner with minimal instructions in the hope of approximating the situation of the animals. The investigators observed that many subjects showed little or no learning over several sessions, accepting instead a large number of very painful electric shocks. When these subjects were asked about the experiment, it became clear that they thought the study was a test of their capacity to tolerate painful electric shock. Given such a set, the idea that the shocks could be or should be avoided had simply not occurred to them. On the other hand, subjects who were told that they could do something to avoid the shocks had relatively little difficulty in discerning and learning the appropriate response.

In these as well as many other studies, not giving the subject explicit verbal information about the task in no way prevented them from forming definite hypotheses about the study and behaving accordingly. It never does. In this particular case, a preexperimental procedure used to set shock level—which "required" individuals to tolerate as high a shock as they could—may have inadvertently served to create the specific set which prevented the acquisition of avoidance behavior. Thus a change of experimental procedure might also have been designed effectively to communicate that avoidance was expected. The basic point remains, however, that the behavior cannot be interpreted without understanding how the experiment is perceived.

One can easily imagine how one might have varied a large number of parameters other than instructions and shown their effects upon the subject's ability to learn to avoid shock. One might eventually have inferred a number of mechanisms or even motives affecting the avoidance learning. This is precisely what we are forced to do when we are working with nonhuman species. Fortunately, with human subjects a relatively simple procedure—the inquiry—designed to elicit their perception of the experiment allows the investigator to understand what is probably occurring. Frequently one finds that the feature of an experiment which is intended by the investigator to represent one set of circumstances outside the laboratory is seen by the subjects in the laboratory as representing an entirely different set of circumstances. Under those conditions the inference drawn from the experimental data is bound to be incorrect.

The inquiry procedure, then, is the simplest technique to find out about the active cognitive processes that the subject introduces into the experimental situation. Its purpose is to help the investigator understand (not measure) how those processes may have affected the results. The inquiry is only one of a family of such techniques that constitute a special kind of control procedure. They are not controls in the classic sense. Rather they focus upon the elucidation of the possible interaction of the subject's cognitive processes and his experimental behavior.

For some time I have tried to find an appropriate term for these techniques. They all share the property of telling us little about the actual variables under investigation but a great deal about the procedures used to study them. For this reason the term "procedural control" has been suggested. It would be appropriate since they characteristically lead to modifications in the experimental procedure. The term "active control" is appealing since it emphasizes the extent to which the subject is required to participate actively rather than respond passively. Another significant aspect is that a proper inquiry procedure alters the role relationship between subject and experimenter. Instead of being an object of study the subject becomes a collaborator, a colleague even, helping to solve the difficult problem of understanding why he has behaved in some particular fashion. The term "collaborative control" suggests itself. Again, the techniques all are designed to clarify the perceptions of the subject and the context of the experimental situation as he perceives it. This idea could be expressed in the term "contextual control." These procedures address themselves to what may be considered the validity of the experimental procedure. They ask whether the operational definition by which a construct is translated into an experimental condition is appropriate. They ask whether a deception in an experiment has been successful. They shed light on the type of extraexperimental situation to which the findings of a given experimental procedure may be appropriately extended. The term "inferential control" would emphasize a basic feature of such techniques, their helping to establish the extent to which the inferential leap from one context to another is justified.

Since each of the suggested terms grasps a particular aspect of the procedure and none of them is fully descriptive, I have opted for the term "quasi control." This is a term which emphasizes that the concept is not of a true control, and it therefore is less likely to bring about confusion with other meanings. As I shall try to illustrate, quasi-control procedures allow inference about the adequacy of an experimental procedure, not about either the independent or the dependent variables under investigation. Thus they are crucial in helping the investigator design a better study which will permit more definitive and valid answers to his questions.

Inquiry Data as the Basis for Manipulating Demand Characteristics

A psychophysiological study by Gustafson and Orne (1965) illustrates the use of inquiry data to elucidate the demand characteristics which might explain confusing experimental findings. The example is useful because it illustrates how, once this situation was understood, it became possible to deliberately manipulate demand characteristics and treat them as experimental variables in their own right. The results of this explicit manipulation enabled us to understand an experimental result which otherwise appeared contrary to findings in nonexperimental situations.

A number of studies in recent years have investigated the detection of deception (more popularly known as lie detection) using the galvanic skin response (GSR) as the dependent variable. In one such study, Ellson, Davis, Saltzman, and Burke (1952) reported a very curious finding. Their experiment dealt with the effect which knowledge of results can have on the GSR. After the first trial, some subjects were told that their lies had been detected, while others were told the opposite. This produced striking results on the second trial: those who believed that they had been found out became harder to detect the second time, while those who thought they had deceived the polygraph on Trial 1 became easier to detect on Trial 2. This finding, if generalizable to the field, would have considerable practical implications. Traditionally, interrogators using field lie detectors go to great lengths to show the suspect that the device works by "catching" the suspect, as it were. If the results of Ellson et al. were generalizable to the field situation, the very procedure which the interrogators use would actually defeat the purpose for which it was intended by making subsequent lies of the suspect even harder to detect.

Because the finding of Ellson et al. runs counter to traditional practical experience, it seemed plausible to assume that additional variables might be involved in the experimental situation. The study by Ellson et al. was therefore replicated by Gustafson and Orne (unpublished study, 1962) with equivocal results. Postexperimental interviews with subjects revealed that many college students apparently believe that the lie detector works with normal individuals and that only habitual liars could deceive a polygraph. Given these beliefs, it was important to the student volunteers that they be detected. In that respect the situation of the experimental subjects differs markedly from that of the suspect being interrogated in a real-life situation. Fortunately, with the information about what most experimental subjects believe, it is possible to manipulate those beliefs and thereby change the demand characteristics of the Ellson et al. study.

Two groups of subjects were given different information about the effectiveness of the lie detector. One group was given information congruent with the widely held belief and told: "This is a detection of deception experiment. We are trying to see how well the lie detector works. As you know, it is not possible to detect lying in the case of psychopathic personalities or habitual liars. We want you to try your very best to fool the lie detector during this experiment. Good luck." These instructions tried to maximize the kind of demand characteristics which might have been functioning in the Ellson et al. study, and it was assumed that the subjects would want to be detected in order to prove that they were not habitual liars. The other group was given information which prior work (Gustafson & Orne, 1963) had shown to be plausible and motivating; they were told, "This is a lie detection study, and while it is extremely difficult to fool the lie detector, highly intelligent, emotionally stable, and mature individuals are able to do so." The demand characteristics in this case were designed to maximize the wish to deceive.

From that point on, the two groups were treated identically. They drew a card from an apparently randomized deck; the card had a number on it which they were to keep secret. All the possible

TABLE 5
Number of Successful and Unsuccessful Detections on
Trial 1 for the Two Subgroups of the *N* Detected and *N*
Deceive Groups

	Told Detected (Subsequently)	Told Not Detected (Subsequently)	χ^2 between columns 1 and 2
" Need to be Detected Group"			
Detected	9	13	$\chi^2 = 1.31$
Not Detected	7	3	n.s.
" Need to Deceive Group"			
Detected	13	11	$\chi^2 = 0.17$
Not Detected	3	5	n.s.
χ^2 between n Detected and n Deceive Groups	$\chi^2 = 1.31$ n.s.	$\chi^2 = 0.17$ n.s.	

Note: *Ss* were not given information about the success of detection until *after* the trial on which these data are based.

A multiple chi-square contingency analysis (Sutcliffe, 1957) was used to analyze the departures from expected frequencies in the entire table. Neither the chi-square components for each variable alone, nor the interaction between variables, were significant.

From L. A. Gustafson and M. T. Orne, "Effects of perceived role and role success on the detection of deception," *Journal of Applied Psychology*, 1965, **49**, 412–417. Copyright 1965 by the American Psychological Association and reproduced by permission.

numbers were then presented by a prerecorded tape while a polygraph recorded the subjects' GSR responses. On the first such trial, the "detection ratios"—that is, the relative magnitudes of the critical GSR responses—in the two groups were not significantly different. When the first trial was over, the experimenter gave half the subjects in each group the impression that they had been detected, by telling them what their number had been. (The experimenter had independent access to this information.) The other half were given the impression that they had fooled the polygraph, the experimenter reporting an incorrect number to them. A table of random numbers was used to determine, independent of his actual GSR, which kind of feedback each subject received.

A second detection trial with a new number was then given. The dramatic effects of the feedback in interaction with the original instructions are visible in Table 6. Two kinds of subjects now gave large GSRs to the critical number: those who had wanted to be detected but yet had *not* been detected, and also those who had hoped to deceive and yet had *not* deceived. (This latter group is analogous to the field situation.) On the other hand, subjects whose hopes had been confirmed now responded less and thus became

TABLE 6

Number of Successful and Unsuccessful Detections on
Trial 2 for the Two Subgroups of the N Detected and N
Deceive Groups

	Told Detected (Previous to Trial)	Told Not Detected (Previous to Trial)	χ^2 between Columns 1 and 2
"Need to be Detected Group"			
Detected	4	14	$\chi^2 = 10.28$
Not Detected	12	2	$p < .005$
"Need to Deceive Group"			
Detected	15	3	$\chi^2 = 15.36$
Not Detected	1	13	$p < .001$
χ^2 between *n* Detected and *n* Deceive Groups	$\chi^2 = 12.96$ $p < .001$	$\chi^2 = 12.55$ $p < .001$	

Note: A multiple chi-square contingency analysis here shows that neither information given nor motivation (*n* Detect vs. *n* Deceive) has significant effects by itself. The relevant chi-square values, calculated from partitioned subtables, are .25 ($p > .95$) and .00 respectively ($df = 1$). However, successful detection does depend significantly on the interaction between information and motivation ($\chi^2 = 30.94; p < .001; df = 1$).

From L. A. Gustafson and M. T. Orne, "Effects of perceived role and role success on the detection of deception," *Journal of Applied Psychology,* 1965, **49,** 412–417. Copyright 1965 by the American Psychological Association and reproduced by permission.

harder to detect, regardless of what their hopes had been. Those who had wanted to be detected, and indeed had been detected, behaved physiologically like those who had wanted to deceive and indeed had deceived.

This effect is an extremely powerful but also an exceedingly subtle one. The differential pretreatment of groups is not apparent on the first trial. Only on the second trial do the manipulated demand characteristics produce clear-cut differential results, in interaction with the independent variable of feedback. Furthermore, we are dealing with a dependent measure which is often erroneously assumed to be outside of volitional control, namely, a physiological response—in this instance, the GSR. This study serves as a link toward resolving the discrepancy between the laboratory findings of Ellson et al. (1952) and the experience of interrogators using the lie detector in real life.

It proved possible in this experiment to use simple variations in instructions as a means of varying the demand characteristics. The success of the manipulation may be ascribed to the fact that the instructions themselves reflected views that emerged from interview data, and both sets of instructions were congruent with the experimental procedure. Only if instructions are plausible—a function of their congruence with the subjects' past knowledge as well as with the experimental procedure—will they be a reliable way of altering the demand characteristics. In this instance the instructions were not designed to manipulate the subjects' attitude directly; rather they were designed to provide differential background information relevant to the experiment. This background information was designed to provide very different contexts for the subjects' performance within the experiment. We believe this approach was effective because it altered the subjects' perception of the experimental situation, which is the basis of the demand characteristics in any experiment. It is relevant that the differential instructions in no way told subjects to behave differently. Obviously, subjects in an experiment will tend to do what they are told to do—that is the implicit contract of the situation—and to demonstrate this would prove little. Our effort here was to create the kind of context which might differentiate the laboratory from the field situation and which might explain differential results in these two settings. Plausible verbal instructions were one way of accomplishing this end. (Also see Cataldo, Silverman, & Brown, 1967; Kroger, 1967; Page & Lumia, 1968; Silverman, 1968.)

Unless verbal instructions are very carefully designed and pretested they may well fail to achieve such an end. It can be extremely difficult to predict how, if at all, demand characteristics are altered by instructions, and frequently more subtle aspects of the experimental setting and the experimental procedure may become more potent determinants of how the study is perceived.

THE NONEXPERIMENT, OR PREEXPERIMENTAL INQUIRY

One of the major logical problems with postexperimental inquiry data is the difficulty of determining whether the subject's behavior was a function of how he perceived the experiment or whether his perceptions of the experiment serve post hoc to rationalize what he actually did. In part at least, this problem is made more acute because, as an experiment progresses, additional information is made available to the subject and he may become aware of the purpose of the study or of some deception in the later stages of an experiment. In that case his awareness will not have affected his earlier performance but may well have affected his later performance. (In many studies where there are strong order effects, different orders of presentation will yield different amounts of information at various points in the experiment.)

One approach to this problem has been suggested by Richard Solomon (personal communication). One would need to run a large number of subjects, only a small percentage of whom would actually complete the study. The others would be used as "sacrifice" groups. The experiment would be stopped for different groups at different junctures in the procedure and an inquiry carried out— perhaps for one group shortly after the beginning, for another perhaps halfway through, for a third perhaps three-quarters of the way through, and so on. In this way it would be possible to establish the subjects' perceptions at different stages of an experimental procedure. Some of the subjects at least would be evaluated before thay had had much opportunity to give behavioral responses, so that one could get an idea of the kind of cues which are made available to the subject by his own behavior. Unfortunately, such a technique is extremely time-consuming and costly.

An alternative procedure does not ask about the demand characteristics inherent in an experimental procedure at various points; rather it tests the overall impact much in the way inquiry does, but it does so without allowing the subject to experience his own response to the independent variable. This technique for uncovering the demand characteristics of a given experimental design is the preinquiry, or "nonexperiment." This procedure was independently proposed by Riecken (1962). A group of persons drawn from the same population as the actual experimental subjects will be selected from are asked to imagine that they are subjects themselves. They are shown the equipment that is to be used and the room in which the experiment is to be conducted. The procedure is explained in such a way as to provide them with information equivalent to that which would be available to the actual experimental subjects. However, they are not exposed to the experimental treatment; it is only explained.

In a nonexperiment on a certain drug, for example, the participant would be told that subjects are given a pill. He would be shown the actual pill, read the instructions destined for the experimental subjects, and then asked to produce data as if he had been subjected to the experimental treatment, that is, had taken the pill. If there are pretests in the study he would be given the pretest instructions first, take the pretests, then shown the pill and given the pill instructions, but not allowed to take it. He would then be told that an actual subject would have to wait a half hour for the pill to take effect. He would then be given the actual posttests, or asked to fill out the rating scales, or requested to carry out any behavior appropriate to the actual proposed experiment.

The nonexperiment yields data similar in quality to inquiry material, but it is obtained in the same form as an actual subject's data. Direct comparison of nonexperimental data and experimental data is therefore possible, but caution is essential. If these two kinds of data are identical, it shows only that the subject population in the actual experiment could have guessed what was expected of them. It cannot tell us that such guesses were the real determinants of their behavior.

Kelman (1965) has suggested that such a technique might appropriately be used as a social psychological tool to obviate the need for deception studies. The economy of such procedures is appealing and working in a situation where subjects become quasi collaborators instead of objects to be manipulated is more satisfying to many of us. Nonetheless it would seem dangerous to draw inferences to the actual situation in real life from results obtained in this fashion. In fact, when subjects in preinquiry experiments perform exactly as subjects do in actual experimental situations, it becomes impossible to know how much their performances is due to the independent variables and how much to the demand characteristics of the experimental situation. (See also Freedman, 1969, in this regard.)

In most psychological studies when one is investigating the subject's best possible performance in response to different physical or psychological stimuli, there is relatively little concern for the kind of problems introduced by demand characteristics. The need to take these factors into account becomes far more pronounced when investigating the effects of various interventions such as drugs, psychotherapy, hypnosis, sensory deprivation, conditioning of physiological responses, and so forth on performance or experiential parameters. Here the possibility that the subject's response may inadvertently be determined by the demand characteristics rather than the process itself must certainly be considered. Equally subject to these influences are studies where attitude changes rather than performance changes are explored. The investigator's intuitive recognition that a subject's perceptions of an experiment and of its meaning are very likely to affect the nature of his responses is probably one of the main reasons why deception studies have become so popular in the investigation of attitude change.

PROBLEMS OF INFERENCE

There is in the literature a very good illustration of the value of the nonexperiment. One of the major attractions of Festinger's (1957) cognitive dissonance theory has been that it makes predictions possible which appear to be counterexpectational; that is, it is commonly thought that the predictions made on the basis of intuitive common sense are wrong whereas those made on the basis of dissonance theory are both unexpected and validated by experimental findings. Bem (1967) has shown in an elegant application of the techniques which I have called the preinquiry experiment that subjects to whom the situation in typical cognitive dissonance studies is described in detail without being really placed in the situation are able to produce data closely resembling those observed. Bem appropriately questions the assertion that the dissonance theory allows counterexpectational predictions. His data effectively make the cognitive dissonance studies which his own nonexperiments replicate far less compelling than they were thought to be by showing that subjects could have figured out the way others respond. It should not be concluded, however, that because Bem was able to show that subjects not exposed to the situation could second-guess the experiment, further empirical studies are unnecessary. On the contrary, his findings show only that the avowed claims of these studies to counterexpectational results were not, in fact, justified, and that a more stringent test is required in future experiments that aim to demonstrate such effects.

In the same way, of course, I cannot agree with Kelman's suggestion that we can build a reliable social psychology on data obtained from subjects' role playing. Certainly it is true that subjects can often correctly role play the kind of behavior that would occur in actual situations. When we are dealing with such a situation and we do the actual experiment, the findings tend to strike us as relatively trivial. This is particularly true because we have, at best, validated our intuitive common sense. However, we are also left with a nagging doubt as to whether the subjects in the actual experiment were not responsive merely to the demand characteristics in the situation rather than to the independent variables themselves. Only when we succeed in setting up an experiment where the results are counterexpectational in the sense that a preinquiry yields findings different from those obtained from subjects in the actual situation can we be relatively sure that these findings represent the real effects of the experimental treatment.

It appears to me then that nonexperiments, or role-playing experiments, which are close relatives, are in essence first cousins of the simple postexperimental inquiry. The data they yield are based upon the active use of the subject's cognitive processes. Such nonexperiments require the subject to think through the situation and figure out how other subjects would behave. Certainly this is an extremely useful procedure to clarify findings obtained in actual experiments, but it does not supplant the need for substantive research. Subjects simply do not always know how they would respond when confronted with the actual situation.

THE PREINQUIRY TO HELP CLARIFY THE DEMAND CHARACTERISTICS

When it is possible to produce the same experimental results despite extreme variations in experimental procedures, or when identical experimental procedures carried out in different laboratories yield radically different results, the probability of demand characteristic effects must be seriously considered. An area of investigation characterized in this way was the early studies on sensory deprivation. The initial findings attracted wide attention because they not only had great theoretical significance for psychology but seemed to have practical implications for the space program as well. A review of the literature indicated that dramatic hallucinatory effects and other perceptual changes were typically observed after the subject had been in the experiment approximately two-thirds of the total time; however, it seemed to matter relatively little whether the total time was three weeks, two weeks, three days, two days, twenty-four hours, or eight hours. Clearly, factors other than physical conditions would have to account for such discrepancies. As a first quasi control we interviewed subjects who had participated in such studies (unpublished study). It became clear that they had been aware of the kind of behavior that was expected of them. Next a preinquiry was carried out, and from participants who were guessing how they might respond if they were in a sensory deprivation situation, we obtained data remarkably like those of the actual studies (Stare, Brown, & Orne, 1959). We were then in a position to design an actual experiment in which the demand characteristics of sensory deprivation were the independent variables (Orne & Scheibe, 1964).

One group of subjects were run in a "meaning deprivation" study which included the accouterments of sensory deprivation research but omitted the condition itself. They were required to undergo a physical examination, provide a short medical history, sign a release form, were "assured" of the safety of the procedure by the presence of an emergency tray containing various syringes and emergency drugs, and were taken to a well-lighted cubicle, provided food and water, and given an optional task. After taking a number of pretests, the subjects were told that if they heard, saw, smelled, or experienced anything strange they were to report it through the microphone in the room. They were again reassured and told that if they could not stand the situation any longer or became discomforted they merely had to press the red "panic button" in order to obtain immediate release.

They were then subjected to four hours of isolation in the experimental cubicle and given posttests. The control subjects were told that they were controls for a sensory deprivation study and put in the same objective conditions as the experimental subjects. Table 7 summarizes the findings, which indicate that manipulation of the demand characteristics by itself can produce many findings that have previously been ascribed to the sensory deprivation condition.

TABLE 7

SUMMARY AND ANALYSIS OF TEN TESTS FOR CONTROL AND
EXPERIMENTAL GROUPS IN PSEUDO-SENSORY DEPPRIVATION

Test and Group	Pretest M	Posttest M	Difference Statistic
Mirror Tracing (errors)			
Experimental	28.1	19.7	$F = 1.67^a$
Control	35.8	15.2	
Spatial Orientation			
Angular deviation			
Experimental	45.7	53.9	$F = .25^a$
Control	52.5	59.1	
Linear deviation			
Experimental	5.3	5.4	$F = 3.34^b$
Control	6.4	5.7	
Word Recognition (N Correct)			
Experimental	17.3	15.6	$t = .50$
Control	15.2	12.3	
Reversible Figure (Rate per Minute)			
Experimental	29.0	35.0	$F = 1.54^a$
Control	20.1	25.0	
Digit Symbol (N Correct)			
Experimental	98.2	109.9	$F = .05^a$
Control	99.2	111.9	
Mechanical Ability			
Tapping speed (*N* completed)			
Experimental	33.9	32.2	$F = 2.26$
Control	32.9	35.0	
Tracing speed (*N* completed)			
Experimental	55.6	52.3	$F = 4.57^b$
Control	53.1	58.4	
Visual pursuit (*N* completed)			
Experimental	5.7	8.9	$F = .22^a$
Control	5.7	9.2	
Simple Forms (N Increment Distortions)			
Experimental	—	3.1	$U = 19^c$
Control	—	0.8	
Size Constancy (Change in Steps)			
Experimental	—	0.6	$t = 1.03^a$
Control	—	0.0	
Spiral Aftereffect			
Duration, seconds			
Experimental	24.4	27.1	$F = .99^a$
Control	15.6	16.1	
Absolute Change			
Experimental	—	7.0	$t = 3.38^d$
Control	—	2.7	
Logical Deduction (N Correct)			
Experimental	—	20.3	$t = 1.64$
Control	—	22.1	

NOTE: F = adjusted postexperimental scores, analysis of covariance; $t = t$ tests; U = Mann-Whitney U test, where plot of data appeared grossly abnormal.

From M. T. Orne and K. E. Scheibe, "The contribution of nondeprivation factors in the production of sensory deprivation effects: The psychology of the 'panic button'" *Journal of Abnormal and Social Psychology*, 1964, **68**, 3–12. Copyright 1964 by the American Psychological Association and reproduced by permission.

[a] Indicates differences between groups were in predicted direction.
[b] $p < .05$, one-tailed.　　　[c] $p < .01$, one-tailed.　　　[d] $p < .001$, nondirectional measure.

245

Of course, neither the quasi controls nor the experimental manipulation of the demand characteristics sheds light on the actual effects of the condition of sensory deprivation. They do show that demand characteristics may produce effects similar to those ascribed to sensory deprivation.

SIMULATORS

The use of the subjects' active cognitive processes to figure out what constitutes "appropriate" behavior can be carried one step further to provide yet another technique for uncovering demand characteristics, i.e., the use of simulators. Subjects are asked to pretend that they are being affected by an experimental treatment which they do not actually receive or to which they are immune. Note that this is merely an extension of the nonexperiment; but, whereas in that procedure the investigator is aware of which subject is which and is likely to treat them quite differently, the simulating technique permits subjects to be run by an experimenter who is in fact unaware of their actual status. As I have already pointed out, for this technique to be effective it is essential that the subject be aware that the experimenter is actually blind as well as that the experimenter actually be blind. The use of a blind experimenter makes certain that any effects due to experimenter bias are held constant across the actual group and the simulating group. We use this technique extensively in the study of hypnosis, and an example of it has already been described. Fortunately, it is possible for unhypnotized subjects to deceive an experimenter by acting as though they have been hypnotized. Obviously, it is essential that these subjects have no special training regarding the variables being studied so that they have no more information than that actually available to the real subjects. The simulating subjects have to guess what real subjects do in an experimental situation in response to instructions administered by a particular experimenter.

This design permits us to separate experimenter bias effects from demand characteristic effects. In addition to his other functions, the experimenter may be asked to judge whether each subject is "real" or simulating. In our work, this judgment tends to be random and unrelated to the true status of the subject; nevertheless, we have frequently observed differences between the behaviors of subjects contingent upon whether the experimenter has judged them to be hypnotized or just simulating. Such differences are likely to be due to differential treatment and bias, whereas differences between actual hypnotized subjects and actual simulators are likely to be due to hypnosis itself.

I would like to emphasize that the simulating group is a special-treatment group. It is not a true control group in the classical sense, though it appears in some ways to be very similar. It is easy to confuse the simulating group with a true control group, since we have a blind experimenter treating two groups in identical ways and the data are being given in the same form by both groups; but they are different. Actually, the simulator is a very close relative of the role player in the nonexperiment. As in the postexperimental inquiry, we are still asking subjects to collaborate with us and to "psych out" how other subjects exposed to the actual treatment might behave. Consequently the inferences from the results of such a quasi-control group must be drawn with extreme caution. If we do not observe differences between deeply hypnotized subjects and simulators, this is not evidence that hypnosis is only a response to the demand characteristics of the situation. It merely indicates that our procedure has been unable to prove that something more is involved.

The problem here is the same as we have discussed with the preinquiry and the nonexperiment. In all probability there are many real effects of hypnosis which can be mimicked successfully by simulators. Thus the failure to find differences says a good deal about the effectiveness of the experimental procedure for studying hypnosis, but little about hypnosis itself. This is much the same situation as that with a patient who successfully malingers by simulating low back pain. His ability to persuade an orthopedic surgeon that his simulated pain is real cannot be taken as evidence that other patients do not have low back pain. It does not establish the nonexistence of the syndrome, but highlights the fallibility of the procedures used to establish the diagnosis.

Only when we are able to demonstrate differences between the behavior of real and simulating subjects can we feel that the experiment is compelling in demonstrating that a given effect is due to the presence of the independent variable. In the case of hypnotic experiments, the limitations of the procedure are such that these differences will either have to involve transcendence of unhypnotized performances or turn out to be counterexpectational in nature.

AN EXAMPLE OF THE USE OF SIMULATORS AS QUASI-CONTROLS

The problem of inference with quasi controls is illustrated in several studies (Evans, 1966; Orne & Evans, 1966) which we have carried out to investigate what happens if the investigator disappears after hypnosis has been induced. This is not an easy question to resolve. The hypnotist's disappearance must be managed in such a way as to seem plausible, truly accidental, and in accord with the implicit agreement between subject and hypnotist that the latter is responsible for the welfare of the former during the course of the experiment. Such a situation was finally created in a study requiring two sessions with subjects previously trained to enter hypnosis readily. It was explained to them that in order to standardize the procedure all instructions, including the induction and termination of hypnosis, would be carried out by tape recording.

The experimenter's task became essentially that of a technician— turning on the tape recorder, applying electrodes, presenting experimental materials, etc. He did not say anything throughout the study, since every item of instruction was given by means of the tape recorder. Each subject came for two such sessions. During the second session, while the subject was deeply hypnotized and tapping his foot in rhythm with hallucinated music, the tape recorder came to a grinding halt, the light on the desk went out, and the experimenter tried in vain to reactivate the machine by flicking the switch. He then muttered under his breath that the fuse must be blown and dashed from the room. The subject's behavior was observed through a one-way screen throughout the experiment in order to discover what happened when the experimenter left the room. Would hypnosis be terminated immediately once the subject was alone, as some theories would predict, or would it take a period of time for the subject to pull himself out of hypnosis, as one would expect if the condition were some special altered state?

Despite the "cuteness" of the deception procedure of the simulated power failure, there was no certainty that subjects would accept it as such. For this reason quasi controls were run. In this particular situation simulating subjects were the most appropriate kind of quasi-control, and they were included without the hypnotist being aware which subjects were in fact deeply hypnotizable and which were unhypnotizable individuals instructed to simulate. The findings were clear-cut: five out of the six deeply hypnotized subjects did not rouse immediately when the hypnotist left. They required varying periods of time to pull themselves out of the state. When they did, they appeared somewhat disoriented and confused. However, five out of the six simulating subjects also continued to simulate hypnosis after the experimenter left the room. In fact, they did "better" than the real subjects and feigned trance until the technician returned half an hour later! During the subsequent postexperimental inquiry it became clear that the simulators caught on to the fact that the power failure was contrived and that they behaved as they thought a hypnotized subject would if there had been a true power failure. The simulating subjects quite cogently pointed out that having been instructed to fool the experimenter, they were on guard lest they themselves be fooled. In contrast, only one of the hypnotized subjects suspected that the power failure was contrived.

Because the quasi-control subjects are a special-treatment group, their purpose is not primarily to provide comparison objects for actual subjects; rather, it is to clarify the adequacy of the experimental procedure. Since the simulators caught on to the fact that the power failure was contrived, it was possible that at some level the hypnotized subjects also had responded to the same cues, even though they did not verbalize such awareness. Therefore, despite statistically significant differences between these two groups, the results did not permit any conclusions to be drawn about the nature of the hypnotic phenomenon. Rather, the behavior of the quasi controls demonstrated an inadequacy of the deception procedure and indicated that the behavior of the hypnotized subjects could not be confidently interpreted at face value.

Having found the deception manipulation wanting, we re-examined in detail the cues which might have allowed the subjects to become aware that the power failure was a planned part of the experiment and that his behavior would actually be observed after it. The kind of nitty-gritty details which most investigators fail to publish and which, even if they wished to, most editors would delete for the sake of brevity, are crucial in this regard. In the study just described, to facilitate observation after the "power failure," the overhead lights remained on and only the bright desk lamp went out as the tape recorder stopped; an obvious one-way mirror to which we hoped (in vain) that the subject would have adapted remained in the room; and, further, a small polygraph continued to run in the experimental room. So we now redesigned the study with considerable attention to such details. The one-way screen was eliminated and replaced by another less well known and care-fully hidden means of observation. When the power failure occurred all the lights in the room were extinguished. Just enough light was filtered into the room through the window curtains from daylight—or from a strategically placed parking light outside at night—to make observation possible. Furthermore, physiological recordings were ostensibly made by means of a large Ampex instrumentation tape recorder and a small polygraph. Both of these machines stopped, along with the lights and the tape recorder, at the power failure. (Actually the wires from the subject were run through to another room at some distance in order to permit continuous recording of relevant data.) When the experimenter left the room the hall lights were out. Every effort was made by scrupulous attention to such details to have the power failure appear genuine.

With these revised conditions simulating and hypnotized sub-jects were run in another experiment by a blind experimenter. This time five out of six simulating subjects stopped simulating the moment the technician left the room, and indulged in exploratory or other private behavior, clearly indicating that they felt themselves to be unobserved. On the other hand, the hypnotized group be-haved much as they had in the earlier experiment, pulling them-selves out of the state only after a considerable period of time had elapsed. This behavior was in line with the data provided during an inquiry, which indicated that both real and simulating subjects accepted the power failure as genuine.

Significant differences were again obtained, but, in contrast to the findings of the first study, those from the second study allow meaningful inference. The behavior of the quasi-controls clearly indicates that the power failure was accepted as genuine, and therefore it is legitimate to accept the behavior of the hypnotized individuals at face value.[8]

DEMAND CHARACTERISTICS IN PSYCHOLOGICAL EXPERIMENTS

In the effort to understand hypnosis, the need to concern oneself with the effect of subtle cues which help to define the subject's appropriate response became abundantly clear. In other areas of inquiry—most notably psychopharmacology—similar effects have long been recognized under the heading of placebo response. These effects, complex yet exceedingly powerful, are ubiquitous. They are

8. An interesting quasi-control has recently been developed to evaluate deception studies. A group of subjects is either informed of the deception or warned to look out for trickery by another experimenter. These subjects are then run by a blind experimenter to see whether they behave differently from uninformed subjects. Such a procedure was used by Holland (1967) in a partial replication of Milgram's (1965) obedience study. A more refined, similar procedure was used by Levy (1967) to study the effect of awareness in a verbal conditioning situation. Most recently, Golding and Lichtenstein (1970) used such a technique to evaluate the effectiveness of interview procedures in detecting awareness of deception in the Valins false heart rate feedback situation (Valins, 1966). They informed some subjects that the heartbeat they would hear, during the experiment to follow, would not be their own. However, neither their behavior in the experiment nor their reports in postexperimental interviews allowed the experimenter to distinguish informed subjects from uninformed individuals.

These techniques are true quasi-controls and therefore do not permit any definitive inference to be drawn about the dependent variables. Certainly it would be inappropriate to conclude from such findings that the uninformed group must of necessity have been aware of the deception. As is the case with all quasi controls, they serve only to clarify flaws in the experimental procedure. In this instance they would show that the particular experimental and inquiry techniques employed cannot discriminate between informed and uninformed subjects. This could be either because the deception was so transparent that even uninformed subjects were aware of the true state of affairs or because an inadequate experimental technique was utilized that was insensitive to true differences between subjects who differed in their awareness of deception. The latter possibility, which implies that the same behavior *could* result from different mental processes in these two groups, cannot be excluded. The Golding-Lichtenstein study, for example, is an effective critique of the techniques that have been used to evaluate subject awareness and indicates the need for improved inquiry methods. The experiment provides a useful paradigm for testing the effectiveness of new inquiry procedures in assessing awareness. However, beyond showing that the evidence of nonawareness based on this inquiry technique is inconclusive, the experiment sheds no light on the extent to which uninformed subjects run with the Valins procedure were, in fact, aware of false feedback.

summarized in the clinical bromide that suggests one use a new drug quickly while it still works.

In industrial psychology "placebo effects" have been recognized since the classic Hawthorne (Roethlisberger & Dickson, 1939) studies, and the investigators' enthusiasm has accounted for initial dramatic successes in a wide range of psychotherapeutic interventions.

It should be emphasized that the phenomena we are discussing here all stem from the individual's recognition that his behavior is under close scrutiny and that changes of some kind are expected. These are not effects of experimenter bias in the sense that the observations of the investigator are distorted or even that he treats the control and experimental groups differently in some subtle fashion. The focus of these effects lies in the perception of the subject more than the behavior of the experimenter. As long as the subject perceives himself to be under investigation, effects of this kind cannot be eliminated.

It is perhaps an irony that in areas of applied research which attempt to solve problems considered by many as mundane, effects of this kind are recognized and taken into account, while in much research carried out in the laboratory they have been systematically ignored.

Demand characteristics, the experimental analogue of the placebo effect of psychopharmacology or the Hawthorne effect of industrial psychology, cannot be controlled in the classic sense; that is, they cannot be eliminated by simply holding the effect constant or by allowing for it in some statistical sense. Rather, they are phenomena in their own right.

Perhaps the problem is best illustrated in psychopharmacology. Studying a drug by comparing it with the effect of placebo does not allow the investigator to determine the effect of the drug alone. Rather, he studies the placebo response plus drug effect as compared to the placebo response without drug effect. Such a design does not permit correct inference about the effect of drugs independent of the subject's awareness that he is taking medication, as has been demonstrated by Ross, Krugman, Lyerly, and Clyde (1962). Since psychopharmacology—in contrast to most laboratory research—is concerned to draw inferences about the effect of drugs on individuals who know they are taking medication, this issue can usually be ignored. Even here, however, a drug effect may function in interaction with the placebo effect, which would not necessarily become apparent in a double-blind study. For example, Fisher, Cole, Rickels, and Uhlenhuth (1964) showed that when meprobamate was compared with a placebo in a double-blind study and the medication was administered with scientific objectivity by the physician, there were no differences between drug and placebo; however, in the same double-blind design, when medication was administered with enthusiasm, conveying the expectation of improvement, meprobamate was clearly superior to the placebo. It would appear that, under some circumstances at least, real drug effects require appropriate "demand characteristics" before they become apparent, or, put in another way, real drug effects may be blocked by situational factors.

Experimental studies with human subjects rarely have utilized independent variables that are as readily manipulated as drugs, nor do we have the advantage of a control procedure even approaching the adequacy of the placebo, yet we are all too ready to extend conclusions from a context where a subject knows his behavior is under scrutiny to contexts where this is not the case. Though this is a problem of little moment to the psychopharmacologist, it is of great moment to the psychologist.

These difficulties are illustrated particularly well by the dramatic and highly original work of Milgram (1963, 1965) in obedience behavior. These studies are important because they address themselves to significant issues and, in contrast to most social psychological research, make an effort to address the question of ecological validity.

In all of the variations of Milgram's research, subjects are told that they are participating in an experiment to study the effect of punishment on memory. Two subjects, one of whom is a confederate, participate together. Each subject draws straws with the other and "by chance" the true subject ends up in the teacher's role. The other subject (the confederate) is strapped into an awesome-looking chair and electrodes are attached to him. Both subjects are always shown the shock generator which permits the administration of shocks from a very low voltage up to 450 volts.

The machine is made all the more awesome by labeling the high end of the scale in red letters, "Danger—Severe Shock—XXX."

Before the beginning of the experiment a shock described as 45 volts is administered to the true subject, presumably so that he knows what the shocks are like. This, incidentally, is an extremely uncomfortable shock. The teacher's role is then explained to the subject—how to present a paired-associate learning task to the learner, how he is to determine the duration of the punishment, and how a higher level of shock must be administered for each failure. Initially the learner is able to answer correctly two out of three times, but he rapidly begins to fail more and more frequently, requiring the subject to administer ever higher levels of shock to the victim: "Starting with 75 volts the learner begins to grunt and moan. At 150 volts he demands to be let out of the experiment. At 180 volts he cries out that he can no longer stand the pain. At 300 volts he refuses to provide any more answers to the memory test, insisting that he is no longer a participant in the experiment and must be freed" (Milgram, 1965, p. 60).

The experimenter remains calm throughout this procedure and instructs the subject to continue. If the teacher says that the learner is no longer responding and therefore there is no point in going on, he is told, "Treat the absence of an answer as equivalent to a wrong answer and follow the usual shock procedure." If the subject does not wish to do so, he is told, "You have no other choice, you must go on." Regardless of the degree of agitation shown by the subject or the anguished screams of the victim, the experimenter remains imperturbable and demands that the subject continue.

Milgram asked 45 psychiatrists what percentage of subjects they thought would continue to the top of the scale in this experiment, and on the average the view was that no more than one in a thousand would persist. However, in a series of studies which examined the effect on obedience of varied parameters such as the relationship between subjects (friends versus strangers), the proximity to the subject (in the next room, in the same room, the teacher being required to hold the learner's hand on the shock electrodes), and the legitimacy of the setting (Yale University versus run-down quarters in Bridgeport), a disturbingly high percentage of subjects nonetheless continued to shock the learners up to the very top of the scale.

Finally, in one particularly dramatic study the learner inquired at the beginning of the study whether the fact that he had some heart trouble would be a problem. During the study the learner began to complain about chest pain and eventually appeared to pass out, with the strong implication that he had had a heart attack. Even under these circumstances a goodly number of subjects continued to administer shocks as directed to the top of the scale.

Milgram concludes that the willingness of subjects to administer shocks in this experiment indicates how easily obedience can be exacted from individuals by a legitimizing context. He implies that a similar mechanism operates in nonexperimental situations where violent and dangerous actions may be demanded and elicited from individuals, and that perhaps these studies help to explain the kind of behavior which occurred in concentration camps.

An entirely different way of viewing Milgram's studies is possible. The Milgram studies are a special instance of deception research, and in all such experiments it is vital that the investigator determine whether it is the subject or he, himself, who is deceived. Elsewhere (Orne & Holland, 1968) we have discussed the cues which indicate to the subject that the situation is basically safe. Of particular importance is the behavior of the experimenter, who sits by without being perturbed despite the moans, groans, and cries of anguish. While one might assume that the experimenter is merely unfeeling, it becomes more difficult to understand that he fails to be disturbed when the subject appears to pass out. The subject cannot help but be aware of the experimenter's culpability should anything happen to one of his subjects.

The superfluous nature of the subject's actual role is another aspect that could well raise doubts in the subject. For he does nothing that could not equally well be done by the investigator himself. Again, the necessarily awesome shock generator which is labeled "Danger—Severe Shock—**XXX**" may well provide cues that the situation is one more of role playing than of actual physical danger for the victim. In short, the labeling paradoxically indicates too much apparent danger for the situation to appear plausible.

For reasons that have been discussed earlier, it is exceedingly difficult to determine the extent to which subjects may have or may not have at some level perceived the many paradoxes in this situation and recognized that it must, of necessity, be completely safe for the apparent victim. The problems of interpretation are compounded by the fact that both subjects who accept the experiment as totally real and subjects who see through the experiment, recognizing that their own behavior is under investigation, are the ones likely to stop, whereas it is the subjects who are partially aware of the situation who are the ones most likely to be obedient. Therefore, awareness of deception is not only difficult to determine but, even if known, is not a simple correlate of obedience.

The problems of inference from such a study are illustrated by a different series of studies which were designed to investigate whether deeply hypnotized subjects can be compelled to carry out self-destructive or antisocial actions. Some years ago, Rowland (1939) showed that deeply hypnotized subjects could be compelled to pick up a poisonous snake with their bare hands, remove with their bare fingers a penny dissolving in a beaker of fuming nitric acid, and finally throw the acid at a research assistant. He also showed that these same subjects in the waking state, as well as other subjects, when asked whether they would carry out these actions, recoiled with horror and said emphatically, "No." This study was replicated by Young (1952) with essentially parallel findings. We (Orne & Evans, 1965) repeated the procedure yet a third time, adding, however, a quasi-control group of simulating subjects. Subjects were run blind. We were able to validate the observations of Rowland and Young that five out of six deeply hypnotized subjects could be compelled to carry out all three of these dangerous, self-destructive, and antisocial actions. However, six out of six simulators also carried out these behaviors.

Once we noted that simulators would carry out the behaviors, we ran subjects who were merely co-opted from the corridors and agreed to participate in a study, and we found that they were also ready to carry out the behaviors. Compliance turned out to be a function of the expectation that the experimenter conveyed in explaining the requirements. If he clearly expected compliance, subjects complied; if he asked whether subjects would carry out these actions, they said no.

Postexperimental inquiries revealed that the distinctions were not so much ones of the command quality of the way the request was made as of its cue quality. If one asks a subject whether he is willing to carry out such a behavior, the appropriate response is, of course, no. He would be foolish to do so. On the other hand, if it is clearly communicated that the experimenter expects him to carry out the actions, it is implicitly but nonetheless effectively communicated that, regardless of appearances, it is safe to proceed. As the experiment was being described, you, no doubt, realized that all kinds of safety precautions must have been taken to prevent the snake from biting and the acid from hurting either the subject or the research assistant. The awareness that I could not afford to have anyone hurt in my laboratory is not limited to this audience. It is shared by our subjects. Their appropriate recognition that the situation was, in the final analysis, totally safe, was a function of the kind of cues communicated in the experimental situation despite the fact that only one subject had the slightest inkling of how one could carry out these actions without either being hurt or hurting someone else.

The inference drawn from the Milgram studies was that, outside of an experimental situation, it would be relatively easy to cause individuals to maim or even kill for some presumed greater good, and it is tempting, of course, to point to the concentration camp situations or even the present war as examples of such eventualities. If one wished to draw conclusions from the Orne and Evans (1965) study, one would have to say that individuals would be prepared not only to hurt others but also to risk serious injury or death themselves. There is no doubt that under some conditions men will behave in precisely such a manner. However, it seems to me that the resemblance of these conditions to the experimental context is phenotypic rather than genotypic. Unfortunately, no evidence is available which allows one to determine the extent to which the Milgram experimental situation was perceived as "real" or the extent to which subjects were convinced that it was basically safe. In order to draw inference beyond the laboratory such information would be crucial. Ultimately, I believe, other kinds of data will be required to shed light on these issues. I do know that in the Orne and Evans study subjects did not for a moment expect that they would be seriously harmed or that they would harm anyone else, despite appearances to the contrary. Perhaps it is the recognition of the inadequacy of the experimental situation to yield answers to questions about antisocial behavior under hypnosis which makes me worry about the meaning of the Milgram experiments.

THE EXPERIMENT AS A TECHNIQUE OF INVESTIGATION

In this discussion I have focused upon my growing awareness of the complexity of experimental research with human subjects. When first confronted with the recognition of the difficulties inherent in working with one's fellow man as an experimental subject, one is tempted to discard the psychological experiment as a means of acquiring reliable knowledge; yet I certainly would not intend such a conclusion and would view it as most unfortunate. The experimental method remains the most effective single technique of exploring a broad range of problems. I would be equally troubled to see these comments taken as justification for replacing rigorous research with casual observation or for a return to armchair speculation. Indeed, it is precisely because of my interest in utilizing the experimental approach as a means of studying psychological mechanisms that I have felt compelled to concern myself with the psychology of the psychological experiment and the motivation of both the subject and the experimenter.[9]

The problems we encounter in psychological experiments may be somewhat more complex but not different in kind from those encountered in many sciences that seek to bridge the gap between laboratory research on a relatively isolated system and the function of that system in the complexity of the real world. No physiologist would assume that observations in vitro may cavalierly be assumed to represent the actual mechanism in vivo. On the contrary, he recognizes that an enzyme system studied in the test tube must then be studied in the liver slide, then in the liver itself, and finally in the total organism. While some of these steps may be telescoped, the translations from studies of relatively simple environments to ones of increasing complexity are required.

Indeed these problems are not confined to studies of living tissue. In aerodynamics, for example, the wind tunnel has become a crucial instrument. Without the opportunity to test variations in

9. For a highly relevant and illuminating discussion, see Aronson and Carlsmith (1968).

design under the controlled conditions of the wind tunnel, where a multitude of complex measurements can be obtained relatively easily and cheaply, modern plane design would not be possible. But it is not possible to take the observations in the wind tunnel and use them uncritically in the construction of an actual airplane. Rather, it is essential to include a series of conversion factors to match Reynold's numbers if one hopes to build a craft that will actually fly. Perhaps because of the staggering complexity inherent in all psychological research we have heretofore avoided concerning ourselves with the development of the conversion factors necessary to allow us to draw inference across situations. Egon Brunswik's (1947) concept of the ecological validity of research represents a rare but incisive effort at emphasizing this issue in the study of perception.

In my view the single most important variable which must be taken into account in psychological research with man is his recognition that he is under observation, that he is the object of study. Appropriately, Webb, Campbell, Schwartz, and Sechrest (1966) have emphasized the virtue of unobtrusive measures as one way in which this difficulty may be circumvented. Certainly, to the extent that we observe behaviors when subjects are unaware that they are being observed, we will eliminate difficulties.

The deception study is another, albeit methodologically difficult, approach to the problems that arise when the subject knows he is being studied; field studies are still a third. Even the judicious use of anecdotal material may, under some circumstances, serve important purposes.

While each of these approaches has considerable face validity and, with appropriate caution, may be extremely useful and important, it must be remembered that these techniques are often so involved, difficult, and complex that one could not ever hope to carry out with them the systematic work of exploring the effect of a given parameter on human behavior and experience. We cannot, for this reason, afford to give up the ordinary psychological experiment as a means of study. It is the only way parametric data can reasonably be obtained. On the other hand, neither can we afford to ignore the effects that are inevitably introduced when an active, thinking individual participates in a psychological experiment.

In recognizing the importance of demand characteristics and their effects in psychological experimentation, it is all too easy to go to the opposite extreme and assume that they account for most, if not all, findings. Such a nihilistic view is at least as naive as that which denies the potential importance of these factors. We cannot afford merely to speculate on their importance in any given set of studies, and it is for this reason that I emphasize quasi-controls as one means by which at least a rough assessment of their effect may be obtained. I would hope that other, more sophisticated techniques will ultimately be devised which will permit the development of systematic conversion factors to allow the translation of the findings from the laboratory to other situations. Finally, we will need to recognize the necessity of demonstrating that psychological mechanisms which have been studied in the laboratory hold in other settings. To do so we will have to recognize that laboratory observations are not of necessity better data—they are only data which are better controlled in a very clear sense but inevitably less well controlled in yet another sense. Ultimately, we seek congruence between the systematic findings obtained in laboratory experiments and those obtained in studies using unobtrusive measures, observations gathered from field studies, experiments in nature, systematized clinical observations, and even ordinary common-sense experience. In such a context, applied research may teach as much about basic psychological mechanisms as laboratory findings may clarify phenomena in the real world.

One would hope that these and other efforts clarifying the methodological issues of experimental research will ultimately lead to a psychology which is oriented to understanding and predicting significant human experience and behavior in extraexperimental as well in as experimental settings.

REFERENCES

Aronson, E., & Carlsmith, J. M. Experimentation in social psychology. In G. Lindzey & E. Aronson (Eds.), *The Handbook of Social Psychology*. Vol. 2. *Research Methods*. Reading, Mass.: Addison-Wesley, 1968.

Ashley, W. R., Harper, R. S., & Runyon, Dale L. The perceived size of coins in normal and hypnotically induced economic states. *American Journal of Psychology*, 1951, **64**, 564–572.

Barber, T. X., & Calverley, D. S. Toward a theory of "hypnotic" behavior: Enhancement of strength and endurance. *Canadian Journal of Psychology*, 1964, **18**, 156–167.

Bem, D. J. Self-perception: An alternative interpretation of cognitive dissonance phenomena. *Psychological Review*, 1967, **74**, 183–200.

Binet, A., & Féré, C. *Animal magnetism.* (Trans.) New York: Appleton, 1888.

Boring, E. J. *A history of experimental psychology.* (2nd ed.) New York & London: Appleton-Century-Crofts, 1950.

Bruner, J. S., & Goodman, C. C. Value and need as organizing factors in perception. *Journal of Abnormal and Social Psychology*, 1947, **42**, 33–44.

Brunswik, E. *Systematic and representative design of psychological experiments with results in physical and social perception.* (Syllabus Series, No. 304) Berkeley: University of California Press, 1947.

Carmichael, L., Hogan, H. P., & Walter, A. An experimental study of the effect of language on the reproduction of visually perceived forms. *Journal of Experimental Psychology*, 1932, **15**, 73–86.

Cataldo, J. F., Silverman, I., & Brown, J. M. Demand characteristics associated with semantic differential ratings of nouns and verbs. *Educational and Psychological Measurement*, 1967, **27**, 83–87.

Charcot, J. M. *Oeuvres complètes.* Paris: Aux Bureaux du Progrès Médical, 1886. 9 vols.

Coué, E. Self mastery through conscious autosuggestion. *New York American Library Service*, 1922. P. 83.

Damaser, Esther. Experimental study of long-term posthypnotic suggestion. Unpublished doctoral dissertation, Harvard University, 1964.

Damaser, Esther C., Shor, R. E., & Orne, M. T. Physiological effects during hypnotically requested emotions. *Psychosomatic Medicine*, 1963, **25**, 334–343.

Du Maurier, G. *Trilby.* New York: Harper, 1895.

Ellson, D. G., Davis, R. C., Saltzman, I. J., & Burke, C. J. A report on research on detection of deception. Indiana University, Department of Psychology, 1952, Contract Nonr 60nr-18011, Office of Naval Research.

Evans, F. J. The case of the disappearing hypnotist. Paper presented at the meeting of the American Psychological Association, New York, September 1966.

Evans, F. J., & Orne, M. T. Motivation, performance, and hypnosis. *International Journal of Clinical and Experimental Hypnosis*, 1965, **13**, 103–116.

Festinger, L. *A theory of cognitive dissonance.* New York: Row & Peterson, 1957.

Fisher, R. M. An empirical examination of the dissociation hypothesis of hypnosis. Unpublished bachelor (honors) dissertation, Harvard University, 1960.

Fisher, S. The role of expectancy in the performance of posthypnotic behavior. *Journal of Abnormal and Social Psychology*, 1954, **49**, 503–507.

Fisher, S., Cole, J. O., Rickels, K., & Uhlenhuth, E. H. Drug-set interaction: The effect of expectations on drug response in out-patients. In P. B. Bradley, F. Flügel, and P. Hoch (Eds.), *Neuropsychopharmacology*. Vol. 3. New York: Elsevier, 1964. Pp. 149–156.

Freedman, J. L. Role playing: Psychology by consensus. *Journal of Personality and Social Psychology*, 1969, **13**, 107–114.

Garfinkel, H. *Studies in ethonomethodology.* Englewood Cliffs, N.J.: Prentice-Hall, 1967.

Gill, M. M., & Brenman, Margaret. *Hypnosis and related states.* New York: International Universities Press, 1959.

Golding, S. L., & Lichtenstein, E. Confession of awareness and prior knowledge of deception as a function of interview set and approval motivation. *Journal of Personality and Social Psychology,* 1970, **14**, 213–223.

Gustafson, L. A., & Orne, M. T. Effects of heightened motivation on the detection of deception. *Journal of Applied Psychology,* 1963, **47**, 408–411.

Gustafson, L. A., & Orne, M. T. Effects of perceived role and role success on the detection of deception. *Journal of Applied Psychology,* 1965, **49**, 412–417.

Holland, C. H. Sources of variance in the experimental investigation of behavioral obedience. Unpublished doctoral dissertation, University of Connecticut, 1967.

Hull, C. L. *Hypnosis and suggestibility.* New York & London: Appleton-Century, 1933.

Kellogg, E. R. Duration and effects of post-hypnotic suggestions. *Journal of Experimental Psychology,* 1929, **12**, 502–514.

Kelman, H. C. The human use of human subjects: The problems of deception in social-psychological experiments. Paper presented at the meeting of the American Psychological Association, Chicago, September 1965.

Kroger, R. O. The effects of role demands and test-cue properties upon personality-test performance. *Journal of Consulting Psychology,* 1967, **31**, 304–312.

Levitt, E. E., & Brady, J. P. Muscular endurance under hypnosis and in the motivated waking state. *International Journal of Clinical and Experimental Hypnosis,* 1964, **12**, 21–27.

Levy, L. H. Awareness, learning, and the beneficent subject as expert witness. *Journal of Personality and Social Psychology,* 1967, **6**, 365–370.

Lewin, K. *Die Entwicklung der experimentellen Willenspsychologie und die Psychotherapie.* Leipzig: Verlag Von S. Hirzel, 1929.

London, P., & Fuhrer, M. Hypnosis, motivation, and performance. *Journal of Personality,* 1961, **29**, 321–333.

Mann, T. *Mario and the magician.* Lowe-Porter (Trans.) New York: Knopf, 1931.

Milgram, S. Behavioral study of obedience. *Journal of Abnormal and Social Psychology,* 1963, **67**, 371–378.

Milgram, S. Some conditions of obedience and disobedience to authority. *Human Relations,* 1965, **18**, 57–76.

Mills, T. M. A sleeper variable in small groups research: The experimenter. *Pacific Sociological Review,* 1962, **5**, 21–28.

Nace, E. P., & Orne, M. T. Fate of an uncompleted posthypnotic suggestion. *Journal of Abnormal Psychology,* 1970, **75**, 278–285.

O'Connell, D. N., Shor, R. E., & Orne, M. T. Hypnotic age regression: An empirical and methodological analysis. *Journal of Abnormal Psychology,* in press.

Orne, M. T. The mechanisms of hypnotic age regression: An experimental study. *Journal of Abnormal and Social Psychology,* 1951, **46**, 213–225.

Orne, M. T. Hypnosis, hypnotherapy, and medical practice. *Tufts Medical Journal,* 1953, **21**, 14–25.

Orne, M. T. The demand characteristics of an experimental design and their implications. Paper presented at the meeting of the American Psychological Association, Cincinnati, September 1959. (a)

Orne, M. T. The nature of hypnosis: Artifact and essence. *Journal of Abnormal and Social Psychology*, 1959, **58**, 277–299. (b)

Orne, M. T. On the social psychology of the psychological experiment: With particular reference to demand characteristics and their implications. *American Psychologist*, 1962, **17**, 776–783.

Orne, M. T. The nature of the hypnotic phenomenon: Recent empirical studies. Paper presented at the meeting of the American Psychological Association, Philadelphia, September 1963.

Orne, M. T. Hypnosis, state or role? Paper presented at the 5th International Congress on Hypnosis and Psychosomatic Medicine, Mainz, Germany, April 1970.

Orne, M. T., & Evans, F. J. Social control in the psychological experiment: Antisocial behavior and hypnosis. *Journal of Personality and Social Psychology*, 1965, **1**, 189–200.

Orne, M. T., & Evans, F. J. Inadvertent termination of hypnosis with hypnotized and simulating subjects. *International Journal of Clinical and Experimental Hypnosis*, 1966, **14**, 61–78.

Orne, M. T., & Holland, C. H. On the ecological validity of laboratory deceptions. *International Journal of Psychiatry*, 1968, **6**, 282–293.

Orne, M. T., & Scheibe, K. E. The contribution of nondeprivation factors in the production of sensory deprivation effects: The psychology of the "panic button." *Journal of Abnormal and Social Psychology*, 1964, **68**, 3–12.

Orne, M. T., Sheehan, P. W., & Evans, F. J. Occurrence of posthypnotic behavior outside the experimental setting. *Journal of Personality and Social Psychology*, 1968, **9**, 189–196.

Page, M. M., & Lumia, A. R. Cooperation with demand characteristics and the bimodal distribution of verbal conditioning data. *Psychonomic Science*, 1968, **12**, 243–244.

Patten, E. F. The duration of post-hypnotic suggestions. *Journal of Abnormal and Social Psychology*, 1930, **25**, 319–334.

Pattie, F. A. A report of attempts to produce uniocular blindness by hypnotic suggestion. *British Journal of Medical Psychology*, 1935, **15**, 230–241.

Riecken, H. W. A program for research on experiments in social psychology. In N. F. Washburne (Ed.), *Decisions, values and groups*. Vol. 2. New York: Pergamon Press, 1962. Pp. 28–42.

Roethlisberger, F. J., & Dickson, W. J. *Management and the worker*. Cambridge, Mass.: Harvard University Press, 1939.

Rosenberg, M. J. The conditions and consequences of evaluation apprehension. In R. Rosenthal & R. L. Rosnow (Eds.), *Artifact in behavioral research*. New York: Academic Press, 1969. Pp. 279–349.

Rosenhan, D., & London, P. Hypnosis: Expectation, susceptibility and performance. *Journal of Abnormal and Social Psychology*, 1963, **66**, 77–81. (a)

Rosenhan, D., & London, P. Hypnosis in the unhypnotizable: A study in rote learning. *Journal of Experimental Psychology*, 1963, **65**, 30–34. (b)

Rosenthal, R. On the social psychology of the psychological experiment: The experimenter's hypothesis as unintended determinant of experimental results. *American Scientist*, 1963, **51**, 268–283.

Rosenthal, R. *Experimenter effects in behavioral research.* New York: Appleton-Century-Crofts, 1966.

Ross, S., Krugman, A. D., Lyerly, S. B., & Clyde, D. J. Drugs and placebos: A model design. *Psychological Reports*, 1962, **10**, 383–392.

Rowland, L. W. Will hypnotized persons try to harm themselves or others? *Journal of Abnormal and Social Psychology*, 1939, **34**, 114–117.

Sarbin, T. R. Contributions to role taking theory: I. Hypnotic behavior. *Psychological Review*, 1950, **57**, 255–270.

Shor, R. E. Hypnosis and the concept of the generalized reality-orientation. *American Journal of Psychotherapy*, 1959, **13**, 582–602.

Shor, R. E. Physiological effects of painful stimulation during hypnotic analgesia under conditions designed to minimize anxiety. *International Journal of Clinical and Experimental Hypnosis*, 1962, **10**, 183–202.

Shor, R. E., & Orne, Emily C. *The Harvard Group Scale of Hypnotic Susceptibility, Form A: An adaptation for group administration with self-report scoring of the Stanford Hypnotic Susceptibility Scale, Form A.* Palo Alto, Calif.: Consulting Psychologists Press, 1962.

Silverman, I. Role-related behavior of subjects in laboratory studies of attitude change. *Journal of Personality and Social Psychology*, 1968, **8**, 343–348.

Silverman, I., Shulman, A. D., & Wiesenthal, D. L. Effects of deceiving and debriefing psychological subjects on performance in later experiments. *Journal of Personality and Social Psychology*, 1970, **14**, 203–212.

Stalnaker, J. M., & Riddle, E. E. The effect of hypnosis on long-delayed recall. *Journal of General Psychology*, 1932, **6**, 429–440.

Stare, F., Brown, J., & Orne, M. T. Demand characteristics in sensory deprivation studies. Unpublished seminar paper, Massachusetts Mental Health Center and Harvard University, 1959.

Stricker, L. J., Messick, S., & Jackson, D. N. Suspicion of deception: Implications for conformity research. *Journal of Personality and Social Psychology*, 1967, **5**, 379–389.

Sutcliffe, J. P. A general method of analysis of frequency data for multiple classification designs. *Psychological Bulletin*, 1957, **54**, 134–137.

Turner, L. H., & Solomon, R. L. Human traumatic avoidance learning: Theory and experiments on the operant-respondent distinction and failures to learn. *Psychological Monographs*, 1962, **76** (Whole No. 559), 1–32.

Valins, S. Cognitive effects of false heart-rate feedback. *Journal of Personality and Social Psychology*, 1966, **4**, 400–408.

Webb, E. J., Campbell, D. T., Schwartz, R. D., & Sechrest, L. *Unobtrusive measures: Nonreactive research in the social sciences.* Chicago: Rand McNally, 1966.

Weitzenhoffer, A. M., & Hilgard, E. R. *Stanford Hypnotic Susceptibility Scale, Forms A and B.* Palo Alto, Calif.: Consulting Psychologists Press, 1959.

Weitzenhoffer, A. M., & Hilgard, E. R. *Stanford Hypnotic Susceptibility Scale, Form C.* Palo Alto, Calif.: Consulting Psychologists Press, 1962.

White, R. W. A preface to a theory of hypnotism. *Journal of Abnormal and Social Psychology*, 1941, **36**, 477–506.

Young, P. C. Antisocial uses of hypnosis. In L. M. LeCron (Ed.), *Experimental hypnosis*. New York: Macmillan, 1952. Pp. 376–409.

Zamansky, H. S., Scharf, B., & Brightbill, R. The effect of expectancy for hypnosis on prehypnotic performance. *Journal of Personality*, 1964, **32**, 236–248.

Zeigarnik, B. Über das Behalten von erledigten und unerledigten Handlungen. *Psychologische Forschung*, 1927, **9**, 1–85.

Chronological List
of Contents of the Nebraska
Symposia on Motivation

1953 (Vol. 1)

Brown, J. S. Problems presented by the concept of acquired drive, pp. 1–21.

Harlow, H. F. Motivation as a factor in new responses, pp. 24–49.

Postman, L. J. The experimental analysis of motivational factors in perception, pp. 59–108.

Nowlis, V. The development and modification of motivational systems in personality, pp. 114–138.

Newcomb, T. M. Motivation in social behavior, pp. 139–161.

Mowrer, O. H. Motivation and neurosis, pp. 162–185.

1954 (Vol. 2)

Farber, I. E. Anxiety as a drive state, pp. 1–46.

Atkinson, J. W. Exploration using imaginative thought to assess the strength of human motives, pp. 56–112.

Ritchie, B. F. A logical and experimental analysis of the laws of motivation, pp. 121–176.

Festinger, L. Motivation leading to social behavior, pp. 191–219.

Klein, G. S. Need and regulation, pp. 224–274.

Nissen, H. W. The nature of the drive as innate determinant of behavioral organization, pp. 281–321.

1955 (Vol. 3)

Maslow, A. Deficiency motivation and growth motivation, pp. 1–30.

McClelland, D. C. Some social consequences of achievement motivation, pp. 41–65.

Olds, J. Physiological mechanisms of reward, pp. 73–139.

Peak, H. Attitude and motivation, pp. 149–189.

Young, P. T. The role of hedonic processes in motivation, pp. 193–238.

Rotter, J. B. The role of the psychological situation in determining the direction of human behavior, pp. 245–269.

1956 (Vol. 4)

Beach, F. A. Characteristics of masculine "sex drive," pp. 1–32.

Koch, S. Behavior as "intrinsically" regulated: Work notes towards a pre-theory of phenomena called "motivational," pp. 42–87.

Marx, M. H. Some relations between frustration and drive, pp. 92–130.

Miller, D. R., & Swanson, G. E. The study of conflict, pp. 137–174.

Seward, J. P. A neurological approach to motivation, pp. 180–208.

Solomon, R. L., & Brush, E. S. Experimentally derived conceptions of anxiety and aversion, pp. 212–305.

1957 (Vol. 5)

Morgan, C. T. Physiological mechanisms of motivation, pp. 1–35.

Lindsley, D. B. Psychophysiology and motivation, pp. 44–105.

Rodnick, E. H., & Garmezy, N. An experimental approach to the study of motivation in schizophrenia, pp. 109–184.

Wittenborn, J. R. Inferring the strength of drive, pp. 191–259.

Sears, P. S. Problems in the investigation of achievement and self-esteem motivation, pp. 265–339.

Osgood, C. E. Motivational dynamics of language behavior, pp. 348–424.

1958 (Vol. 6)

Bolles, R. C. The usefulness of the drive concept, pp. 1–33.

Estes, W. K. Stimulus-response theory of drive, pp. 35–69.

Spence, K. W. Behavior theory and selective learning, pp. 73–107.

Littman, R. A. Motives, history and causes, pp. 114–168.

Eriksen, C. W. Unconscious processes, pp. 169–227.

Malmo, R. B. Measurement of drive: An unsolved problem in psychology, pp. 229–265.

1959 (Vol. 7)

Schneirla, T. C. An evolutionary and developmental theory of biphasic processes underlying approach and withdrawal, pp. 1–42.

Hess, E. The relationship between imprinting and motivation, pp. 44–77.

Cattell, R. B. The dynamic calculus: Concepts and crucial experiments, pp. 84–134.

Levin, H., & Baldwin, A. L. Pride and shame in children, pp. 138–174.

Whiting, J. W. M. Sorcery, sin, and the superego. A cross-cultural study of some mechanisms of social control, pp. 174–195.

Janis, I. L. Motivational factors in the resolution of decisional conflicts, pp. 198–231.

1960 (Vol. 8)

Barker, R. G. Ecology and motivation, pp. 1–49.

Taylor, D. W. Toward an informational processing theory of motivation, pp. 51–79.

Toman, W. On the periodicity of motivation, pp. 80–95.

White, R. W. Competence and the psychosexual stages of development, pp. 97–141.

Heider, F. The Gestalt theory of motivation, pp. 145–172.

Rapaport, D. On the psychoanalytic theory of motivation, pp. 173–247.

1961 (Vol. 9)

Falk, J. L. The behavioral regulation of water-electrolyte balance, p. 1–33.

Teitelbaum, P. Disturbances in feeding and drinking behavior after hypothalamic lesions, pp. 39–65.

Pfaffmann, C. The sensory and motivating properties of the sense of taste, pp. 71–108.
McKeachie, W. J. Motivation, teaching methods, and college learning, pp. 111–142.
Sarason, S. B. The contents of human problem solving, pp. 147–174.
Birch, D. A motivational interpretation of extinction, pp. 179–197.

1962 (Vol. 10)

Vinacke, W. E. Motivation as a complex problem, pp. 1–46.
Brehm, J. W. Motivational effects of cognitive dissonance, pp. 51–77.
Kelly, G. A. Europe's matrix of decision, pp. 83–123.
Epstein, S. The measurement of drive and conflict in humans: Theory and experiment, pp. 127–206.
Bandura, A. Social learning through imitation, pp. 211–269.
Deutsch, M. Cooperation and trust: Some theoretical notes, pp. 275–319.

1963 (Vol. 11)

Rogers, C. R. Actualizing tendency in relation to "motives" and to consciousness, pp. 1–24.
Sears, R. R. Dependency motivation, pp. 25–64.
Miller, N. E. Some reflections on the law of effect produce a new alternative to drive reduction, pp. 65–112.
Pribram, K. H. Reinforcement revisited: A structural view, pp. 113–159.
Magoun, H. W. Central neural inhibition, pp. 161–193.

1964 (Vol. 12)

Hilgard, E. R. The motivational relevance of hypnosis, pp. 1–44.
Walker, E. L. Psychological complexity as a basis for a theory of motivation and choice, pp. 47–95.
Logan, F. A. The free behavior situation, pp. 99–128.
Edwards, A. L. The assessment of human motives by means of personality scales, pp. 135–162.

Mandler, G. The interruption of behavior, pp. 163–219.

Schachter, S., & Latané, B. Crime, cognition, and the autonomic nervous system, pp. 221–273.

1965 (Vol. 13)

Kendler, H. H. Motivation and behavior, pp. 1–23.

Leeper, R. W. Some needed developments in the motivational theory of emotions, pp. 25–122.

Premack, D. Reinforcement theory, pp. 123–180.

Hunt, J. McV. Intrinsic motivation and its role in psychological development, pp. 189–282.

Campbell, D. T. Ethnocentric and other altruistic motives, pp. 283–311.

Guilford, J. P. Motivation in an informational psychology, pp. 313–332.

1966 (Vol. 14)

Holt, R. R. Measuring libidinal and aggressive motives and their controls by means of the Rorschach test, pp. 1–47.

Burke, C. J. Linear models for Pavlovian conditioning, pp. 49–66.

Masling, J. Role-related behavior of the subject and psychologist and its effects upon psychological data, pp. 67–103.

Dethier, V. G. Insects and the concept of motivation, pp. 105–136.

Helson, H. Some problems in motivation from the point of view of the theory of adaptation level, pp. 137–182.

Malamud, W. The concept of motivation in psychiatric practice, pp. 183–200.

1967 (Vol. 15)

Berlyne, D. E. Arousal and reinforcement, pp. 1–110.

Scott, J. P. The development of social motivation, pp. 111–132.

Katz, I. The socialization of academic motivation in minority group children, pp. 133–191.

Kelley, H. H. Attribution theory in social psychology, pp. 192–238.

Pettigrew, T. F. Social evaluation theory: Convergences and applications, pp. 241–311.

1968 (Vol. 16)

Grossmann, S. P. The physiological basis of specific and nonspecific motivational processes, pp. 1–46.

McClearn, G. E. Genetics and motivation of the mouse, pp. 47–83.

Levine, S. Hormones and conditioning, pp. 85–101.

Heckhausen, H. Achievement motive research: Current problems and some contributions towards a general theory of motivation, pp. 103–174.

Lazarus, R. S. Emotions and adaptation: Conceptual and empirical relations, pp. 175–266.

Aronfreed, J. Aversive control of socialization, pp. 271–320.

1969 (Vol. 17)

Bindra, D. The interrelated mechanisms of reinforcement and motivation, and the nature of their influence on response, pp. 1–33.

Wike, E. L. Secondary reinforcement: Some research and theoretical issues, pp. 39–82.

Black, R. W. Incentive motivation and the parameters of reward in instrumental conditioning, pp. 85–137.

Aronson, E. Some antecedents of interpersonal attraction, pp. 143–173.

Cook, S. W. Motives in a conceptual analysis of attitude-related behavior, pp. 179–231.

Zimbardo, P. H. The human choice: Individuation, reason, and order versus deindividuation 1970 (Vol. 18), impulse, and chaos, pp. 237–307.

King, J. A. Ecological psychology: An approach to motivation, pp. 1–33.

Mason, W. A. Motivational factors in psychosocial development, pp. 35–67.

Denenberg, V. H. The mother as a motivator, pp. 69–93.

Berkowitz, L. The contagion of violence: An S-R mediational analysis of some effects of observed aggression, pp. 95–135.

Maddi, S. R. The search for meaning, pp. 137–186.

Orne, M. T. Hypnosis, motivation, and the ecological validity of the psychological experiment, pp. 187–265.

Alphabetical List
of Contents of the Nebraska
Symposia on Motivation
by Author

Aronfreed, J. Aversive control of socialization. 1968, **16**, 271–320.

Aronson, E. Some antecedents of interpersonal attraction. 1969, **17**, 143–173.

Atkinson, J. W. Exploration using imaginative thought to assess the strength of human motives. 1954, **2**, 56–112.

Bandura, A. Social learning through imitation. 1962, **10**, 211–269.

Barker, R. G. Ecology and motivation. 1960, **8**, 1–49.

Beach, F. A. Characteristics of masculine "sex drive." 1956, **4**, 1–32.

Berkowitz, L. The contagion of violence: An S-R mediational analysis of some effects of observed aggression. 1970, **18**, 95–135.

Berlyne, D. E. Arousal and reinforcement. 1967, **15**, 1–110.

Bindra, D. The interrelated mechanisms of reinforcement and motivation, and the nature of their influence on response. 1969, **17**, 1–33.

Birch, D. A motivational interpretation of extinction. 1961, **9**, 179–197.

Black, R. W. Incentive motivation and the parameters of reward in instrumental conditioning. 1969, **17**, 85–137.

Bolles, R. C. The usefulness of the drive concept. 1958, **6**, 1–33.

Brehm, J. W. Motivational effects of cognitive dissonance. 1962, **10**, 51–77.

Brown, J. S. Problems presented by the concept of acquired drive. 1953, **1**, 1–21.

Burke, C. J. Linear models for Pavlovian conditioning. 1966, **14**, 49–66.

273

Campbell, D. T. Ethnocentric and other altruistic motives. 1965, **13**, 283–311.

Cattell, R. B. The dynamic calculus: Concepts and crucial experiments. 1959, **7**, 84–134.

Cook, S. W. Motives in a conceptual analysis of attitude-related behavior. 1969, **17**, 179–231.

Denenberg, V. H. The mother as a motivator. 1970, **18**, 69–93.

Dethier, V. G. Insects and the concept of motivation. 1966, **14**, 105–136.

Deutsch, M. Cooperation and trust: Some theoretical notes. 1962, **10**, 275–319.

Edwards, A. L. The assessment of human motives by means of personality scales. 1964, **12**, 135–162.

Epstein, S. The measurement of drive and conflict in humans: Theory and experiment. 1962, **10**, 127–206.

Eriksen, C. W. Unconscious processes. 1958, **6**, 169–227.

Estes, W. K. Stimulus-response theory of drive. 1958, **6**, 35–69.

Falk, J. L. The behavioral regulation of water-electrolyte balance. 1961, **9**, 1–33.

Farber, I. E. Anxiety as a drive state. 1954, **2**, 1–46.

Festinger, L. Motivation leading to social behavior. 1954, **2**, 191–219.

Grossman, S. P. The physiological basis of specific and non-specific motivational processes. 1968, **16**, 1–46.

Guilford, J. P. Motivation in an informational psychology. 1965, **13**, 313–332.

Harlow, H. F. Motivation as a factor in new responses. 1953, **1**, 24–49.

Heckhausen, H. Achievement motive research: Current problems and some contributions towards a general theory of motivation. 1968, **16**, 103–174.

Heider, F. The Gestalt theory of motivation. 1960, **8**, 145–172.

Helson, H. Some problems in motivation from the point of view of the theory of adaptation level. 1966, **14**, 137–182.

Hess, E. The relationship between imprinting and motivation. 1959, **7**, 44–77.

Hilgard, E. R. The motivational relevance of hypnosis. 1964, **12**, 1–44.

Holt, R. R. Measuring libidinal and aggressive motives and their controls by means of the Rorschach test. 1966, **14**, 1–47.

Hunt, J. McV. Intrinsic motivation and its role in psychological development. 1965, **13**, 189–282.

Janis, I. L. Motivational factors in the resolution of decisional conflicts. 1959, **7**, 198–231.

Katz, I. The socialization of academic motivation in minority group children. 1967, **15**, 133–191.

Kelley, H. H. Attribution theory in social psychology. 1967, **15**, 192–238.

Kelly, G. A. Europe's matrix of decision. 1962, **10**, 83–123.

Kendler, H. H. Motivation and behavior. 1965, **13**, 1–23.

King, J. A. Ecological psychology: An approach to motivation. 1970, **18**, 1–33.

Klein, G. S. Need and regulation. 1954. **2**, 224–274.

Koch, S. Behavior as "intrinsically" regulated: Work notes towards a pre-theory of phenomena called "motivational." 1956, **4**, 42–87.

Lazarus, R. S. Emotions and adaptation: Conceptual and empirical relations. 1968, **16**, 175–266.

Leeper, R. W. Some needed developments in the motivational theory of emotions. 1965, **13**, 25–122.

Levin, H., & Baldwin, A. L. Pride and shame in children. 1959, **7**, 138–173.

Levine, S. Hormones and conditioning. 1968, **16**, 85–101.

Lindsley, D. B. Psychophysiology and motivation. 1957, **5**, 44–105.

Littman, R. A. Motives, history and causes. 1958, **6**, 114–168.

Logan, F. A. The free behavior situation. 1964, **12**, 99–128.

Maddi, S. R. The search for meaning. 1970, **18**, 137–186.

Magoun, H. W. Central neural inhibition. 1963, **11**, 161–193.

Malamud, W. The concept of motivation in psychiatric practice. 1966, **14**, 183–200.

Malmo, R. B. Measurement of drive: An unsolved problem in psychology. 1958, **6**, 229–265.

Mandler, G. The interruption of behavior. 1964, **12**, 163–219.

Marx, M. H. Some relations between frustration and drive. 1956, **4**, 92–130.

Masling, J. Role-related behavior of the subject and psychologist and its effects upon psychological data. 1966, **14**, 67–103.

Maslow, A. Deficiency motivation and growth motivation. 1955, **3**, 1–30.

Mason, W. A. Motivational factors in psychosocial development. 1970, **18**, 35–67.

McClearn, G. E. Genetics and motivation of the mouse. 1968, **16**, 47–83.

McClelland, D. C. Some social consequences of achievement motivation. 1955, **3**, 41–65.

McKeachie, W. J. Motivation, teaching methods, and college learning. 1961, **9**, 111–142.

Miller, D. R., & Swanson, G. E. The study of conflict. 1956, **4**, 137–174.

Miller, N. E. Some reflections on the law of effect produce a new alternative to drive reduction. 1963, **11**, 65–112.

Morgan, C. T. Physiological mechanisms of motivation. 1957, **5**, 1–35.

Mowrer, O. H. Motivation and neurosis. 1953, **1**, 162–185.

Newcomb, T. M. Motivation in social behavior. 1953, **1**, 139–161.

Nissen, H. W. The nature of the drive as innate determinant of behavioral organization. 1954, **2**, 281–321.

Nowlis, V. The development and modification of motivational systems in personality. 1953, **1**, 114–138.

Olds, J. Physiological mechanisms of reward. 1955, **3**, 73–139.

Orne, M. T. Hypnosis, motivation, and the ecological validity of the psychological experiment. 1970, **18**, 187–265.

Osgood, C. E. Motivational dynamics of language behavior. 1957, **5**, 348–424.

Peak, H. Attitude and motivation. 1955, **3**, 149–189.

Pettigrew, T. F. Social evaluation theory: Convergences and applications. 1967, **15**, 241–311.

Pfaffman, C. The sensory and motivating properties of the sense of taste. 1961, **9**, 71–108.

Postman, L. J. The experimental analysis of motivational factors in perception. 1953, **1**, 59–108.

Premack, D. Reinforcement theory. 1965, **13**, 123–180.

Pribram, K. H. Reinforcement revisited: A structural view. 1963, **11**, 113–159.

Rapaport, D. On the psychoanalytic theory of motivation. 1960, **8**, 173–247.

Ritchie, B. F. A logical and experimental analysis of the laws of motivation. 1954, **2**, 121–176.

Rodnick, E. H., & Garmezy, N. An experimental approach to the study of motivation in schizophrenia. 1957, **5**, 109–184.

Rogers, C. R. Actualizing tendency in relation to "motives" and to consciousness. 1963, **11**, 1–24.

Rotter, J. B. The role of the psychological situation in determining the direction of human behavior. 1955, **3**, 245–269.

Sarason, S. B. The contents of human problem solving. 1961, **9**, 147–174.

Schachter, S., & Latané, B. Crime, cognition, and the autonomic nervous system. 1964, **12**, 221–273.

Schneirla, T. C. An evolutionary and developmental theory of biphasic processes underlying approach and withdrawal. 1959, **7**, 1–42.

Scott, J. P. The development of social motivation. 1967, **15**, 111–132.

Sears, P. S. Problems in the investigation of achievement and self-esteem motivation. 1957, **5**, 265–339.

Sears, R. R. Dependency motivation. 1963, **11**, 25–64.

Seward, J. P. A neurological approach to motivation. 1956, **4**, 180–208.

Solomon, R. L., & Brush, E. S. Experimentally derived conceptions of anxiety and aversion. 1956, **4**, 212–305.

Spence, K. W. Behavior theory and selective learning. 1958, **6**, 73–107.

Taylor, D. W. Toward an informational processing theory of motivation. 1960, **8**, 51–79.

Teitelbaum, P. Disturbances in feeding and drinking behavior after hypothalamic lesions. 1961, **9**, 39–65.

Toman, W. On the periodicity of motivation. 1960, **8**, 80–95.

Vinacke, W. E. Motivation as a complex problem. 1962, **10**, 1–46.

Walker, E. L. Psychological complexity as a basis for a theory of motivation and choice. 1964, **12**, 47–95.

White, R. W. Competence and the psychosexual stages of development. 1960, **8**, 97–141.

Whiting, J. W. M. Sorcery, sin, and the superego. A cross-cultural study of some mechanisms of social control. 1959, **7**, 174–195.

Wike, E. L. Secondary reinforcement: Some research and theoretical issues. 1969, **17**, 39–82.

Wittenborn, J. R. Inferring the strength of drive. 1957, **5**, 191–259.

Young, P. T. The role of hedonic processes in motivation. 1955, **3**, 193–238.

Zimbardo, P. H. The human choice: Individuation, reason, and order versus deindividuation, impulse, and chaos. 1969, **17**, 237–307.

Subject Index

Arousal and social learning, 57–60
  nonfilial responses, 58
  response integration, 58
  signal learning, 59–60

Biological needs of personality, 149
Black conformity and protest, 176–179
Bruner-Goodman effect, 195, 196

Conformism, 155–162
  biological and social reactionism, 155–157
  definition, 155
  as existential premorbidity, 159
  pragmatism and materialism, 157–158
    effect on interpersonal relations, 158–159
  precipitation of stresses, 159
    disruption of social order, 161
    repeated confrontations, 161–162
    research, 169 ff.
    threat of imminent death, 160–161
Contagion of violence, 95–133
  aggression-enhancing effect of observed violence, 102–103
  conclusions, 131–133
  conditioning model of impulsive aggression, 103–105
  contact sports, perceived aggressiveness in, 112–114
  crime statistics, 99
  elicited versus disinhibited reaction, 104

emotional arousal, 120–123
  frustration, 120–122
  multiple-range tests, 121
examples of behavioral contagion, 97–100
film group studies, 123–127
frequency of violent crimes, 100
identification with film characters, 127–129
imitation concept, 100, 102
Kennedy assassination, 99–101, 105
learning as basis of contagious imitation, 104
mass media stimuli, 96, 110 ff.
  characteristics of available target, 114–120
  contact sports, perceived aggressiveness in, 114–120
multiple causation, 100
National Commission on Causes and Prevention of Violence, 95–97
news stories as stimuli, 98
oversimplified diagnoses, 96
perceptual-cognitive behavior, 102
propriety of observed aggression, 123–127
reflex contagious behavior, 104–105
reinforcing quality of aggression, 129–131
social facilitation concept, 100, 102, 103
Speck murders, 98, 99, 105
S-R generalization and aggressive "meaning," 105–110

279

Contagion of violence (*contd.*)
"suggesto-imitative" assaults, 97–98
television as stimulus, 95–97
theoretical analyses, 102–105
types of reaction, 103
weapons as stimuli, 107–110
Whitman Texas Tower murders, 98, 105
Crusadism, 147–148

Deprivation syndrome, 48–51, 60–61
Development, ideal and nonideal, 168–169

Ecological psychology, 1–30
behavioral factors in distribution, 2–5
cause-effect systems, 2
descriptive studies, 3
localization in time and space, 4
manipulation of perceptual selectivity, 3–4
perception of environment, 2–3
sampling and censusing of populations, 5
temporal units or sequences, 4–5
comparative methods, 5–8
basis, 6
goal, 5, 6
levels of genetic differences, 6–7
techniques of genetic manipulation, 7–8
definition, 1
deermice studies. *See Peromyscus, below*
light reinforcement in *Peromyscus*, 18–25
effect of early light treatment, 23–25
explanations, 19
licking in water experiments, 20
periodic activity, 22–23
species differences, 19
Peromyscus (genus), 8–30
age of eyelid separation, 9–12
eye size, 12–13

habitat selection, 16–17
light reinforcement, 18–25. *See also subentry above*
locomotion, 16
motivation, 26–29
selective advantage of trait, 29–30
orientation, 15–16
periodicity, 17–22
predator detection, 17
ranges and localities, 9
social behavior, 17–18
species distribution, 9
vision, 13–15
Peromyscus (species):
californicus, 13, 20
crinitus, 21, 22, 28
enemicus, 13, 19–22, 24, 27, 28
guardia, 9, 28
leocopus, 13
maniculatus and subspecies, 9–13, 15, 16, 19, 20, 22, 25, 27–29
polionotus, 13, 19, 24, 27–29
sejugis, 9
stephani, 28
primary aim, 3
summary, 30
Existential sickness, 139–148
crusadism, 147–148
definition, 139, 148
nihilism, 145–147
vegetative syndrome, 140–144
in literature and films, 141–143
psychotherapy for, 144
shift in symptomatology, 143–144

Filial behavior, 52–55

Government as integration, 175

Hippie movement, 181–182
Humanistic protest, 180, 181
Hypnotic research, 189–220. *See also* Psychological experimentation
amenable to laboratory research, 189

Hypnotic research (*contd.*)
  Ashley-Harper-Runyon design, 195–198
  Bruner-Goodman effect, 195–198
  Carmichael-Hogan-Walter effect, 194–195
  catalepsy of dominant hand, 191–192
  compliance as inadequate explanatory mechanism, 201–202
    increment in, 203
  confused public picture, 190
  consistency in behavior, 192
  demand characteristics, 194–201
  determination of core phenomena, 192–193
  effect of laboratory instructions on behavior, 204–207
    on responses to subsequent requests, 207–208
    on subject's wish to please, 202–204
    after trance, 204
  endurance in and out of hypnosis, 203
  historical review, 190–191
  hypnotic age regression, 194–195
  inconsistent nonexperimental behavior, 218–220
  nature of hypnosis, 190–217
  posthypnotic phenomena, 209–213
    response to interpersonal versus intrapsychic needs, 213–217
  prior knowledge of hypnosis in subject, 192
  relationship between subject's wish to please and subsequent response to suggestions, 208–209
  shaping of behavior by hypnotist, 193–194
  as special form of interaction, 220

Ideological protest in reeducation, 177
Imagination as psychological need, 151–152
Imminent death in conformism, 160
Impulsive aggression, 103

Individualism as ideal personality, 162–168
  creativity, 167–168
  doubt as sign of health, 166–167
  exploration of other forms of expression, 164–165
  freedom from conformist stresses, 167
  intimacy substituted for contract, 164
  monsterism as threat, 165
  pseudoexamples, 165–166
  research, 169 ff.
  self-definition, 163
  world view, 163–164

Jack the Ripper murders, 98
Judgment as psychological need, 152
  values and preferences as goals, 153

Kennedy assassination, 99–101, 105
King, Martin Luther, assassination, 98

Materialism in conformism, 157, 158
Meaning. *See* Search for meaning
Mesmerism, 190
Mother as motivator, 69–92, 150. *See also* Psychosocial development
  conclusions, 92–93
  dependent variables:
    activity in open field, 71
    fighting behavior, 70–71
    plasma cortisone, physiological reactivity, 71
  manipulation of maternal environment, 69–70
  modification of aggression and activity, 72–80
    of plasma and corticosterone and activity in Swiss-Albino mouse, 80–89
  peer group composition before and after weaning, 70
  procedure during infancy, 71–72
  rat mothers and rat aunts: effects on aggression and activity, 89–91
  summary, 92

National Commission on Causes and Prevention of Violence, 95–97
Nihilism, 145–147
Nonfilial social behavior, 55–57

Observed aggression. *See* Contagion of Violence

Psychological experimentation, 187–190, 220–260. *See also* Hypnotic research
  demand characteristics:
    cues to, 227
    functioning of, 224–227
    inquiry data for manipulating, 235–239
    preinquiry for clarifying, 242–246
  distortion from observations, 188
  episodic, 188–189
  man as focus of interest, 188
  mesmerism, 190
  motivation of subject, 220–224
  nonexperimental or preexperimental inquiry, 239–242
  postexperimental interview, 230–232
  motivation of subject, 220–224
  problems of inference, 242–243
  quasi controls, 189, 232–235
    simulators as, 248–251
  rules of the game, 229–230
  simulators, 246–248
    as quasi controls, 248, 251
  techniques of investigation, 258–260
Psychological needs of personality, 151–152
Psychosocial development, motivational factors, 35–65
  adaptation: developmental tasks, 35–37
    contact of infant with mother, 35–37
    preparation for adult function, 37
  arousal and social learning, 57–60
  causation, filial and exploitative behavior, 42–48

chimpanzee experiments, 45–48
  motivational consequences, 44–45
  motivational determinants, 42–44
  reinforcing properties, 48
central problem, 35
clinging in filial attachment, 52–55
deprivation syndrome:
  abnormal postures and movements, 49–50
  disturbed communication, 51
  elements, 48, 60–61
  gross motivational disturbance, 50–51
  poor integration of motor patterns, 51
developmental trends, 37–42
  affective-social responses, 40–41
  commerce with world, 38
  inferred from filial responses, 37–38
  mother-directed and other-directed, 39
  relationships between trends, 42
epilogue, 64
filial attachment, 52–55
mother as social object, 61–63. *See also* Mother as motivator
nonfilial social behavior, 55–57
postulates, 52–61
role of social objects, 61–64
studies of Old World primates, 35 ff.
summary, 64–65
waning of filial behavior, 55

Reductionism, biological and social, 155–157

Search for meaning, 137–183
  conclusions, 182–185
  conformism as premorbidity, 155–162
  contemporary social concerns, 175–182
    black conformity and protest, 176–179

Search for meaning (*contd.*)
  Hippie movement, 181–182
  ideological protest in reeducation, 177
  unrepresentativeness in government, 175–176
  white protest, 179–182
  core of personality, 149–155
  biological needs, 149
  expression of needs essential, 155
  psychological needs, 151–155
    effects of deprivation, 154
    evolutionary argument for, 154
  social needs, 149–151
  existential sickness, 139–148
  ideal and nonideal development, 168–169
  individualism as ideal personality, 162–168
  inherent in man, 153
  model for personality theorizing, 138–139
  paramount in view of personality, 139
  peripheral personality, 138, 149
    ideal, 139
    nonideal, 139
  personologist's approach, 138
  premorbidity of nonideal peripheral personality, 139, 149

psychopathologies of meaning, 139
reductionism, 155–156
relevant research, 169–175
Skinnerian concept of rewards, 137
  as ultimate problem, 137
social concerns, 149–151
  as ultimate problem, 137
Social concerns in search for meaning, 175–182
Social needs of personality, 149–151
Social objects in psychosocial development, 61–64
Society as integration, 175
Speck murders, 98, 99, 105
Sports as factor in aggressive violence, 112–114
Symbolization as psychological need, 151
  recognition as goal, 152–153
Sympathy protest, 180

Television and spread of violence, 95–97

Vegetative syndrome, 140–144

War protest, 180
Weapons as stimuli to violence, 107–110
White protest, 179–182
Whitman Texas Tower murders, 98, 105

Author Index

Acker, C. W., 103
Adams, L., 5
Ali, M., 178
Anderson, P. K., 6
Arendt, H., 166
Aronfreed, J., 102, 103, 105
Aschoff, J., 22
Ashley, W. R., 195–198, 200

Baker, R. H., 9
Barker, R. G., 1
Baldwin, J., 177
Bandura, A., 102–104, 110, 114
Barber, T. X., 203
Battle, E., 172
Bem, D. J., 242
Benjamin, L. S., 61
Berger, S. M., 104
Berkowitz, L., 95, 107, 111, 113, 114, 117, 119, 120, 122, 123
Berkson, G., 44, 50, 60
Berlyne, D. E., 19
Bernstein, S., 55
Binet, A., 190
Bitterman, M. E., 7
Bolles, R. C., 4
Boring, E. J., 190
Brady, J. P., 203
Brenman, M., 218
Brightbill, R., 203, 209
Broadhurst, P. L., 6, 29
Bronson, G. W., 61
Brower, L. P., 29
Brown, J., 244

Brown, J. M., 239
Brown, R. L., 129
Bruell, J. H., 6
Brunswik, E., 259
Burke, C. J., 235
Busch, R. A., 81

Calverley, D. S., 203
Campbell, C. B. G., 7
Campbell, D. T., 259
Campbell, E. Q., 172
Camus, A., 141, 145, 146
Carmichael, L., 194, 195, 225
Cataldo, J. F., 239
Caul, W. F., 58
Caviness, J. A., 59
Chaney, D., 129
Charcot, J. M., 191
Cleaver, E., 177
Clyde, D. J., 252
Cole, J. O., 253
Coleman, J. S., 172
Conn, L. K., 170
Cook, L. M., 29
Corwin, R., 123, 125
Costa, P., 173
Coué, E., 191
Craig, K. D., 107
Cromwell, R., 172
Crowne, D. P., 169–171
Croze, H. J., 29

Damaser, E. C., 200, 204, 210, 212
Davis, R. C., 235

284

Dement, W., 154
Denenberg, V. H., 3, 69, 72, 76, 82, 83, 85, 86, 88, 90
Dickson, W. J., 252
Douglass, F., 177
Draper, W. R., 4
Du Maurier, G., 192
Durkheim, E., 161

Eisenberg, J. F., 6
Eisenhower, M. S., 97
Eliot, T. S., 142
Ellson, D. G., 235, 236, 238
Emerson, R. W., 165
Erlenmeyer-Kimling, L., 29
Eron, L. D., 129
Evans, F. J., 171, 200 n., 204, 215, 216, 248, 256, 257

Falls, J. B., 17
Fantz, R. L., 55
Feldinger, I., 174
Féré, C., 190
Festinger, L., 240
Fisher, R. M., 200 n.
Fisher, S., 215, 253
Fiske, D. W., 150
Fitz-Gerald, F. L., 61
Fraczek, A., 109
Franck, D., 29
Frankl, V., 166
Freedman, J. L., 241
Fuhrer, M., 201, 203, 218
Fuller, J. L., 6

Garfinkel, H., 188
Geen, R. G., 117, 119, 120, 123
Geer, E. P., 127
Gibson, J. J., 59
Gill, M. M., 218
Ginsberg, B. E., 6
Golding, S. L., 251 n.
Goranson, R. E., 126, 127
Gore, P. M., 172
Graves, T. D., 172

Guilford, J. P., 174
Gustafson, L. A., 235, 236

Hall, K. R., 8
Halloran, J. D., 129
Haltmeyer, G. C., 80
Hamilton, W. J., 4
Hansen, E. W., 39
Harlow, H. F., 43, 55, 61, 62, 150
Harlow, M. K., 61
Harper, R. S., 195–198, 200
Harris, V. T., 17
Hartley, R., 110
Hartmann, D. P., 131
Hebb, D. O., 58
Heironimus, M., 123, 125
Heisenberg, W., 188
Hilgard, E. R., 207, 213
Hill, J., 18
Hill, S., 43
Hirsch, J., 29
Hnatiow, M., 106
Hobson, C. J., 172
Hodos, W., 7
Hogan, H. P., 194, 195, 225
Holland, C. H., 251 n., 255
Hollander, E. P., 169
Hollis, J. H., 44, 58
Honzik, C. H., 16
Hooper, E. T., 8
Horace, Q. H. F., 146
Hudgens, G. A., 72, 76, 77, 82
Hull, C. L., 187, 201, 203, 209

Impekoven, M., 29

Jackson, D. N., 227
James, W., 171
Jenkins, O., 170
Jones, L., 177
Joslin, J., 16
Julian, J. W., 171

Kahn, T., 172
Karas, G. G., 80

Katkin, E. S., 171
Kaufmann, J. H., 39
Kavanau, J. L., 16, 19
Kellogg, E. R., 210, 212
Kelman, H. C., 241, 242
Kelson, K. R., 8
Kettlewell, H. B. D., 6, 29
King, D. L., 61
King, J. A., 1, 13, 14, 19
King, M. L., 178
Klapper, J. T., 110
Klopfer, P. H., 27
Knurek, D., 107
Kolin, E. A., 174
Krebs, C. J., 7
Kroger, R. O., 239
Krugman, A. D., 252
Kubie, L., 154

Ladwig, G. W., 172
Lang, P. J., 106
Layne, J. N., 9
Lefcourt, H. M., 172
LePage, A., 107, 122
Lettvin, J. Y., 18
Leuba, C., 58
Levine, S., 80
Levitt, E. E., 203
Levy, L. H., 251 n.
Lewin, K., 226
Lichtenstein, E., 251 n.
Lichtman, C. M., 171
Lit, A., 14
Liverant, S., 171
Lloyd, M., 5
Lockard, R. B., 8, 19
Loew, C. A., 106
London, P., 201, 203, 208, 209, 218
Lovaas, O., 106, 130
Lumia, A. R., 239
Lyerly, S. B., 252

Macaulay, J., 99
Macaulay, J. R., 109
Mackinnon, D. W., 174

Maddi, S. R., 137, 138, 140, 149, 155, 160, 167
Malmo, R. B., 58
Mann, T., 192
Marler, P. R., 4
Marlowe, D., 169, 170
Mason, W. A., 35, 44, 45, 53, 55, 58, 60, 64
Maturana, H. R., 18
McCall, P. B., 19
McClearn, G. E., 8
McCormack, S., 43
McCulloch, T. L., 53
McCulloch, W. S., 18
McPartland, J., 172
Menzel, E. W., Jr., 56
Mesmer, F. A., 190, 198
Messick, S., 227
Milgram, S., 251 n., 253–255, 257, 258
Miller, A., 142, 161, 168
Miller, R. E., 58
Mirsky, I. A., 58
Mood, A. M., 172
Moody, P. A., 18

Nace, E. P., 213

O'Connell, D. N., 200 n.
Odell, M., 171
O'Neal, E. C., 122
Orne, E., 208
Orne, M. T., 187, 191, 194, 198, 200 n., 201, 203, 204, 207, 213, 215, 216, 221, 225, 230, 235, 236, 244, 248, 255–257
Osgood, C., 153
Oslapas, R., 81

Page, M. M., 239
Paschke, R. E., 83, 88, 90
Patten, E. F., 210, 212
Pattie, F. A., 218, 219
Pavlov, I. P., 187
Peterson, R. C., 96
Phares, E. J., 171

Pigg, R., 106
Pitts, W. H., 18
Price, L., 174
Propst, B. S., 174

Rahmann, H., 14, 15
Rahmann, M., 14
Rawlings, E., 123
Ribble, M., 150
Rickels, K., 253
Riddle, E. E., 194
Riecken, H. W., 240
Robel, R. J., 29
Rodwan, A. S., 171
Roeder, K. D., 29
Roethlisberger, F. J., 252
Rogers, C. R., 165, 168
Rosenberg, K. M., 83, 85, 86, 88
Rosenberg, M. J., 221
Rosenblatt, J., 83
Rosenblum, L. A., 62
Rosenhan, D., 201, 208, 209
Rosenthal, D., 172
Rosenthal, R., 225, 227 n.
Rosenzweig, M. L., 5
Ross, S., 252
Rothenbuhler, W. C., 6
Rotter, J. B., 171, 172
Rowland, L. W., 256
Rueping, R. R., 55
Runyon, D. L., 195–198, 200

Sackett, G. P., 56, 59
Saltzman, I. J., 235
Sarbin, T. R., 201
Scheibe, K. E., 244
Schiff, W., 59
Schwartz, R. D., 259
Scott, J. P., 6
Sechrest, L., 259
Seeman, M., 171
Shakow, D., 172
Sharf, B., 203, 209
Sharpe, L. G., 44
Sheehan, P. W., 215, 216

Shor, R. E., 200 n., 207
Shulman, A. D., 227
Silber, R. H., 81
Silverman, I., 227, 239
Simpson, H. M., 107
Sisemore, D. A., 16
Smith, M. B., 180
Solomon, R. L., 232, 240
Southwood, T. R. E., 5
Spitz, R. A., 150
Staats, A., 107
Staats, C., 107
Stalmaker, J. M., 194
Stare, F., 244
Stengel, K., 150
Stricker, L. J., 227
Strickland, B. R., 170–172

Tamarin, R. H., 7
Tannenbaum, P. H., 120, 122, 127
Tarde, G., 97, 98
Thomas, E. L., 103
Thurstone, L. L., 96
Tinbergen, N., 4, 29
Tolman, C. W., 104
Torrey, C. C., 55
Tryon, R. C., 29
Turner, L. H., 113, 232, 233

Uhlenhuth, E. H., 253

Valins, S., 251 n.
Vestal, B. M., 14, 15

Walk, R. D., 16
Walter, A., 194, 195, 225
Walters, R. H., 102–104, 114
Webb, E. G., 259
Weinfeld, F. D., 172
Weiss, W., 110
Weitzenhoffer, A. M., 207, 213
Wertham, F. C., 110
Wheeler, L., 102, 104
White, R. W., 191, 201
Whitten, W. K., 17

Wiesenthal, D. L., 227
Wilcock, J., 6
Wilcoxon, H. C., 16
Willington, A. M., 170
Willis, R. H., 169
Winakur, J., 5
Winn, H. E., 7

Yerkes, R. M., 43
York, R. L., 172

Young, P. C., 256

Zamansky, H. F., 203, 209
Zarrow, M. X., 72, 76, 77, 82, 83, 85, 86, 88, 90
Zeigarnik, B., 215
Zimmerman, R. R., 55
Zoob, I., 174
Zubek, J. P., 150
Zuckerman, M., 174